Stealing Tesla's Weapons

LAWRENCE ROBERTS, MA

Order this book online at www.trafford.com
or email orders@trafford.com

Most Trafford titles are also available at major online book retailers.

Print information available on the last page.

ISBN: 978-1-4907-7209-7 (sc)
ISBN: 978-1-4907-7213-4 (hc)
ISBN: 978-1-4907-7212-7 (e)

Library of Congress Control Number: 2016905342

Trafford rev.   04/06/2016

 www.trafford.com

North America & international
toll-free: 1 888 232 4444 (USA & Canada)
fax: 812 355 4082

Contents

DEDICATION

"When I spoke of future warfare I meant that it should be conducted by direct application of electrical waves without the use of aerial or other implements of destruction. This means, as I pointed out, would be ideal, for not only would the energy of war require no effort for the maintenance of its potentiality, but it would be productive in times of peace. This is not a dream."

Dr. Nikola Tesla, New York Times, April 21, 1908

Friday, January 8, 1943

The Next Day

Hotel New Yorker - 34ᵗʰ St at Eighth Ave

Standing outside the hotel suite door, the cleaning lady wiped the sweat from her brow. After two deep breaths, she began wringing her hands, while staring at the 'Do Not Disturb' sign, hanging from the doorknob outside Dr. Nikola Tesla's suite. The nervous woman grabbed the sign for an anxious moment then let it go, afraid of what secret power Tesla might have used. Her tired, sagging shoulders weighed heavy as she helplessly stared at the warning sign swaying from side to side.

Peeking through the door cracked open across from the hallway was a pair of thick glasses, looking up and down as Fitzgerald frantically scribbled notes on her every move. In his report to his Captain, the new recruit noted he was not a spy but a physicist who was drafted.

There was good reason for hiding and watching Suite 3327. The Army realized the impact of Tesla's weapon and knew other countries had seen it too. Before he was drafted into Army Intelligence, Fitzgerald was certain the technology to end all wars was behind the door. On his first assignment for A.I., he was taught how to control breathing so she would not hear being watched. The technique made him dizzy so he wrote, "I maintained silence by breathing through my mouth". Spying was prickly to the raw trooper.

Straight out of boot camp his assignment was Army Intelligence. There was no time for gradual anything during a war. The first week Fitzgerald was deciphering the notes of a genius and a few months later he was following a suspicious maid.

Fitzgerald was not exactly conscripted; he was chosen. He had not finished his dissertation but sure in hell was in the Army now. They made him wear their black rimmed G.I. issued glasses. There were other reasons he hated thick specs. The G.I. pair could not focus well at middle distances, like the other side of the hall. However as Fitzgerald learned his military specialty code was as a researcher and all Army orders were correct, every time any Officer said they were.

Fitzgerald watched the maid nervously gape up and down at the door, resting on one leg and then the other. The frumpy matron was unmindful of her right hand twisting the cleaning towel hard around her left wrist. She cut off the circulation and he could see her fingers turned sallow. Oblivious she continued to gaze afraid, frozen into a mindless gaze with wilting fingers.

The young spy was afraid she was damaging herself. He feared Tesla was going to open the door any second. She stopped twisting the towel to wipe her brow. She stared at the door.

He recalled the gracious meeting he had with Tesla last year. They were both tall soft spoken men, Fitzgerald a fourth the Doctor's age. Tesla articulated a precise metric. Fitzgerald remembered spending months afterwards practicing Tesla's pacing to sound smarter.

Fitzgerald later confessed "After years of graduate study, I still could not keep up with his mind". The old genius told me that, "We have to let go of power to enjoy it."

In his notes the old man noticed his nervous maid. Tesla explained, "The maid came inside the suite for no apparent reason.

She looked through various stacks of notes and took not one." Given she stole nothing and was quite neat he did not consider her nosey ways important.

Fitzgerald's assignment was to maintain and report on the advanced technology created by Nikola Tesla. With each day, Fitzgerald was becoming more worried. There was a cloud growing, creating an increasing distance in the old man's ways. Tesla's brilliant intellect cared less and less about every day details. Fitzgerald considered the Doctors well-being to be, well, he personally felt he was the only one who cared.

The maid had a file as a wartime threat. Fitzgerald presumed she would return. Katy had plenty of reason to fear the Tesla's door. The 33rd floor maids at the Hotel New Yorker knew that failing to clean each and every guest's room was grounds for termination. Today, she stood still outside, shivering, frightened of her job and what else she had to do.

The frumpy worker jumped back, when the hallway lights flickered. She had reasons to fear some old eccentric who lived in this hotel for years. The staff whispers about the mastermind who created the generators of their brightly lit ballrooms. They say he could make lights blink anywhere, any time he wanted. They were sure he had something to do when the lights blinked as WWII battled on.

In later testimony, Katy read from her diary. She had spoken with the tenant in 3327 three times in the last two years. The first time, Tesla cautioned her about the suite's arrangements and the placement of each item. In a second brief discussion, he politely asked her "where might I purchase pigeon food?" Then there was the third time when he politely asked her not to clean that day. The maid felt uncontrollably beguiled, yet afraid of him. He looked straight through her with his deep-set, crystal blue piercing eyes. Every maid knew the gaze of this reclusive genius could look right through others. Some whispered the eyes could continue to pierce into a person's soul. Everyone kept their distance.

Most maids were terrified of his stare. Katy could not remember any maid daring to approach the mastermind.

He was extremely neat and precise. If she sneezed, Katy was sure he would see the marks. Everywhere throughout the suite, the meticulous eccentric placed the same note neatly on top of every project and each tidy stack:

MAID

Please do not disturb anything here or
clean or dust. I will attend to this myself.
Clean bathtub and toilet and leave towels.

The two rooms in Tesla's suite were always in perfect order. She learned to work around the stacks of carefully written notations on every table. Cleaning this room took longer than any other on the Hotel floor. Years of cleaning taught Katy to sweep away from his sacred piles. The housekeeper later confessed she had fingered through the bundles of documents but, none of the words or diagrams made much sense. Katy stumbled every time she struggled to say out loud, 'Projecting Concentrated Non-Dispersive Energy through Natural Media'.

After thumbing through the mounds of documents, she always double-checked to make sure the papers appeared untouched. If one page was out of order, he would have noticed. He kept every sheet well organized.

Last week A.I. searched her room. Her diary told two stories. The other one was being alone and accidentally meeting a well-groomed stranger. She hated her one room home. Her letters to no one were written by a worn woman; she was tired out long before the war, and was wearing down because of the hostilities. After her pet dachshund, *Poodee* died she stayed home and wrote bad poetry. The wishful writer submitted weekly poems and kept a stack of boxes in the corner to store the dead mail. Rejection letters were better than nothing.

Her second narrative was recounting her love, a spruce, slightly older man wearing an ascot she met near home. In his polished accent he asked "I am new to this country can a gentlemen carry the lady's small grocery bag for some advice?" His name was

George. What kind of wonderful man would ask "would you ever forgive my broken English?"

His eyes begged for her love while he humbly offered. "You write poetry perhaps you would honor me with a reading. Is your poetry at your home close by?"

The first night, they ate spaghetti and laughed at her stories of the hotel. "Yes, Dr. Tesla is on my floor and when I clean he doesn't even know I am there. His mind is always in the clouds."

Although she was shy, the dapper man only had to lay his hand on hers for her latest poem "roses are red violets are blue, I met a man and it was you. No, that is the new one. The old one reads, "Wish I was young and could fly into the blue." He could only smile. Looking down so as not to see his answer she asked "Is it alright to use the same word twice?" He said "A poet is always free, waiting only with wonder."

She loved his European ways. After she sprayed the hotel's best talcum powder underneath her hotel sheets and over her worn mattress he stayed the night. Early the next morning, they went shopping and this wonderful man filled her tiny kitchen with food. When Katy told him she didn't like rice, he put a real $20 bill in the Uncle Ben's carton and placed it in the rear of her ice box, for emergencies.

After George told her about his arriving in America to recover his stolen documents, she was surprised to learn this concerned Tesla. "What a wonderful happenstance" Katy bragged she could tell him all about the strange geezer in 3327. "Can you fancy that?" She was proud to help her new lover. Listening to George was her joy, inspiring her to spend time alone, filling every piece of paper with simple poetry.

George wanted her to bring him certain stacks of papers with diagrams from suite 3327. He explained "you are helping me and America when you look through every one of those heaps of notes before the enemy gets them."

Katy swore she would bring back documents to help George deliver his contract for the American war effort. When he held her she could hardly breathe. He promised "Let me buy you some of those black nylons. You know the kind, with the black line going all the way up the back of your leg." The forlorn maid wrote he was a dream come true and all hers.

She dragged home that evening to find George impatiently waiting, tapping his foot hard. Obviously, she did not have any papers, much less the ones he wanted. He was a righteous European lover who excited her. The unyielding George angrily explained, "You disappoint me and endanger your country!"

Katy broke down in tears. After he left, she took solace in her diary. Leaving the frightened maid alone to fear what the old genius might do if he found out she was searching his room.

The Army rented Private Fitzgerald a hotel room across the hallway. He watched a week for nothing, at least until yesterday, when the 'Do Not Disturb' sign appeared on the door during the night.

Fitzgerald was certain she came to steal from his ward even though he had not seen Tesla for days. There were strict orders not to alarm the elderly man.

That afternoon an A.I. messenger delivered the background file on a one Kathryn 'Katy' O'Brian. The maid had lived alone for 34 of the last 48 years. At sixteen, her one child was given up for adoption. Her life was as the hotel housekeeper. No driver's license and she did not finish high school. The hotel withheld her taxes; she paid her rent on time and never missed a day of work, except for the long ago problems with her teenage pregnancy and the bastard child the Sisters of St. Joseph took in.

Today was Katy's second time to steal for George. Taking a long breath, the maid trembled while turning the key to Tesla's suite. The door creaked open and she took one step in. Fitzgerald heard her gagging. While opening the door wider she started to shake. Covering her mouth Katy could not stop from walking inside.

A pungent stench struck her like it had been thrown. She stopped for a breath, clutching a nearby chair. Wanting desperately for this whole thing to be over, Katy put her head down with a towel over her nose and wrapped her right arm around, just below her watering eyes and staggered past the table with dozens of patents neatly stacked into sorted piles.

From across the hall Fitzgerald could hear her choking. The maid called out from beneath her arm, "Dr. Tesla, I need to clean your room." There was no answer. The room was exactly as it appeared last week, only colder.

There were only two rooms inside suite 3327. The front room contained Spartan furniture, numerous file drawers and an eight-foot tall black safe standing in the corner. On the tall hat-rack she noticed the expensive but tattered top hat, cane, suitcase and embroidered bag. They were expensive when they were new, many decades ago.

Taking a deep breath Fitzgerald stepped out into the hallway and hid outside Tesla's door to peak in. From across the hall Fitzgerald could smell the pungent odor of death.

With short, frightened steps she headed to the bedroom. Katy stuttered, "Dr. Tesla… I need to clean your room. Hello?" Struggling for a deep breath, she inched towards the next room with her hand extended as if it was dark. Before she was able to cross the floor, the stench became overwhelming.

Turning, she stumbled into the small chamber pot, fumbling the faucet handle, the confused woman splashed water on her face. Gasping for air, the frightened maid stood, inhaled deeply, pulled her dress straight and moved quickly into the bedroom before freezing at the doorway.

On the antique brass bed, the old man lay naked, except for his socks. His pale white skin hung in loose folds draping the frail skeleton down along obvious bones. His famous blue, deep set eyes remained wide open, staring blankly at the broken ceiling fan. His quiet body reeked of death.

With both hands Katy grabbed her face, frantically trying to hold her head steady. She fumbled and fell into the chair next to the doorway. The maid slowly twisted the cleaning towel around her wrist, struggling to catch her breath.

Katy couldn't turn away from Tesla's empty stare. She was confused by the heat in the room, he had always kept cold. The maid staggered over to the overheated wall furnace and twisted the knob off.

Fitzgerald ran back across the hall as she turned around. Staggering out into the hallway, choking the distressed woman leaned against the far wall to stay up.

Always listening for anything to talk about the other 33rd floor maid, hefty Alice Thompson stopped cleaning and lumbered out into the hallway. Alice's yell echoed, "What's the matter, doll? Get another whiff of that ammonia?"

Still gasping, Katy struggled to yell, "CALL THE DESK! T-Tesla's dead!"

Across the hall, Fitzgerald stood in shock. He cared deeply and his notes made repeated references to the genius' fragile age. The signs were there. He was acting so very old. There was nothing anyone could do. It was meant to be. Fitzgerald's mind raced with possibilities and impacts. During graduate school, Fitzgerald had studied hundreds of Tesla's patents and deeply admired his genius. The former doctoral student knew he understood more of the science than all the others. The problem was the A.I. private did not know what to do now.

Down the hallway, Alice put her hands over her heart, turned and ran back into her open suite. She telephoned the news to the front desk.

Katy wrapped a towel around her nose before turning back into the room. Fitzgerald followed and stopped outside to watch from the door. She was confused between the numerous piles of papers, showing confusing and complex diagrams. Reading through the farthest pile, Katy struggled not to stammer and fumbled the words out loud, "The Art of Telegeodynamics".

Even though she was on the telephone inside the room down the hall Alice's yelling was frightening. Katy dropped a slipping pile and turned back to the closest table, Katy struggled to read 'A Method of Producing Powerful Radiations'. She looked back and forth between the piles. Not wanting anyone to notice later and confused about everything, she grabbed the bottom section from each one of the four piles. Katy yanked off her apron and wrapped up the three inches thick of documents. She turned and ran out the door.

One step ahead of her, Fitzgerald ran back inside his room.

Katy looked down the hall and heard Alice. Turning away, she shuffled quickly to the end of the hall, stumbling out the nearby Fire Exit staircase.

Fitzgerald was a scientist without training on what to do with dead bodies and screaming women. After the maid left, he ran into Tesla's suite and back into the bedroom, gagging even though he covered his mouth. He wanted to say something but he could not. The once great genius now lays there, a skeleton covered with flaccid skin.

A large black binder stamped U.S. GOVERNMENT lay on the table near the body so the agent secured it. Fitzgerald's eyes were watering so badly he was forced back outside.

He could hear Alice down the hall hollering her latest gossip into the telephone. "Yeah Gracie he sure up and died."

Fitzgerald ran to the Fire Exit and looked down the endless staircase and the lady wheezing. After scrambling down three floors of stairs Katy had stopped and struggled to catch her breath. She looked over the rail, sighing at the remaining thirty floors and then continued down. Fitzgerald removed his shoes and started down the stairs after her.

The frantic woman slipped, cussed and scurried down the endless flights of steps. Her moans drove her downward. Hugging her package tightly, the lover talked to the papers "He will be so proud of me."

She cursed all the way down to the South door, where the alarm was always disconnected for cigarette breaks. At this hour, no one was there. The panting thief nearly fell into the alley, gasping for air while staggering down the alley. Katy fell between five garbage cans and lost control crying.

***

The straight laced desk manager, Reginald Otis immediately called the Coroner's Office. He later explained to the U.S. Army investigating officer about the insolent bureaucrat who said he will send 'a meat wagon' to pick up Tesla's body. "How dare you?" Reginald criticized the fool for slighting any of his noble guests. The language had lost so much since his family squandered their fortune but one never loses good breeding. "A gentleman of Dr. Tesla's stature should be carried with respect, don't you agree?" He challenged the coroner.

Reginald's demand was an engrained drool, seasoned by an ever so proper upbringing. After hanging up the manager turned to the guest ledger files. As he lifted the room folder the shocking truth was an unwarrantable list of overdue room bills for Suite 3327. He later admitted in his debriefing to discretely cursing his employer. It was common practice; he was going to be held accountable. The newspaper detailed his losing far too much, assuring the end of this career, at least in New York.

The Nikola Tesla room account folder listed an emergency contact name, Mr. Kenneth Swezey. Reginald remembered this modern day Sancho Panza, who constantly praised the eccentric old Tesla. Swezey was always egging the Desk Manager on his ridiculous thoughts of bouncing rays off the moon. What people knew and thought about each other mattered little now; after all, the genius who made such dreams come true had just died.

During the next debriefing Reginald recollected seeing Tesla's performance at the 1893 Chicago World's Fair. Even before Tesla's show, his English Nanny told the eager lad the horrible truth about the infamous and macabre war with Edison.

The lively old lady prefaced the story by explaining this narrative of American history was such an embarrassment. And then her voice got louder in case others wanted to hear. *"Not so very long ago, the Hawker came and set up a stand on busy 4ᵗʰ Street, right in the middle of town."*

As a lad, Reginald would worry to the point of tears when Nanny shook. She always did while recounting the growing story, *"The flashy dressing man would have his young assistant set up two* metal plates: the one labeled 'DC' would have a small dog strapped to it, and on the other metal plate a large cat was strapped over the label 'AC'.

The carnival Hawker proclaimed, "Listen up. What you are about to witness will save your life. DC means 'direct current' and the very words sound straight and safe, like America. Of course they are safe. They are from the greatest inventor in all America, no, no, yes, yes in the entire world, Mr. Thomas Alva Edison." The hawker in his brown checkered suit looked at each person, sure he had everyone's attention while inhaling another long breath before continuing, "Now hear ye, hear ye, I will demonstrate, and prove to every last one of you beyond a reasonable doubt, the dangers of this here foolhardy notion of European electricity invading your home."

The crowd would always inch forward when he paused to gasp at his punctuations. His basset hound long face had teeth so big they seemed to snap when he talked. "Are you going to trust some new-fangled foolhardy experiment with the safety of your family?"

With planned timing, a few men working for the huckster shouted a few loud approvals. "Think of your children. I'm here to educate you folks for your own protection. This new-fangled AC can burn your homes down while you're sleeping! What responsible parent with any country sense would want crazy alternating currents where your babies sleep in their cribs?"

After an anxious moment while taking another long breath for dramatic effect, the prepaid peddler adjusted his bowler before flipping the DC switch. The hot plate labeled DC caused the dog to scratch a flea.

Everyone laughed. The dog howled to the crowd, to everyone's delight. The proud man in the checkered suit knew he controlled the show.

Then with great fanfare, the macabe marketer warned the growing crowd to step back. He told the children "take another step back" and they all took two steps back before shoving to the front. The barker announced "This here is alternating current." And look at any one fool enough not to be scared. Challenging the throngs,

"Don't you have to agree, the name 'alternating' sounds crazy as a loon? We all know what a loon is, don't we? Yesiree...

"Ladies, gentlemen, girls and boys, I surely apologize for showing god's truth. I'm sure you will agree with the necessity for me, the humble messenger, delivering a grave warning to save your life." The barker then flipped the switch labeled 'AC'. The sleeping cat jumped and hair went on end. Shrieking and crying, he stopped before he was burned on the skillet, leaving a scorched, smoldering carcass. Everyone gasped, women fainted and babies cried. The hawker declared, *"Forgive the herald for warning you of the danger of AC electricity. You need to thank the messenger. Thank me for saving your homes and your children's lives, Yesiree."*

Quite offended, Reginald's nanny was far and away too well trained for such riffraff. Dressed in her couture visiting gown for the long journey inland, Nanny ignored her old dress had become quite tight with age. Quite indignant over Edison she complained the entire flip flap was the most god-awful show she ever saw. Only with labored disdain, she retold that story many times to everyone on the railcar who would listen.

During Christmas holidays Reginald's gabby nanny took him all the way to Chicago for the World's Fair. Never had the boy or anyone else seen so many people in one place. The newspapers wrote one in three Americans came to visit these reconstructed marble castles holding testimony to the wonders of technology. For a lad, each new exhibit proved ever more marvelous.

The searchlights reflected off the fountains and the colors made prisms keeping the millions in awe. There was a train that hung from a wire and driven entirely by this new-fangled electricity. Nanny told Reginald all this electricity was the AC kind, the very same one invented by that foreigner Tesla. There was a wheel 250-feet in diameter where a guy named Ferris it set up so it could spin people around using this AC electricity. Edison's DC electricity was nowhere to be found but there was a skidoo of a show with that contraption Edison called a Kinetoscope, it could make pictures move.

As his mind floated back to happier times, Reginald could only think of the Fair's most popular exhibit - Nikola Tesla Alternating Current Show.

Under one big top, large crowds sat in bleachers around a big circle. In the middle of the arena was a huge metal platform, with an operator dressed like an undertaker. The man in black stood between a switch and a huge meter that measured from zero to one million volts of alternating current - AC. And it was the real deal.

Critics and Edison's team of hucksters attempted to pan the show for using no more than 200,000 volts AC but, all agreed every one of Edison's cats were fried by far less.

When the Tesla show began, the lights under the circus tent were dimmed. The audience became silent. The tall, rail thin man dressed in a white tuxedo wore the highest, white top hat ever seen in these parts. He walked out in white shoes with six-inch cork soles. Clad in all white, the young, dapper Tesla surely enjoyed the wonder of the crowds but they went quiet not sure what to do or how to respond. Some people gasped, some laughed and some told others to be quiet. Walking slowly onto the top of the large metal plate labeled AC, Tesla held his cane aloft until the crowd became silent. When he tossed his cane to the side, his assistant flipped the switch.

The huge plate vibrated, creating an ephemeral light emanating from Tesla's body. The aura discharged splinters of luminosity while emitting halos and glimmers of pure light. After the longest few seconds of Reginald's young life, the switch was prematurely turned off for the lad in awe. The heavenly lights vaporized. The full house was stunned silent. Tesla stepped down and bowed graciously and the crowd exploded into jubilation, ecstasy and screaming with admiration. The boy never forgot the wonder of the electric man in the white hat.

Nanny let Reginald have two nickels and he spent one on a science magazine. He read how Tesla put the maximum amount of voltage, vibrating a million times per second through his body. The genius knew and applied the secrets of electricity, the frequency harmonized with the rate of recurrence of the human body. He had worked out the mathematics to secure his personal safety. The lad remembered reading that fascinating story to both of his house butlers.

Even as the years past, Reginald saved the newspaper article about the most popular show at the World's Fair. It read *an actual flame is produced by the agitation of electrostatically charged molecules. The curious spectacle can be seen of puissant, white ghostly flames that do not consume anything bursting from the ends of an induction coil, as though it were the bush on holy ground.*

Reginald recollected that one special memory. The one dream surviving the agonizing Depression, long after memories of his family money being lost had faded.

***

Later that day, Reginald met with Mr. H.W. Wembly, Assistant Medical Examiner of the County Coroner's office. After briefly investigating the body of Dr. Nikola Tesla he mumbled, "Excuse me, I have completed my preliminary autopsy."

Impatient to learn what more problems were to threaten his job from his delinquent tenant, Reginald demanded, "And?"

Without a breath the coroner finished the sentence, "And, Nikola Tesla died of a coronary thrombosis." He stood there staring and waiting, apparently proud of the report's brevity.

The Desk Manager glared impatiently "And?"

The diminutive Wembly adjusted his heavily starched collar before reporting. "There were no suspicious circumstances beyond that, except Nikola Tesla evidently was from an Orthodox background and died on the Orthodox Christmas. At 10:30 PM on January 7th, 1943, Nikola Tesla, an 87-year old man died of natural causes. It is all simple as that, simple as death."

Reginald was silent for a moment, and then concluded, "And, so it is." He added, "Be good enough to make sure the body is removed promptly."

Waiting for a nod of acknowledgement, the medical examiner countered, "We need to identify and contact the closest relative".

Reginald dismissively flicked his fingers. "Don't tell me my job. You just do yours."

The frail examiner shook his head and left. Turning back to his desk, the manager dialed the five-digit telephone number listed on the guest ledger. Fortunately, someone answered "Hello?" Reginald asked "Mr. Kenneth Swezey?"

"Yes, May I help you?"

"I regret to inform you your friend Nikola Tesla, has passed away."

After a pause, Swezey chocked back his sobs by asking, "How?"

Reginald responded most professionally, "Quietly and naturally in his bed."

"Thank you," Swezey exhaled softly.

"My condolences, sir"

"Thank you, good bye."

Reginald hung up.

***

Both the OSS and FBI notes were clear; Kenneth Swezey was later verified as an American patriot. His name does not deserve impugning even though he was under investigation. This was wartime and A.I. kept an agent watching him.

Swezey hung up looked at his wall clock to see the time: 9:55 and immediately called their mutual friend, Dr. Paul Rado at New York University. Ken was the rare person who knew Rado's real name was Radosavljevich. During the war, such knowledge was best left unspoken.

Professor Rado knew one of Tesla's two known relatives, who understood the need for protocol. He called King Petar's headquarters at 745 Fifth Avenue. The Serbo-Croatian minister agreed to notify Tesla's nephew, Sava Kosanovic, son of Marica Kosanovic, Tesla's distant sister.

After Rado informed Kosanovic, the diplomat answered crisply, "Yes, yes, I knew it was going to happen soon." Kosanovic rubbed his nose. "Thank you for your kindness, Nikola thought highly of you as well. If you will excuse me now, I must attend to urgent matters." Kosanovic quietly waited for the painfully long chattering condolences to end. He hung up.

Besides A.I., only Kosanovic and the FBI knew about Tesla's other nephew, Trbojevich, who was born in America and far less foreign thinking. Trbojevich didn't want to get involved with politics, Tesla or the government; he wanted to be left alone.

But this was war time. There were good reasons J. Edgar Hoover and A.I. operated on the certainty all Yugoslavs were suspects. Only three years earlier, Regent Paul had agreed to a pact with Hitler, committing Yugoslavia to join the Axis. The palace revolt only reinforced OSS views. It did not matter the Serbian military had plotted a successful coup, replacing Prince Paul with the seventeen year-old King Petar II. It was too little, too late. The war had already started by March 1941. The very young Prince was unable to protect or hold his country together. The Balkans was exploding into flames and innumerable race and ideology wars.

The Americans did not trust the Serbs, Croats, Montenegrins, and Fascist, Communist or any others. And none of the factions trusted each other.

From the beginning of the war, the nephew Sava and Nikola spoke only to boost each other's sense of nationalism and to argue politics. They discussed and debated over the dailies. They only agreed on one point, their homeland was being ravaged by Nazi attacks and Partisan revolts. They shared the same sorrow. No nation lost a greater percentage of its entire people than the Yugoslavs during this world war.

Fitzgerald had been briefed on this Kosanovic fellow. During the war, A.I. didn't need permission to wiretap a foreign agent. They maintained lists of all Southern Slavs living on the East Coast. Everyone knew Yugoslavia was dominated by fratricidal wars, regional battles, and ideological warfare. It didn't matter if they were Serbs or Croats, Communist or Nazi's; Hoover and the Generals classified all Slavs as suspects.

Tenements, 53rd St

Fitzgerald's notes repeated his views, 'I did not join the Army Intelligence to become a gumshoe'. Since he was not given a choice, his only option was to catch up with Katy. The winter wind was merciless. Unable to wrap a coat tight enough, the faster he ran, the more he slipped.

The streets were oily from the continuing stream of passing construction trucks. Katy struggled not to fall as she walked home carrying a small bag of groceries. The sidewalk was as grimy as the street. Half a block behind her while attempting to gasp for air, Fitzgerald rested his hand on a nearby abandon car. The glove stuck to the half frozen oil and he had to leave it to keep up with her.

Fitzgerald ran and caught sight of her as Katy saw George at a distance. She was nervous and frantically looking herself over, holding her breath to prop up her chest, trying very hard to walk faster to her lover.

He was the wiry, immaculately dressed gentleman standing next to her staircase. He wore thin, expensive gold spectacles, a well-trimmed moustache and a spruce hat. Fitzgerald did not need A.I. to tell him this was all wrong.

As Katy approached her stairway, he recited a poem. His full lips recited flowing words that were never to leave Katy's mind. She memorized every word;

> *And flits on to confess,*
> *His great loves and small*
> *He tells each affair,*
> Each tender adventure ...
> Casanova is here."

Katy had never been so happy. This was the first day she ever wanted to come home. It was obvious she remained in denial about what was waiting. Fitzgerald wrote 'George was a dapper looking and suave man who most assuredly had encountered an exaggerated number of the Continent's finest women.'

Now, he had chosen her, who cares why. Katy walked slower to relish the moment, before her words tripped over her tongue. She was willing to say anything. It didn't matter he was older. He was striking and wanted her.

Katy never stuttered before or since. She wrote and rewrote one fact in her diary 'he knew how to wear an ascot with a hat'. Her writing repeated dreamy thoughts 'he wants me'. She didn't care if he had demands. She knew they very well could be hers. These were not exactly stolen papers; they were being returned to their rightful owner, George. It was wonderful how bliss absolved her confusion.

While Katy nervously walked towards him, George smiled, watching this middle-aged maid struggle to stand tall. She pulled her blouse tight and held her breath to expand her chest. She held the grocery bag to her side. He extended his hand and led her up the stairs.

What she did not know and what A.I. just learned – George was an actor, traveling incognito since the war. His real name was Claudius DiDomenico. He had effectively modified his dialect to sound like the German George Viereck. Like a pro, both of the accents were tailored in America.

The real George Viereck was locked safely away in a federal prison. As a corporate spy, Claudius certainly knew what he wanted. He didn't care about the war. He was being paid by Marconi Radio in Europe to subvert a court case in America, a Supreme Court case. He had to make numerous contacts quickly and to this end, DiDomenico assumed the identity of George Viereck for a specific reason.

A.I. had already identified the Italian agent. Katy was never to realize he was the spy, Claudius, who had assumed a prisoner's identity.

Fitzgerald learned A.I. was ill equipped to deal with a corporate spy. The rules require they be treated as civilians, who were criminals. A.I. had to learn a new angle to beat the bad guys under old rules. The new rules were to ignore the old rules.

Katy's seedy tenement was easy for our technical plant man, Donald J., the cagiest engineer in A. I. He took a little getting used to as his deep voice did not fit his wiry body. He was the only man Fitzgerald ever met who spoke in a rapid baritone. Fortunately

Donald J. seldom talked, he just worked at tinkering. He hid a microphone in the hallway and three more inside the room while drilling, two disguised peepholes to monitor Katy and her lover. The two never knew A.I. was next door and would have an agent being nauseated by their naked, writhing bodies fumbling through sex.

As Katy walked up to the stairs George put his hand out and turned her to the stairs. She was uneasy near George and stumbled. With little effort he caught her by the shoulders and whispered "Falling are we?" He obviously enjoyed her hunger.

The matron of dirty rooms dropped her head down for a moment. She stood frozen before her blushing face glanced upwards to say, "Good day."

His Roman nose and Mediterranean eyes were most expressive and appeared to care. "My precious Katy, you don't look well, shall we go inside and get you something to drink?"

Her stuttering started when she looked up "Yeah… that would be better than apple sauce." They laughed together.

Slowly George put his thin arm around Katy's thick shoulders, turning her towards the staircase leading up to her apartment. She could not stop trembling, not with his hand remaining on her shoulder, she struggled to straighten.

Attempting the first step up the stairs, Katy lurched. His quick hand dropped to her waist and caught hold. He pulled a little extra, with the familiarity of a lover. Katy gasped an anxious breath before her head struggled to steady. George calmly took the grocery bag from her hand while extending tender support, one awkward step after another.

Her hands shook, attempting to put her key into the outside door lock. George put his hand around hers and guided the key into the hole. She willingly and nervously accepted, "Thank you."

"Relax Katy. It's good to see you. Why don't you buy that dress covered with all those yellow Roses? The one you told me about? I'm on the level."

"I… know, I mean, I will." "Watch that step."

"Thanks, I'm sorry, thank… you."

They stopped inside the foyer to check the mail but there was none. Side by side, they continued down the stale boarding room hall to her narrow door. The air would have been musty were it not for the chill. George softly removed his deft hand. She looked long at him quietly, helplessly. George held her wrist, guiding the key go into her keyhole. The agent could hear her groan. The warped door needed a little shove to open.

The apartment door swung open to a small studio, with the bathroom door left open. George put his hand on her tense arm and led her over to the only chair, an overstuffed, well-worn sofa. The hotel was going to throw it away but, it ended up being Katy's bonus last year. The manager offered her three dollars in cash. She wanted the couch with a few pieces of furniture to call her own. George guided her into the chair, "Here, sit down for a moment. Can I offer a glass of water?"

The deep chair hugged her hips. That wasn't the reason she struggled to breathe, "Yes, please. Her eyes followed his every step over to the sink.

His thin stripped suit was tailored to assure his pants flowed without losing their crease. This man, this man in her room, with one motion picked up the glass and filled it without a splash. It was more amazing for the faucet splattered every time she used it.

Returning George raised one eyebrow, ever so slightly. Tipping towards her as if he were toasting a goblet to the queen, Katy smiled. He gracefully bent over to hand her the water. "Here drink this, you will feel much better."

Katy timidly looked up to accept the water. He guided her hands and helped the water reach her trembling lips. Kindly George lifted the glass away and looked into her eyes, "Now, do you feel better?"

"Yes." Katy struggled to hold the glass. George pulled the wooden chair over next to her and sat down in one movement.

He was suddenly stern and demanded "Where are the papers?"

"In the drawer."

"Which drawer?"

"The drawer under the hot plate next to the ice box."

George returned to the sink to pull open the drawer. He picked up the three small piles of neatly typed notes, then smiled broadly, "Good, good, good job, Katy. I knew we would enjoy working together." He paused, "Why do you keep papers in that drawer and not the silverware?"

"I don't have any silverware."

"You do not have any silverware, we will have to fix that." He nodded knowingly.

She explained like it was an apology "I just have those knives forks and spoons from the hotel. They're in the sink."

"We will have to buy you some silver before you have me over for dinner" He offered.

He carefully put the four small piles in order and murmured the title, "A Method of Producing Powerful Radiations". Looking over at her, George smiled. "Would you like some more water?"

Accidentally spilling the water from her nearly empty glass, Katy jumped up and sputtered, "Sure, sure yeah. I would like some very much. Are y-you, I mean did I do good?"

"Yes, my dear they are the right ones but, not quite all of them. Where are the rest?"

"The rest?"

"Of course, my dear, what did you leave behind?"

"I... I don't know. There were so many piles of papers and all looked important. I..." Katy turned away.

George stared at her, reassuring his pigeon,

"Well, not to worry Katy, you did fine."

Turning halfway back she stammered "Really?" Smiling, George asked, "My sweet Katy, are you sure I can trust you?"

"Anything I mean yes, yes, you can."

George pulled out his wallet and picked out two twenty dollar bills, placing them carefully into her hand. He quietly, forcibly articulated each word; "America is going to trust you take this money and buy you the dress and then find that one setting of silver you will always cherish. Now, the hard part is you must never, ever tell any-one I gave it to you or you will put our country in harm's way. You wouldn't do that, would you?"

With eyes darting back and forth between George's soft gaze and the money, Katy blurted, "Yes, No, No."

"Good girl you know what you have to do?" "Shall I go back and get the rest?"

"I do not think that would be a good idea just now. In fact promise me that you will not discuss this with anyone and swear you won't go back into that room until I tell you, okay?"

Sure, okay, whatever you want."

"Good girl. Now I need to go and revisit my old friend's apartment."

"Do you know Dr. Tesla?"

"Of course that is why I want his personal belongings protected. And that is why, I must trust you to never tell anyone… there is a war going on."

"Sure, I know. I read you know."

Elgin Ship Building Company - 24th St.

In later years Fitzgerald regretted his photographic memory. When young, he was full of the 'bop'. He later wrote; "Age has taught me better. This is now, that was then. Life is a long time." His reports were detailed and far too wordy.

Fitzgerald's notes on the interested party meeting were extensive. After turning on the light of the small New York office of the Elgin Ship Building Company of New Orleans, Fitzgerald walked over to the side of the window and slowly studied 24th Street. Across the street, underneath the canopy shadow, a hefty figure moved along the walls. His shadow flickered across the rows of brownstones. Carrying an attaché, he lumbered under the canopied porch. Fitzgerald pulled the curtain closed and sat behind the desk.

His notes read: 'I was assigned all potential leads regarding Tesla. The service wanted educated supervision of the project. It didn't matter whether I signed on for any of these assignments. The fact was my vote didn't count. As the most qualified Tesla expert, my knowledge was meant to be utilized by the Service for this one. A dead genius leaves many a sleepless night behind for those who have to chase after the world's most awesome weapon.'

'Opening the center desk drawer, I carefully slipped in the black binder entitled, *Government*. Putting my feet up on the Spartan desk, directly over the drawer, I turned on the radio. I rotated the dial until I heard Benny Goodman's clarinet spinning a young man's heart with George Gershwin's 'Somebody Loves Me'. I locked my hands behind my head and leaned back, whistling.

'Looking back, I have no idea why I ignored the first knock. Minutes after the second knock, the office door opened slowly. The president of National Latex Corporation of Dover cautiously put his head through the opening.

"Come in, Mr. Spanel." Spanel opened the door wider, looked at each side of the room, and walked in quickly. After pulling the door behind him shut, he walked over with his hand out. "Good evening, Mr. Fitzgerald."

Not sure how seriously to take this assignment. This rich guy was looking for Tesla's inventions and A.I. only needed those bringing money or solutions.

He sat on the only available chair, a wooden one and was overly polite. "If I may call you Fitzgerald, I deeply regret the untimely death of your mentor. I have been on a long drive. May we dispense with formalities?"

"By all means Mr. Spanel" I offered, "How may I help you?"

Pulling out a newspaper article, Spanel carefully unfolded the copy, revealing the *New York Times* head-line, 'Death Ray for Planes'. He looked up for my reaction.

Fitzgerald didn't blink.

Spanel asked, "If I may read you what this newspaper says, perhaps you could enlighten me with the rest". As an experienced CEO he read with authority, "The Teleforce would operate through a beam one one-hundred millionth of a square centimeter in diameter... which could melt any engine... ignite the explosive aboard any bomber... A dozen... plants... would be enough to defend the country against all possible aerial attack."

Pausing to look over his glasses he asked, "You say you worked for this Dr. Tesla and saw this happen? Where is the prototype?"

Thinking to himself, Fitzgerald hated he wasted another evening on some fools dream before explaining. "It's real hot stuff. If it existed, I'd know about the humdinger."

Realizing he was not being taken seriously, Spencer's tone became stern "Can you build it?"

Fitzgerald threw his feet down to the floor and leaned forward to determine how committed his resources were. "We need a 'box-man' fast to get into Tesla's safe. I have his notes and can build the prototype if we can locate the weapon and pick it up soon."

The CEO stared without moving.

Fitzgerald explained, "Did you know we are working at MIT on the resolution of certain problems regarding the dissipation of energy from rapid fire weapons?"

Spencer became a bit too excited. "I heard your explanation at the engineering conference last year. How long would it take to build a working model?"

"If I can build my team, we can end the war in 18 months."

He asked like he had it "How much?"

"Two million... to start," Fitzgerald answered without blinking.

"Two million dollars, do you realize there's not a corporation in America that can raise that kind of seed money?"

It didn't matter, this was the war. "It will require a government contract and I repeat two million to start."

Fitzgerald never figured where he got off lecturing "I know what you mean by beginning money and that you engineers are all alike. In truth, you really need three times that amount."

Fitzgerald lowered his voice as he acknowledged "But, the return on investment would be incalculable." The young physicist expounded the obvious, "It would dictate the victor of any war. After all, how much does, say, an air corps cost?"

Spencer sunk into deep thought. He scratched his chin before asking, "What other insurmountable problems are there?"

"The FBI office in Washington has the attention of J. Edger Hoover himself and he can make it happen or make sure it will never happen."

After moving his chair closer to the desk, Spanel leaned forward "I have discussed this with the FBI. This is of grave national interest to our country, wouldn't you agree?"

"I have also discussed the matter with our intelligence." We sat back and took new note of each other.

"Do you have weapon's documentation?"

"Of course" Fitzgerald said with the arrogance of youth. Spanel was no fool "How did you come by this document?"

"I was the last one to be with Dr. Tesla. I was the last one to hear his wishes."

Spanel lifted his attaché case onto the desk. He was constantly moving, balancing the papers on his knees even though his huge belly robbed him of a lap. Spanel looked down at a newspaper article before pulling out another, "The four basic principles to the death beam are; number one, a method for producing rays in free air without a vacuum; number two is a way to generate a very great electrical force, three is a method of amplifying the force; and number four is a method for producing a tremendous electrical propel-ling force." He asked, "Is this correct?"

"Absolutely."

Reading from the Times article, the CEO was closing his deal, "What you are saying here is that you have each and every one of the documents, covering all four areas?"

Fitzgerald answered, "I have seen his notes." Spaniel greed was clear "Can you build it?"

"Will Rogers once declared, 'It ain't brag if it's the truth', and the fact is there is no one more qualified on this planet." Fitzgerald was hoping to bait him to finance the project. Spanel's left hand covered his chin as he continually stroked his cleft, "We will need clearance from the FBI."

"What do you have in mind?"

Spanel's thick eyelashes lifted as he spoke. "If we bring to Mr. Hoover's attention that Tesla's nephew Sava Kosanovic is giving family papers to the Axis powers in support of his exiled King Petar. He will lose control of Tesla's papers."

"And I know how to tip Hoover's mitt." Fitzgerald offered, "Call me when you have the money."

George Viereck's - 1001 Madison Ave

A.I. had learned where George lived on Madison and was fortunate to have found a vacancy next door. Even though the stateside budget was thin, the apartment was secured for ninety days and put Donald J. to work wiring the recording in every room.

George was cagey with his alter ego or stage name or whatever was going on in his conspiring mind. Without an ID Claudius had subleased a Manhattan suite under the perplexing pseudonym George Sylvester Viereck. Most interesting, A.I. was surprised he did not need any false identification to rent in George's name. Ample cash proved to work quickly during the war, especially in these overpriced brown-stones.

After moving in, Claudius would put on heavy boots and practiced marching across the chevron-patterned floor to Mussolini's Fascist Marching Song. He high kicked across the art deco interior and knew he could bill Marconi in London. The walls and ceiling of a window alcove were covered in silver leaf, and orange and yellow linen cushions contrasted with the violet, green and gray of the draperies and with the black glass fireplace mantle bordered with beetle green wood and Formica. In spite of his Jumping around his apartment in stage leaps, never revealed where Donald J. hid his work.

Claudius preferred staying in character as George. He wrote it was the only time he was not lonely. After closing his diary he pulled out the stolen documents from the cabinet. The little Italian was usually nervous, and this new style of indirect lighting confused his aging eyes. George accidentally dropped the papers on the silver-gray carpet. Without his glasses, he fumbled to pick up the schematics. His unfamiliarity with handling papers proved telling. He cursed himself in Italian, *"Troiaio"* after crumpling one of the pages.

With a deep breath, he pulled himself up on the swivel chair covered in bright Chinese red leather. He loved his décor, he often talked to it. The dining room's black and white colors created a busy background behind the shiny black round table. Deco decorum was all too confusing and repeatedly tricked his bifocals but it was so very vogue. After hours of searching through the three-inch pile of assorted documents, he found a title page. The actor couldn't interpret the endnotes of manuscripts as profound as a 'Method of Producing Powerful Radiations'. He sat back and stared at the wall and said "Nikola Tesla what can you tell me?"

A.I. was astounded by the background materials found in his room. Claudius wrote about one night where the intellectuals' lived. Back then, George would still have been living on W113th Street, off Riverside Drive. The writer was often the host parties where everyone came early and none would dare depart until the next morning. This was the time where music and dancing was subordinated to talk and discussion. Tesla was prone to entering the room quietly. A stranger would hardly have been aware of his presence. That night was spellbinding with the lean man whose eyes and ideas blazed like a blue light for it was a night among friends.

That night, Nikola recounted his life story simply and with quiet eloquence. He told of his platonic affairs of the heart. Tesla spoke with guileless simplicity about his work preceding the bandit Marconi and his deep belief that the Supreme Court would soon rule him as originator of wireless communications. The royalties for the radio could be substantial. The world's greatest inventor quietly confessed he needed the money.

Having no illusions, Claudius prepared well for the forthcoming court trial of Tesla versus Marconi and the invention of the radio were why his generous patrons sent him to New

York. It was a matter of wartime convenience that payments came through London. Marconi Radio had offices in England. They realized the limitations of Guglielmo Marconi's experiments with the radio and Tesla's role in their history would dictate their personal future and fortunes. Tesla's lawsuit had to be stopped. The Marconi court case seemed to have no relationship with George's court case, except here, now that Tesla is dead. Claudius was enamored with secretly using George Sylvester Viereck's identity, stealing the weapon and assuring contact with Nazis in New York. The rare opportunity to live a challenging role was his reward, for Claudius was a disciplined student of his acting profession.

Alone in his room, he practiced George's poetry that worked so very well with Katy,

> *"Shall be my pillow, mindful that the thorn.*
> *Still pricks and rankles when the rose dies"*

Claudius wrote that he well understood the opportunity and limitations of playing George. As he expected on September 21st, the United States Court of Appeals for the District of Columbia agreed with the District Court that George Viereck violated at least one element of the federal Propaganda Agency Act. His jail time was expected to be lengthened.

The case must have been an interesting read for Claudius; it certainly was for the A.I. agents scouring his notes. Even though George failed to register 'their' way, he did register and file every one of those supplemental statements. The fact his reports were not exactly true didn't change the fact the British lies were far worse. The Brits wanted to drag the U.S. into the war to save their own fish and sticks, just like they had done in the last war. Actually they sold Americans on the idea that entering European combat would make the last war the last war not the root cause of the next War. The U.S. bit the British bait every time. George wrote he knew the British were to blame for fingering him. The British needed American weapons and needed them all. And so it was. The U.S. government sided with the British. For his advocating peace, George was railroaded for sedition and, for what? He was guilty of trying to keep the U.S. out of the war? In those days

Washington made all major legal decisions and enemies were instantly generated.

George's battle was already lost. The District of Columbia grand jury indicted him on July 24, 1942. Along with twenty-eight assorted, conspirators, isolationist, anti-Communist, anti-Semites, Fascist, German Bundists and mixed rabble-rousers with their violations of the Sedition Act breaching sections of both the Espionage Act of 1917 and the Smith Act of 1940. A.I. was secretly pleased George did not really belong in jail.

Fitzgerald questioned the report "how can they claim he did not reveal his activities? He made his reports. George did not hate Americans or Jews. He registered his $500 a month stipend from both the Munich Newspaper and the German Library of Information. He had been a professional journalist for decades, what did they expect? Sure, he organized and, sure, he was active in 'Make Europe Pay War Debts', 'Islands for War Debts' and 'War Debts Defense." Fitzgerald's' answer was simply "so?"

The Court saw only that one book, with the fearful title "Spreading Germs of Hate". The real George had been a professional journalist for decades, what did they expect? George supported his homeland, Germany. Hitler provided the populist response to the insufferable Treaty of Versailles. The petty and vindictive treaty never ceased humiliating every German who loved their homeland. George was born a German before he became a journalist.

***

Claudius sat, alone, with his head resting on his light oak table. It didn't matter where anyone was sitting. He felt utterly alone. If George was freed, Claudius knew he would have to flee. The case before the Supreme Court was scheduled for February 1st. That was next month.

Certainly Tesla knew Viereck would never be a traitor. Nikola understood what it was to be a patriot who loved his homeland. With every news reel from Europe, Hitler was testing the mettle of every proud German patriot in America with blood ties to the Fatherland. The real George remained in prison while the forces of war continued to move forward.

After staring at the wall Claudius picked up his leather attaché and pulled out his newly acquired documents. Smiling broadly, he let his thumb run up the sides and fanned the pages.

There was no one in the room when he said "George I am sorry you are in prison and I feel your pain. Do you even know your close friend Nikola was dead?" Claudius waved his arms with grandeur. "Enough of this nonsense for I am George." To the A.I. spotter's surprise, as the first tear rolled down George jumped up, hurried to the sink and washed his face. Returning to admire the documents, with a long breath the *Uomo universal*, the man of all arts realized what he had and sat back down at the table with his grand prize.

Three sharp knocks on the front door startled him. George first walked to the mirror to review his presentation. The knuckles outside rapped ever harder.

"Yes, yes," George walked to the door. Glancing back at the table, he saw Tesla's papers. Momentarily muddled he turned and hurried back to hide the documents in the pantry. With one last deep breath before answering, he pulled his jacket tight and opened the front door.

A broad, powerfully built blond—the true model of an Aryan superman—stood for a second, quickly scanned the room and then, without hesitation or invitation, marched inside. The German's black three piece suit was immaculate, stretching to accommodate his beefy build. The smaller Italian hurried to move aside. George shook for a moment then cleared his throat and satirically offered, "Come in, come in."

Turning, the German visitor glared directly into the small nervous eyes, he demanded "Who are you?" He didn't wait for an answer until he asked the second question. "Why are you pretending to be George Viereck?"

Even though he anticipated this meeting, George was taken aback by the muscularity and force of this visitor. The Nazi seemed to suck the air out of the room while inspecting personal details. Barely able to apologize from his sudden dry mouth, George gagged for a moment. "Excuse me I caught something in my throat." George vainly attempted to clear while speaking, "I wanted to meet you. I was quite sure this charade would bring you to me."

The German had a deep voice with a punctuated sharpness "You have succeeded. You have not answered my question. What do you want?"

Even though Claudius had been on stage most of his life, he stammered when depending on his own lines. "I want to offer you the greatest weapon ever created."

The officer demanded, "Who are you?"

"My name is Claudius, a representative of the Marconi Company."

Looking him up and down the German asked, "I understood Marconi was in the radio business, not the weapon business."

"We are however… we have an opportunity here. Are you interested?"

"I don't believe you have anything of value. Show me what you have."

Looking miffed George stood straighter, "What is your name?"

"Wilhelm Von Haak. Call me Wilhelm." He extended his huge hand with the certitude of a European nobleman.

"Very well please come in, make yourself comfortable."

Von Haak walked across the room while continuing to study the odd room of dark furniture and chestnut floors. He was trained to analyze people through their living quarters. The ivory walls had a brass *torchere* set off the ample moonlight pouring through French doors, an effeminate trait. Von Haak looked at little man. Training produced a polite smile, "Shall I call you George?"

George returned the gesture with a nobleman's nod, "And, so I shall be honored to call you Von Haak."

The German instinctively snapped his heals as he facetiously answered, "When in America, do as the American's"

"As you wish, come, let's sit in my study." George led him down the hall to his private quarters. Von Haak asked about multiple timepieces under an early 1900s print framed in black lacquer. "Why does a grown man need two clocks?"

"Ambiance" the Italian said with a touch of arrogance.

There seemed a subconscious cadence between the two. They walked into the back library and sat in the chairs across from each other. Von Haak looked around at the study, which was filled with lamps, each with a different nude female holding a uniquely shaped light globe. The expansive fireplace burned below the chevrons and curves of a gilt eagle's wings, sitting on a similarly gilt mantel, featuring Egyptian symbols carved in bas-relief.

Von Haak said "Living a pretentious life is not healthy. You have a very nice home. I see the Fatherland is well represented."

Not sure what the Nazi really meant, George sounded defensive "I was earning far more as a journalist."

"The war requires much from each of us." Von Haak pulled out a fag and pounded it against the pack.

Too nervous to ask him not to smoke, George cringed as the flame lit the Lucky Strike. The host quickly placed a teacup saucer on the table next to the German.

Von Haak slowly inhaled the cigarette before observing, "You now assert you were a spokesman for the Fatherland and now you have the opportunity to be a master spy, don't you?" He took another slow drag, without looking at his trembling host.

Switching hands to cover his nose, George was uncomfortable with the cigarette's thick, heavy blue-gray smoke floating past him. George stood and walked over to the Motorola to put on a platter and asked, "May I offer Wagner's *Das Rheingold,* as the Gods enter into the Valhalla?" After receiving a subtle nod, George turned back to set the arm down on the spinning 78. Sitting back down, the two Europeans relaxed while the symphony filled the air and after a few relaxing minutes, George used his forefinger as a wand in harmony.

Quietly enjoying George's fidgeting, Von Haak pretended to care. "Yes, yes it has been much too long to be away from our classics." Von Haak snubbed the cigarette on the food plate.

The small Italian continually adjusted his position, sinking into the reclining chair. After considerable straightening up, he struggled to look more relaxed. George blurted, "You know the Supreme Court hearing is soon."

The visitor continued dissecting the room while maintaining the conversation, "Yes, yes, we have been following it closely."

"Every grand jury and every trial has been lost by your agent, George." Claudius leaned forward.

Von Haak's eyes locked onto the set of distant drawers. "Yes, yes but, now George will have the opportunity to stand before the American Supreme Court. The good German is not guilty of breaking the law. Is that not correct?"

Raising his voice in measured tones Claudius pointed out, "I assure you the court has noticed there is a war. And in war, the scales of justice always favor the accuser."

Von Haak turned sharply and locked his eyes on his host "We sympathize with George's plight and have maintained a stipend benefiting him for nearly a decade."

Without the energy to hold his shoulders erect any longer, sagging Claudius dutifully agreed, "I appreciate what the Fatherland has provided. We want you to know the Marconi Company continues to work diligently for success of the Axis powers."

Von Haak asked "What is your progress?" Feigning obedience, Claudius spoke his words perfectly, "You are aware, Dr. Nikola Tesla died yesterday."

"Of course, we were saddened by the death of his genius. We were quite disappointed by our failure to recruit him."

"He applied his genius to everything his contracted sponsors asked of him." Claudius purposefully sounded defensive as he began his sales presentation.

Hesitant at first Von Haak maintained his composure before challenging, "You are telling me you know he had a weapon capable of winning the war. You need to reexamine your own mind. What we need is to win the war. What we need is to have the finest armaments in the world. What we have is the genius and resolve to achieve this end. What we need is for all loyalists to do their duty."

George blurted out his words in one breath "What I mean is that his death ray weapon was completed."

Von Haak had the eyes of a predator and the patience of a floating falcon. Without the least emotion he asked "I presume you know where this weapon is hidden?"

For the first time, Claudius looked directly at Von Haak to study his reaction as he lied, "He never built it."

"How do you know such a weapon will achieve all that it claims?"

"I personally know of his genius," Claudius explained with great confidence.

"Insufficient."

The Italian felt the power of his role, "Were you to have known Tesla's brilliant mind you would know everything he created in his brain defined the annals of science? He wrote over 800 patents... created in his mind, lying in bed at night thinking, focusing, having the brilliance to think one single thought while understanding and redefining every permutation and ramification."

He continued, "Do you know he wrote every patent from his photographic memory? His memory of each creation was written after focusing for days on one thought. His creation of light, the radio we are listening to and the knowledge of power itself." It seemed as if Claudius paused for a pregnant moment expecting audience adoration of some nature.

The Nazi showed no emotions. "Yes, yes, most interesting history. I am sure you know your target well. We shall judge what is useful. Where is this project... now that Tesla is dead?"

"He had written extensive preparations for his patent."

Von Haak asked, "You know where he keeps these documents?"

"Of course."

With a glint in his eye Von Haak concluded "Upon building such a weapon Germany's problems will disappear. The fool Americans antiquated Constitution makes little sense. This prosecution of Viereck is strictly for publicity to bolster their sagging morale and has no chance of succeeding. Only a fool would take their ploy serious. The aspirations of the Fatherland are critical and nothing else matters."

Surprised to hear that the German knew his alter ego, George asked "Wilhelm, when did you meet Viereck?"

"We met in Berlin over ten years ago. Why?"

"You seemed preoccupied by him."

"Why would the subject come up now?"

"There are rumors, vicious rumors, about death camps. What do you know of this Heir Rippentrop?"

The falcon turned to his prey and without emotion put the fear of the Führer in the little Italian. Von Haak stated "I resent such a tone and would advise against taking such an attitude again."

After a glance at Von Haak, Claudius looked down. "Forgive me if it came out that way, for I only was pained by these rumors of civilian detention centers."

Von Haak asked, "Is your concern with the Jews?"

Claudius carefully alleged, "My concern is with an image history will never erase nor forgive. My concern is with Jews, Slavs, Gypsies and children. My concern is with those who cannot understand that I remain 99 percent with the Fuhrer and 100 percent with the Axis alliance, regardless of what direction the American court takes. My heart will always be dedicated to the rebirth of Europe and that will never waiver."

Von Haak spoke with the cadence of a storm trooper "Ninety-nine percent, George? Claudius or whoever you are you a making a dangerous mistake."

Standing George asked. "What if those stories are true?"

"My Fuehrer has achieved victory in defiance of their false propaganda. And you of all people should know the value of such twisted propaganda is to the American war effort." Von Haak studied the swaggering Italian walking around the room.

With the authority of Mussolini, Claudius lifted his chin. "The Americans could have created far better propaganda than pretending to support the Jews. The American's won't even let the Jews on the same beach. They are hypocrites. I have far more

Jewish friends than any American I know." His voice gained strength explaining "The American's are all complicit anti-Semitics. Whereas it must be said I will always preserve my intellectual integrity. If I write about the new Germany, I shall do so with unfettered support."

Stopping in front of the curtain, he grabbed one side and swept it open, letting the sun temporarily blind Von Haak. Turning, he walked towards the German covering his eyes. "But I shall retain a sense of detachment. As far as *Il Duce*, my Mussolini, is concerned, we have a stupendous achievement in fashioning a new economic and social world out of the wreck of the old. Our countries owe their leaders everything. Let's just hope Fascism never has to rewrite our own history, like the American's have." Abruptly Von Haak stood. Claudius looked over and asked, "Forgive me. May I offer you a drink?"

In one of his blitzkrieg mood swings, Von Haak smiled "Let us take a page from our training manuals on how to act like an American. We should drink a martini." Von Haak smiled.

"Yes, yes I think I will, Wilhelm." George laughed nervously at his own play on words. He walked quickly to the liquor cabinet. After stirring the Dry Gin into two short stemmed glasses of tonic and ice, George handed one drink to Von Haak and toasted the three pictures on the far wall, purchased at the auction from the real George's estate. The actor had hung pictures of Kaiser Wilhelm, Joseph Goebbels and Adolph Hitler on the far wall. The Nazi raised his drink and toasted, "To our beloved Germany."

They drank in unison and as set their glasses down, Von Haak looked intensely into the salesman's eyes, "Now, my friend, tell me about this death ray. Is this the same weapon the old inventor, Dr. Tesla, bragged years ago to every newspaper that would listen?"

George said assuredly, "I do not know where he was in his development. I do know the weapon is real."

"We have developed Von Braun's rocketry and find it superior to any long distance weapon."

George protested "This weapon has infinite energy. Each city can have a force field that could repel an incoming airplane at a range of 250 miles."

"How is it you know this for sure?"

George lied with conviction, "Because I have seen Telsa's plans and documents."

"Do you have them?"

"I know where they are."

"Where?"

"I am going to pick them up tonight."

"I must accompany you." Von Haak snapped his order,

"No, it is too late. I cannot change any plans now. The American FBI and military agents are everywhere."

"I don't worry about fools," Von Haak declared with disdain.

"I do. It has not gone beyond notice they have kept Germany from creating any national presence. Were you not the one who was supposed to have developed the agent network across America, years ago?"

Von Haak sipped the last of the martini before looking at the lesser Italian. "This is the second time this evening you have used an offensive tone, Heir Viereck. I understand the pressure put upon you and must insist that you deliver such documents to me to transport to Germany immediately. Do you understand me clearly?"

George stood and explained "My work has been beyond repute. I will give my last breath for Italy, beyond that I can only do what I must. For now, I must focus on obtaining these papers. I will contact you when possible. I have far greater respect for the abilities of the Americans than you do." Von Haak took a step forward causing only a slight stammer before the Italian continued, "I have no intention of endangering this project. If you would forgive me, I have much work to do. Please do not let whoever is following you, see you leave. Unless you want to put the entire project in danger, you will excuse me now.

Wilhelm returned to the front room. George followed at a safe distance. Von Haak asked, "Why two clocks?" George readily lied, "To remind me."

"Two of everything," Von Haak concluded. "It has been too long since you have visited Europe."

"Have friends stopped giving presents?" George seemed to enjoy the taunt.

With only a parting look Von Haak turned sharply toward the front door and marched out.

Feeling like he has not exhaled for an hour, exhausted, George picked up the first of his three newspapers, the *New York Times*, and sat down to read, unable to help himself from reading the appraisals of the war out loud, "Germany's Sixth Army is holding Stalingrad, diverting several Soviet armies. The newly promoted German Field Marshal Friedrich von Paulus appears defeated already as the Soviet claim 91,000 prisoners of war. The prisoners were marched out of Stalingrad and placed on trains at Saratov and sent to Tashkent. Only half of those that reached Saratov survived. In the Stalingrad area, over 209,000 German prisoners have been killed or captured."

The odd little man threw the newspaper up in the air before congratulating himself out loud, "The German's are mine and the price is my choice. Standing up, he rubbed his cheek, "I must not rely upon her… competence."

Governor Clinton Hotel - 371 7th Ave

The problem was A.I. failed to find out about the nephew's ploy until after he stole the package and was gone. Later, A.I. was able to turn the Night Manager, who sang like a canary.

Viewers were sparse this late at night. Kosanovic and two short, muscular companions exited out of Manhattan's Pennsylvania Station. They all wore suits and the one with the long scar carried a bulky attaché case. They waited until the road was clear before crossing the corner at H Ave and 31st Street. The three marched into the Governor Clinton Hotel.

While crossing the lobby under the ornately paneled ceiling, Kosanovic searched the balcony for curious eyes. The restaurant stretching along the Seventh Avenue facade had three customers at this late hour. None of who seemed to care to watch the well-tailored tall man with a diplomat's cane or two stocky Slavs wearing suits for the first time in their lives.

The front desk manager, Harvey Palanski, was writing at his desk with his office door left open. Later during his FBI interview, Mr. Palanski admitted he was not surprised when these three men marched in. He greeted Kosanovic with an outstretched hand. The two others stayed in the background. As Harvey stood to greet his guest, the Yugoslav shook his hand with more grace than he had experienced, "Thank you for seeing us at this late hour."

Harvey asked, "Just exactly how can I help you gentlemen?" The man with the scar closed the door and sat down watching his cohort, next to the exit. Harvey continued to glance over at the guarded door until the Diplomat declared, "This is a matter of great urgency. I am the only living relative of a former tenant of yours, one Nikola Tesla. Do you remember him?"

"Very well" The manager turned and pulled an older ledger book off the shelf. He opened to the page devoted to, Nikola Tesla on his desk between them. "You are no doubt aware of his unpaid bill and are holding a package belonging to him. I see you remember. Good. I need to make sure it is safe and appreciate your concern."

"Oh, no, sorry, sir I would really like to help you but I cannot." Harvey accentuated every word with wide hand waves. "You will need to make full restitution that you must understand has exceeded $400. We must also satisfy the demands of the court"

Kosanovic interjected, "Harvey, may I call you Harvey? This container in your custody may be very dangerous. Are you aware of that risk?"

Harvey flicked his left index finger. "I don't have to go back there and no one has handled that package for quite some time. Best to leave sleeping dogs lie."

Kosanovic continued, "This problem is of grave importance to my family. Would you kindly consider a gift of our appreciation, perhaps a substantial gift?"

Harvey's finger froze. "Substantial?"

Kosanovic pressed his advantage "What would you consider substantial?"

Harvey said, "I am really quite busy. If you would be so kind as to pay the rather substantial bill, plus interest, then perhaps. Any less is out of the question."

Kosanovic smiled. "And, I trust you understand the need for discretion? If you would simply let us examine the package to ensure its safety, we would be satisfied my uncle did not leave you in danger."

Harvey asked, "Who are these two joes? Are they Americans?"

Kosanovic said, "These friends of mine escort me in this strange neighborhood. I brought them to protect the cash I have brought for you. You can respect that, can't you?"

Clasping his hands, Harvey forced a smile. "Of course security is fundamental to my position. But and I emphasize but, you must understand my position is quite sensitive. I cannot participate with any illegal activities."

Kosanovic said, "My two friends have different specialties, one carries the money and the other carries, as you American's call it, the stick. We want simply to give you the carrot. Can you please accommodate my family concerns?"

Harvey pulled out his handkerchief, "What is substantial?"

Kosanovic flipped his left hand with the palm up.

"You will keep your collateral. Would you consider $200 cash?"

"I know I would consider $400 for my risking my job. Wouldn't you agree?"

They both knew that was a month's salary.

He offered $200. cash, "Can you bring it in here and give us two minutes of privacy? We will return it to you intact and no one else ever needs to be involved. Do we have an agreement?"

"You have the cash here, now?"

With a glance from Kosanovic, the man with the attaché pulled out 10 twenty dollar bills and fanned them.

The manager stared hard at the cash, before standing and turning. "I will take one of your men to the package. Allow me a moment to assure our privacy is guaranteed."

"Of course." They moved towards the door.

Harvey glanced over at the other, thicker man and then looked back at the money. "It is good that it is a weekday, as we are empty at this hour." He handed the brown paper package to Kosanovic. "Perhaps, I should receive the money now."

Waving his hand Kosanovic agreed "Of course. My friend will give it to you."

Kosanovic ordered the second accomplice "Set the case next to the package." Reaching into the case, Kosanovic pulled out an electronic box and laughed. "My friend, allow me to introduce you to a Wheatstone bridge, a wonderful little contraption for those with electronic skills. In our case, the Wheatstone bridge is a superb mechanism for the Americans to curse."

He carefully opened the package wrap. It was disconcerting. The tape was cracked with age. Kosanovic said, "Get me the scissors." The scissors were retrieved and a delicate cut was made while carefully removing the wrap. "Hand me some tape."

The tape was lifted away. The package was not much larger than a shoe box, holding a precision instrument intertwined in some novel fashion. The meticulous man carefully removed the instruments and put a common electrical device, a Wheatstone Bridge into the package and carefully rewrapped it to make it appear it was never opened. Holding up the box, Kosanovic read out loud, "Prototype." He carefully set his prize down to wrap it. Kosanovic told his fellows, "I fear this is only part of the puzzle. Fortunately this happens to be quite a significant part. No time now. Here put this in the case and let no one near it until we return to the Sokol. We can place this inside the gymnasium for the day."

As they walked out the explanation to Harvey fell on deaf ears. Kosanovic said "Your package is now disarmed and our conscience is clear, as long as you keep your part of our agreement." The diplomat took a step toward Harvey. "You don't want to explain your income to your Internal Revenue Service and you don't want to explain to my friend here that you lied to us. Are we in agreement?"

Harvey anxiously shook Kosanovic's hand and the two never crossed paths again.

Later when confronted by the FBI, the manager testified he only went along with Kosanovic out of fear and recommended the FBI raid the Yugoslav Community center.

East River Drive

A. I. had a team watching the Italian, George. There was one close call as he almost found a microphone in his bed-room but, was too preoccupied to see it after a trip wire knocked over a lamp. Except for that time, the team was on strict watch-and-wait orders. A.I. was ordered not to make moves against any of them. The rules of war in the States were different. The Army had to show some deference to local laws yet, with a primary concern of exposing the enemy. During hostilities every action was difficult. Field Agents were warned quite strongly not to impact the civilians.

A.I. was not sure if he had more of Tesla's schematics hidden. After sneaking down to the neighborhood garage, George pulled out of the underground drive in his two-tone sedan. Scanning the street, he quickly spotted the two men wearing hats sitting in the 1940 brown Ford coupe. Hurriedly turning into traffic gave George the advantage on the next turn.

Once around the corner, George turned left into the alley and sped down the long dark trail. He was at the end of the block before the headlights turned into the alley behind. Hitting the throttle, George turned right onto the street and right at the next corner. He then turned left and right onto 36th, to shake the tail.

Donald J. had installed a radio transmitter inside his car and connected to his battery. George drove into the alley behind Katy's apartment. Her apartment lights were out. It was nearly midnight by the time he knocked on her door. After the second rap, he could see a light under the door and hear her drag her slippers. Her sleepy voice croaked, "Who is it?"

With a whisper, "It's George. It's important, open the door."

The double bolts snapped, one by one. Katy held the last lock open and peaked through her chained door. "Oh, George it is you, Oh, I'm not dressed to s-see anyone."

George ordered, "Katy, open the door and run into the bathroom."

Katy unbolted the door chain and then scampered towards the cubby hole of a toilet and sink room. George entered quickly; snapping her awake with teasing glances and giggles from Katy. She slowly closed the door, showing a glimpse of her nipple.

George turned the room light on; fondly remembering the Murphy bed was opened from the closet. How complicated it was for George to be here. Quietly closing the front door George was exhausted and dropped into a chair. His tired back welcomed settling in for five minutes. Noting his watch tick past Midnight he called, "Katy?"

From behind the toilet door Katy apologized "I am so sorry I had no idea you were coming."

Struggling to sit up straight George explained "Forgive me dear. We must talk for a moment."

"Please. I am putting on my makeup as fast as I can."

George buried his face into his hands and leaned forward to put his elbows on his knees. He repeatedly fell asleep only to snap awake.

It seemed like too many minutes later when Katy stumbled out of the bathroom with her new bathing suit, just like the one Betty Grable wore on her poster. Not at ease in her new high heels,

Katy turned awkwardly around and tried to hold her smile. She stammered "Do you like what you bought me?"

George looked blankly at this sweet woman who should have never worn a swimsuit with spiked heels twenty years and forty pounds ago. She was wearing the tight outfit now and waiting for him to speak.

Staring for a second too long, George surprised himself. He found her exciting in some raw way. "Katy, you are full of surprises."

"Do you like it, do you or do you think I ought not to wear it?" She asked with the hope of a poet's heart.

"Katy, I think you should wear whatever makes you feel good, don't you?"

"I shouldn't spend so much on this, with a war going on and all"

George knew that Katy wanted him to sweep her off her feet and carry her to bed. His taste in women was cultured, young, thin, and beautiful. Katy was none of these. She was needy, raw and lusty, and George was more excited than he had felt in years. She was also the woman who held the key to his life. The thought startled him "Katy that looks great. Perhaps we can go swimming someday."

Katy giggled. "Oh, no I never swim."

"Very well, perhaps you can put a robe on; after all it is past midnight."

"You don't like it, do you?"

"Please understand there is a matter of great urgency we must discuss and, I find you in, ah, sexy outfit, ah, most distracting. Please." George repeatedly adjusted his seat.

"Oh, I'm so sorry." Her pale skin flushed pink. Rolling over the edges of the suit, her hanging skin revealed age and a lifetime of manual labor. She stumbled in her high heels back into her bathroom.

George called through the bathroom door, "Katy, please, just slip a robe on and come back out. I'm in a terrible hurry."

The thump against the bathroom door could have been caused by any number of her awkward moves. George looked too tired to survive this evening.

Through the closed bathroom door, Katy's muffled voice struggled to answer while she was changing, "OK, yes sir, right away."

George sat back down. He sunk into the worn sofa so deeply he couldn't reach the armrest. By the time Katy's bathroom door opened, George's arms noticeably ached.

Katy came out wearing her robe and her pile-on wig. "W-why are you here, George? I'm sorry I mean, ah... what? Do you want your money back? I am sorry but I spent it. I thought you wanted me to."

"Well, Katy, we do have a problem. What you brought me wasn't exactly what I asked for, do you understand?"

"I... I am so sorry. I did not know what to do. Did I do wrong? It will take me a year to pay you back."

George enjoyed lying. "Unfortunately my dear, this is not my money. It is the... government's money and this national emergency is more important than... than anything, do you understand?"

"What emergency?"

"Katy, we must... I must get the remainder of the documents you left behind."

"I'll go back tomorrow and get the rest."

"Unfortunately, tomorrow will be too late. I need you to go back into the apartment tonight. You must get me the key. Don't worry, no one lives there now."

"I could get fired real easy for that."

"You will not be fired. Nevertheless your mission is of vital national interest and we must do it at once. Enough now go put your uniform on and we'll drive down to the hotel now. Hurry along now. There will be a nice bonus for you."

Katy scampered back into her bathroom. After a few minutes she returned, dressed in her well-worn uniform. Taking her arm, George escorted her out, down the hall backstairs and back through the alley. He led her quickly over to the side of the auto he used for work, the two-tone 1942 Studebaker. George opened Katy's door and she slid into her seat smiling.

This was the first time Katy had ever ridden in a new coup to the Hotel New Yorker. She rolled down the window, ignoring the cold wind coming in from the harbor. She put her head out the window and beamed with glee.

Pulling up on 34th Street, across the street from the hotel, George turned off the motor. "Now, put the window up." Like a child being scolded, Katy obeyed. He continued, "You must go get the key to the room and bring it here. You must not let anyone see you, do you understand?"

"Yes sir." In her diary Katy wrote she had never been so frightened in her whole life.

George commanded, "Good girl. Be careful and hurry back." Reaching across her lap, George lifted the handle and opened her door. They both held the moment, an inch apart, feeling each other breathing. George said "go".

Katy stepped out of the auto. At the corner, she rested against a streetlight pole and then stood up straight once she realized George was watching her. Walking quickly, Katy entered through the employee's side door.

Walking down the familiar hallway was not reassuring. Katy was unnerved by the sensation of going into her work area and not knowing what to do. She waved to a couple of the other maids milling around the coffee pot. Her supervisor, Rita would not be in until six in the morning, giving her plenty of time.

Katy walked over to the key locker. Looking both ways, hoping no one was looking she lifted the handle and jumped at the creaking sound.

Reaching in through the row of keys, she unfastened room 3327. Returning the ring to its floor hook, the maid clinched her fist around the key. Walking too fast and then too slow the frantic woman finally made it out the side door. She rushed down the short alleyway and into the street. George waved to catch her attention, Katy slid into the Studebaker. It pulled out into the midnight traffic.

Holding the key up with great pride, Katy announced, "See I got it, I got it just like you told me to. There is nothing to worry about, they will not miss it because they will change his lock tomorrow, now that the old man's dead and all."

The Italian looked at her and ordered "Let me have the key."

Katy placed the key in his open palm, letting her hand rest on his for a brief moment. George pulled away and pocketed it.

Pulling up in front of Katy's apartment, George trotted down the hallway, walked in and forced a smile.

He ran the back of his finger across the sad woman's cheek. "You did a good thing here, Katy." Placing a twenty-dollar bill into her hand, George winked. "Buy two sets of silver, will you?"

Katy tried to respond but could not until she blurted out, "Do I know what I should do?" Turning away, Katy opened her door and stumbled out of the auto.

George waved and sadly drove back to the hotel. Pulling up around the corner of the New Yorker, he unexpectedly parked the car. Looking into the rearview mirror, the thief stopped as he examined a new wrinkle.

He stared at his reflection and with a long breath; the old actor pulled a flashlight from the glove box. Stepping out through the winter night he grabbed his wool jacket lapels tightly.

Picking up an abandoned newspaper, George opened the pages wide and held it high, pretending to read. Walking slowly towards the elevator, he pulled his monocle from his pocket to glance at the floor dial above the door. After the long wait and a slow ride up, George turned down the hall, towards Suite 3327.

George paused at the sight of the 'Do Not Disturb' sign still hanging on the knob. He took the last few steps to the door and put the key in. The door creaked.

George pulled out his flashlight and pointed below the windows. He scanned the room. Walking into the bedroom, he recognized the box near the antique bed.

Aiming the flashlight, George read the label out loud, "Teleforce Accelerator".

Lifting the box proved far more taxing. George failed on his first attempt. He set the flashlight in his pocket and pointed the beam towards the door. Squatting down, he lifted the box with a grunt. He walked to the front room and set the box on the dining table.

Setting the flashlight on the box, he struggled to carry it to the front door. Walking out, he turned toward the nearby fire escape.

Looking down the endless floors, George turned back into the hall and set the box down. He picked it up and headed for the elevator. After a few minutes, he regained his breath and pushed floor '2'. Getting off on the second floor, George pulled the fire alarm. The siren blared. He calmly carried his prize down the last flight, and then darted out the open fire escape door.

Saturday, January 9th

The Inventory

FBI Field Office - West Broadway

As Fitzgerald walked up to the door it was opened by a young agent. A bespectacled man stood straight as a commandant and ordered "Have a seat."

Fitzgerald walked past the Field Director's desk and offered his hand, "I trust you have received my credentials?" There were many times back then Fitzgerald later admitted he could have used more tact.

With a quick handshake and a short smile, Foxworth glared and was bothered by the fact the A.I. contact was too young. He said "Yes, I have. Be assured, this office will always extend whatever support you require. I understand you have spoken with the manufacturer, Abraham Spanel?"

Fitzgerald turned to scan his bookshelves and without looking over recited the standard line. "The only reason is to assure you our sole purpose is to make sure a very dangerous weapon does not fall into the hands of the enemy." It's always interesting the way people react when you quietly scrutinize their book case.

The Field Director looked uncomfortable as Fitzgerald thumbed through his copy of *Mein Kompf.* Foxworth was hesitant for the first time as he asked "Is this the weapon Abraham Spanel is shopping his story around the agencies?"

Looking directly at him for the first time Fitzgerald said "The scientist Tesla developed a weapon of such magnitude that it could turn the tide of war."

Without a blink the Director asked "And, how have you and A.I. come by this information?"

Fitzgerald did not know how much he was authorized to tell the FBI. Yet he needed their resources "During my graduate work I worked with Professor's Keenan, Woodruff and Kay at M.I.T. We had developed a solution to certain problems regarding the dissipation of energy from rapid-fire armaments."

The Special Agent focused, "What does this have to do with Tesla?"

"I met with Dr. Tesla repeatedly in the last few months in the hope of better understanding our radiation problems. I learned how far he has progressed in developing his work with the Teleforce weapon. He has also developed a rather novel and brilliant application of his patented spiral-flow turbine."

"What documentation do you have?"

"When I visited Dr. Tesla, we spent hours pouring over his notes on his prototype. I am sure with the proper funding we can have it built in time to end the war. With due respect, my academic skills are not why I am here." Admittedly on a fishing expedition, I asked, "And, why are you here?"

"As should have been explained to you…" Foxworth cut Fitzgerald off. "I have not had any direct conversations with Mr. Spanel or anyone else you may be referring to. I need you to confirm the reports coming in from Washington."

Fitzgerald was sure he was on a hunt for information and only had orders, not clearance. He explained A.I.'s interest in the matter "You understand, whether Teleforce principals are developed by our government or not, we must not let the foreigners get their hands on them."

Foxworth asked, "Do you have any specific evidence the Nazi's are conspiring to steal Dr. Tesla's work?"

It was surprising he had not done more homework. These interagency information games seemed the common parlance. Fitzgerald was not planning on doing this backroom work for life and wanted to go back to the university. He reported "Dr. Tesla's nephew, Sava Kosanovic is a diplomat working for the Yugoslav embassy. He has direct ties with Josip Broz Tito."

Foxworth added "You mean the Moscow trained partisan leading the Stalinist coup against their King Petar?"

Nodding in agreement Fitzgerald explained "And I have reason to believe the Nazi sympathizer George Viereck has visited Dr. Tesla in the last month. This partisan is already facing prison for sedition. Our enemies seem to have a better grasp on the work of this American genius than the American military does. Does that concern you?"

Foxworth showed his true colors. "We still have a constitution in this country. I cannot arrest men on suspicion of thinking about something that does not exist, can I?"

"No, sir but you can protect documentation and have it reviewed for the sake of national security, can't you?" Fitzgerald asked.

Foxworth said, "What direct evidence do you have of foreign agents working to steal this weapon?"

The A.I. report read "In 1922 Tesla addressed the Friends of Soviet Russia at the Grange Hall in Springfield Massachusetts," Fitzgerald continued. "In 1937 Tesla received $25,000 from the Russian government through their communist shell corporation, Amtorg, a well-known front for the Reds".

While looking at his wristwatch Foxworth nodded.

Fitzgerald worried what would happen if no one understands until it is too late? "Since then, Tesla has received 600 dollars a month from the Yugoslavs. That's a tidy sum from a country that is begging us to increase our Land Lease loans, wouldn't you say?"

"What would we be protecting if he has been working with them all along?"

"Dr. Tesla was first and foremost an inventor, one that has been railroaded more than once, I might add. He would not give any secrets away unless he was guaranteed the ability to build it himself without interference."

"What happened?" Foxworth asked.

Fitzgerald had to have him believe in the genius Tesla. "Politically, they couldn't afford to give into his demands. He would allow them to give him money and he would stay in New York. They wanted him to move but no, he would not. Both the Germans and Russians offered to give him whatever he wanted if he would work in their country. Tesla never did.

What does that prove?" The old cop asked "His greatest point of pride was his American citizenship papers. Dr. Tesla would never go to work for either dictatorship and he refused them. Now the Nazi's will see their chance to swoop in and steal what they couldn't buy. Am I making myself clear?"

"What are you proposing?" the Director demanded. Fitzgerald answered aggressively,

"We need to impound Dr. Tesla's property immediately. I'll volunteer to search through and provide you with the evidence of this weapon."

The Field Officer concluded, "I understand the need for quick action during a war but, I don't understand your physics. I haven't lost sight of our big picture here. Fitzgerald, you go with Agent Allen there and provide us with a complete written report. I need to make a call to Washington. Let's follow this."

After they left, Foxworth pulled out a large manila file entitled Nikola Tesla. Foxworth opened and quickly reviewed every sheet. He scanned the high-lights, "The memorandum J. Edgar released entitled 'Slavic Espionage' was specific. The first suspect was Kosanovic; heir to the Tesla estate... this diplomatic guest could make a certain type of materials available to the enemy...." And the report concluded, "There is no way to ascertain where Kosanovic's alliances actually reside."

This was not a matter of educated opinions or meaningless conclusions. This was war. "Was it King Petar, the titular head of the country, or Tito the fast rising Stalinist, or the Fascist factions dominating much of the country? They were all unacceptable. All that matters is Sava Kosanovic is working with one or more of the parties."

Calling in Agent Harless, Foxworth ordered, "I want you to telegram the director the following message and mark it 'Urgent' Copy?"

The copy A. I. received read as follows, *'B.g. - High Security Risk – Nikola Tesla – Deceased. Nikola Tesla, one of the world's more productive inventors in the electrical field. During his lifetime, he invented modern electricity. He developed the transmission of electrical power, without wires.*

NB: Priority – Tesla announced what is commonly called the 'a force field capable of shielding an entire city. Field reports the notes and records of known experiments and formulas, together with designs of machinery are among Tesla's personal effects. Action required preserving them or keeping them from falling into enemy hands.... *Stop."*

The agent escorted Fitzgerald out of the office.

Allen looked tired and like one of those lawmen who just shot somebody but now had to pull desk duty during the investigation. Fitzgerald learned the Field Director ordered a background review on him.

Hotel New Yorker
Eighth Ave at 34 Street

By this time, A.I. had intersecting teams on both the nephew and the apartment, initially confident in the timely respond to this top security issue. Unfortunately once each stakeout was in position the guys realized they were already doing what everyone thought they were only planning. Except one late night A.I. seriously discussed setting fire to the apartment to prevent others from stealing anymore of Tesla's materials but, feared uncontrolled damages and it was too crazy.

Donald J. and his team drilled holes on each side of the suite. They were jack of all technicians for jury rigging. After rubbing the paint scrapings onto a small screen, Donald J. camouflaged the hole with the perfectly-blended color partition. It looked so good they decided risking two portals in the each room and one for the bathroom. There was one Agent downstairs.

The January morning was bitterly cold, with burning wind coming in from the ocean. Swezey waited just inside the Hotel New Yorker's lobby. Across the street, on the corner of Thirty-Fourth Street and Eight Avenue Kosanovic was heading towards the New Yorker. The magnificent hotel's majestic walls, blended into the unornamented facade of alternating vertical bands of gray brick and windows. The walls were deeply etched, with lighted courts producing a powerful play of light and shade accentuating his Slavic features. His gloomy silhouette appeared as Kosanovic entered the lobby.

Swezey met him and the two quietly walked into the open elevator.

They stopped and walked to the Tesla's place. Room 3327 was unattended and unlocked with the 'Do Not Disturb' sign hanging from the knob. Kosanovic spoke for the first time. "No one is in the room".

Walking quickly through the suite they both quietly nodded as the Coroner removed Tesla's body.

Swezey went into the bedroom, looking for missing items and nearly stumbled into the wall. He opened the window to breathe before calling Kosanovic, who remained outside the bedroom intently thumbing through the innumerable stacks of notes and diagrams. Swezey yelled, "Sava ... Sava, come here!"

Kosanovic nearly dropped the huge stack of documents including, The New Art of Projecting Concentrated Non-Dispersive Energy through Natural Media. Swezey pointed to the spot where Tesla had kept that one locked box near his bed. The dull carpet left a bright square declaring where a container once rested.

Kosanovic was barely audible when he concluded, "They stole from him. They will tell lies about him. There was always someone stealing his every idea. The hungry jackals have already descended upon him. They have begun to devour his genius, even before he is buried."

Swezey interrupted "Or perhaps, he wanted them to know what they could control."

"What are you implying, Ken?"

Swezey replied "Tesla proved he could change the fabric of space and time."

"Are you suggesting what I think you are saying?"

"I am not sure."

Kosanovic had to ask "You're sure he developed the weapon or anti-weapon?"

"It was not a weapon as much as a shield. I'm sure he had tested it. I know he proved every one of his hundreds of inventions worked first time, every time." Swezey spoke with the surety of a witness.

Kosanovic had evidently discussed this possibility with his uncle. "The thieves were quicker than anticipated."

Swezey whispered "I am sure it was his choice. He knew as soon as he died the same vultures that had open contempt for him when he was alive were now willing to steal from him after he dies." Swezey walked slowly to the side of the empty bed and quietly pulled a blanket over the mattress. "I will surely miss you. You were one of the great ones."

Kosanovic looked over at the cabinet and saw empty cracker cans stacked on the shelves. "Where is his black binder, the one he always put her and entitled, *Government?*"

"What?" Swezey asked.

"Surely you saw his notebook. It had all of his observations on the weapon, the myriad of modifications he learned from his prototype."

"Are you sure it is not in the safe?"

Shaking his head Kosanovic said, "He kept it by his side, constantly. He relied less on his memory and more on his notes for the last few years. My government has been providing him with an honorarium for the past six years, more of a stipend to keep him alive."

Kosanovic continued searching through each of the stacks then jumped at the knock at the door. Picking up three diagrams Kosanovic quickly folded each one as he walked to the door. He slipped the papers into his inside jacket pocket and reached for the doorknob the moment of the second knock.

Opening the door Kosanovic asked "And you are?"

"Special Agent Fitzgerald and I'm here to represent the government's interest."

"How may I help you?" Kosanovic gave a diplomat's practiced smile.

"I understand Nikola Tesla's body has been removed?"

"Yes and how does this concern you?" Kosanovic's tone was even and stern.

"His room bill is considerably overdue." Fitzgerald did not appreciate his attitude and even though he knew all about him, he asked "Who are you"?

"Sava Kosanovic, Nicola's nephew. What is your government interest in my deceased uncle's hotel bill? You have no authority here. Only I do."

Fitzgerald never liked European titles, they were too pretentious. "Aren't you also the wartime president of the Eastern and Central European Planning Board for the Balkan countries?"

"Yes, I am but how do you know me and I… not you?"

Fitzgerald walked in past him while asking, "May I come in? We are concerned about the national defense issues Tesla was working on."

Kosanovic asked in a way one was sure there would be no answer "What weaponry in particular?"

Fitzgerald was not practiced in hiding his disgust for spies legally working inside his country, "Perhaps you saw the articles published by most major newspapers, the Times, the Sun and the Inquirer about his weapon research?"

Kosanovic asked "Are you referring to the Teleforce proposals your government rejected?"

"I'm concerned, in particular, with a 50 million volt beam that can vaporize airplanes 250 miles away." With folded arms Fitzgerald walked around the room, inspecting

The Yugoslav enjoyed taunting him, "Allow me to repeat myself. Do you mean the proposal your government rejected?"

Fitzgerald knew another agent was watching and maintained his composure. "I don't have to explain to you that half of your and your uncle's country is controlled by the fascists and the other half by the communists. Surely you can understand our concern, considering we don't like either of them."

Kosanovic answered in a regal tone. "Yugoslavia is ruled by King Petar and at war with Germany."

Fitzgerald pointed out "Your King Petar has no support against Germany and is about to be overthrown by Tito's guerillas."

"My uncle was a personal friend of King Petar."

Fitzgerald said "I know he was on the King's payroll."

Kosanovic took a breath and measured his words. "My country honors our greatest inventor of this century and you..., you have no right to speak in that manner before my uncle is buried."

Fitzgerald fired back "The body has been removed." A. I. was working with both hands tied and rhetorically tossing Kosanovic off with a local colloquialism, "Are you falling out?"

The diplomat was offended and demanded, "What does that mean?"

"If you were an American you would know." Fitzgerald went on, "Make any declaration you choose. We are in a war and my authority is absolute in the matter of Dr. Tesla's munitions."

Kosanovic had his uncle's piercing eyes. "If you are here to pay respects, you may start. If you are here to steal his notes then I need to see your court papers."

Ignoring him, Fitzgerald turned and walked into the bedroom. "Mr. Ken Swezey, I'm with the Army and it is an honor to meet you."

Swezey put his hand out to shake while tilting his head slightly "How do you know who I am, Mr. Fitzgerald?"

Holding Swezey's hand in a firm handshake as if to seek his help, Fitzgerald reminded him "Should we understand what is happening in our own country?"

Swezey was taken by the gesture and said "I assure you I think about the war every day. I must confess I am a bit surprised to see you show up."

Fitzgerald explained "Please, we have been watching Dr. Tesla since before this war started."

"Why?"

If anyone else would have asked the question it would have meant one thing but, from a science columnist of the New York Sun, he had a different meaning in mind. Fitzgerald hoped to connect with him. "Why? He's capable of creating speeds greater than light, calling them cosmic rays and causing them to operate a 'motive device'. Our government has assigned someone to guard against his being molested, kidnapped or tortured by our enemies."

The reporter was also Tesla's old friend. "Isn't that what he has been saying for a decade? In fact, you must know he has offered his services to the American government. Why did you wait until he has passed away?"

Fitzgerald asked, "Do you believe he finished the weapon?"

Leaning forward, Swezey whispered "Of course, I believe him. His intellect was without limits. The problem is that he often kept it in his mind. You have to understand he was first and foremost an inventor.

He successfully wrote over 800 major patents and I doubt he had more than a couple of hundred dollars to his name. People cheated him. They stole his inventions. Who do you think invented the radio? Marconi spent years hiding in a boat in the middle of the ocean to avoid the courts. Mark my word, this year the Supreme

Court will conclude once and for all that Mar-coni stole his ideas from Tesla. And most importantly, I saw it."

This revelation worried A.I. because of Tesla's benefactors, "We know you are a personal friend. We also know he sold secrets to Amtorg for $25,000 in 1937."

Swezey's voice rose with more emotion than most civilians "In 1941 our government paid the Russians $92 million for $41 million dollars' worth of shipments."

Fitzgerald countered "They are our allies." "Then why are you questioning Dr. Tesla's work?"

Swezey asked. "Dr. Tesla was selling secrets to Amtorg in 1935, before the government was working with them.

Fitzgerald added, "Only one communist corporation is authorized to work openly in America and has developed multi-million dollar grants to Moscow. Amtorg's the backbone of the Soviet Purchasing Commission and, yes, we all know, is the legalized hideout of the Russian secret police – GSU and the NKGB. This is our federal policy after Hitler invaded Russia."

Swezey became agitated. "He didn't sell anything abroad without first offering the technology to America.

You let Amtorg work in New York since before the Depression. What's wrong with expanding electrical power to countries suffering from the Depression?"

Fitzgerald growled "They were not our allies in 1935. Swezey's face became red as he ordered the agent, "Nikola did nothing wrong in 1935 or 1939 or... Respect him or leave now."

With or without Swezey, Fitzgerald needed them all to be nervous about whatever they were doing. "Right after I am satisfied there are not weapons or the plans for whatever type of weapon that may be revealed."

"It's not Nikola I am worried about." Kosanovic walked in and asked "Are you arguing over his grave before the funeral?" Swezey looked down.

Fitzgerald looked at Kosanovic to ask, "Will you be representing Tito when he completes his Communist takeover?"

Sitting down on the brass bed, Kosanovic was unconcerned with what American's thought. "I am representing my uncle at this moment, thank you."

Fitzgerald asked, "Did you know Dr. Tesla was working with Amtorg Corporation when Tito was studying in Moscow?" A.I. background on Kosanovic came across Gregory Bessedovsky's writings on Amtorg. After the Russian decided not to return to Moscow and stand trial for 'counter-revolutionary activity' he found his new life with his now famous 'singing' testimony about Amtorg.

The A.I. report read: "After crude Soviet attempts to operate a semi-legitimate corporation in America had failed, it was decided to resort to subterfuge and organize a so-called private trading company. The chief stockholders of the company were selected high officials from the Soviet commerce department, who were sent to New York especially for that purpose. To allay all suspicion, it was agreed the chief stockholders should be naturalized American citizens, former Russian immigrants and older residents of America. Their stock remained in the possession of the president of Amtorg. Nonetheless, they are the legal owners of the stock and can at all times demand that the stock be turned over to them. Later on, the Politburo took an additional precaution. The intended members of the Board of the Directors of the Amtorg were required before leaving Moscow to sign personal notes for double the face value of their shares."

Kosanovic had also visited Amtorg at their headquarters on 261 Fifth Avenue. He had contact with the Latvian spy, Alexuim who came here under a bogus passport. The Soviet secret police had many powers; the GPU didn't need Amtorg, beyond making it easier to follow one of their prime directives - keep dossiers on Amtorg employees. And, A.I. knew Kosanovic was being followed if not recruited by them.

As Fitzgerald continued with his interview Kosanovic asked, "How could spies possibly missed getting together in the middle of the Great Depression, given Amtorg is in New York?"

Fitzgerald replied "Same nationalities." Kosanovic snapped, "Don't be ridiculous, Tesla has nothing in common with Tito." He stood and began to pace around the room. "You don't even know if Tesla did sell anything to the Russians, do you?

Kosanovic countered "I saw no evidence of your malicious rumor. I did see evidence of your gifts to Russia." "If your only interest here is to goad me, then you are a fool. Yugoslavia like you, must maintain our alliances with the Russians until Germany is crushed." Walking over to the tripod Kosanovic turned the mounted camera, focused carefully and clicked off two pictures of the safe. He didn't look up as he spoke, "Nothing is simple here. The men who once kept a distant awe of Nicolas Tesla's thoughts will now do anything to grab his skull right off his neck."

Swezey picked up all three packages of stale Nabisco crackers, and pulled out his handkerchief to clean the area. He placed the crackers in the wastebasket then stared at the telephone. Tesla's last admirer walked over and called the locksmith. After hanging up the telephone, he announced. "The safe will be opened at two this afternoon."

Fitzgerald stepped closer to Swezey and quietly pointed out "Please understand, there is a national interest here."

From across the room Kosanovic declared, "There is a family interest here, and..."

Swezey interrupted, "Gentlemen My friend Nikola just died. We are in his bedroom."

Fitzgerald looked at Kosanovic and declared, "All the property in this room is property of the U.S. government."

With diplomatic sneer Kosanovic countered "That is for the court to decide. You have no right to declare any such thing."

Bluffing Fitzgerald declared, "The wartime act gives me the power."

Kosanovic's body went rigid as he turned toward the bathroom, "Excuse me gentlemen." He walked into the small room and closed the door behind.

Kosanovic quickly slid his hand inside his jacket and pull out three sets of documents to inspect before returning them. Bending over the sink, Kosanovic splashed water on his face to regain his composure.

A.I. had no legal right to intercede; only 'Watch and Wait'. When Kosanovic opened the door he saw Fitzgerald searching through the neatly stacked piles of documents. The Nephew walked up next to him and explained "Neither these nor any other documents in this room belong to you. In fact you have no right to be in his apartment."

Fitzgerald set the papers down and asked "Or what?"

Kosanovic had his uncle's deep piercing, questioning blue eyes that revealed nothing.

The prolonged silence was broken with a knock at the door. Swezey walked over to open it "Hugo."

We could hear Hugo ask "Ken is it true?"

"Yes, yes, my dear friend, please come in." Hugo Gernsback walked in and bowed slightly, respectively towards Kosanovic while asking, "How is my old ally holding up?"

Kosanovic smiled slightly and shared his thoughts "It seems the government who ignored my uncle for all of these years is now all too anxious to pick over his bones. I have asked the government agent to leave. He has ignored me." The diplomat turned to the Agent "Mr. Fitzgerald, before I introduce you to the famed science editor and publisher Hugo Gernsback, I will ask you to leave my uncle's home during our bereavement."

Fitzgerald took a breath, gave Hugo and Ken a respectful nod, and then walked out.

Hugo discretely stepped aside before walking into the room. The rap on the door startled everyone and Swezey walked over and opened it for another old friend, Clark was the director of the museum and a laboratory at RCA. On the verge of tears Hugo turned away to keep him busy, "We are here at this moment in history. Without a shade of doubt, Nikola Tesla... has no equal in the annals of the intellectual world." He paused to regain his composure before continuing; "I am going to hire a friend to prepare the death mask. I already fear what the government and others have planned for our old friend. Given the body has been removed quickly I must say, I too must move quickly." Hugo hurried out of the room, leaving the door opened.

As Hugo was walking out the manager, Reginald escorted the locksmith into the room. "Gentlemen, as the hotel manager, I am legally responsible for any and all activities relating to the death of my tenant. I deeply regret this time and carry the greatest respect for him."

Clark walked out of the bedroom to watch, "Let's see what the genius treasured."

The locksmith took only a few moments to open the large safe.

"Your safe was easy to enter." Kosanovic asked, did the hotel provide it?"

Reginald responded, "This is the certified man who installed it for Dr. Tesla as well."

The inner safe door opened easily. The worker pulled out inventory consisting of several honorary degrees stacked neatly; a volume of the greetings on Tesla's seventy-fifty birthday; a set of keys, and a gold Edison medal. Underneath were Nikola Tesla's citizenship papers. In his report, the locksmith dutifully wrote the witnesses names; Sava Kosanovic, together with Clark, an archivist for RCA, Kenneth Swezey, a popular science writer, and an unknown employee of Shaw Walker & Co, together with three hotel staff, opened the safe and examined its contents. They removed some items and locked the safe with a new combination.

With everyone's blessing in a nod or a wink, Kosanovic took three family pictures and Swezey kept the 1931 testimonial autograph book from the commemoration of Tesla's 75th birthday. Kosanovic reached inside his jacket to verify the documents were still there, then quickly left.

Manhattan Warehouse and Storage
52nd St and 7th Ave

The Office of Alien Property Attorney was at work on Saturday because the supervisors were home and the young attorney had no seniority. He was learning the unwritten rules of bureaucracy and was startled by the telephone. The aspiring attorney answered directly "OAP."

"Is Gorsuch in?"

"No sir. It's Saturday."

"Very well then you need to fulfill the following emergency orders. I'm calling from Washington and I am Special Agent L. Smith with the FBI. I'm notifying you will receive written instructions by wire as soon as we hang up. Listen carefully, a one Dr. Nikola Tesla recently died and was reputed to have invented and in possession of the so-called death ray. This is a significant military device capable of destroying incoming warplanes by projecting a beam into the skies and creating a field of energy, causing incoming planes or tanks to disintegrate. There is reason to believe German agents are in pursuit of the device and documentation."

The young attorney explained "I know of Tesla and he is a naturalized citizen. Whereas... do you understand we are the Office of Alien Property."

"Don't you have cases of his materials in storage already?"

"I believe so."

"Then what is your problem?"

The young attorney recited "There is no legal precedent for the OAP or any other government agency to take possession of a naturalized citizen's estate."

Agent Smith's words from Washington were neither loud nor rude but were very sharp. "Unless you can personally guarantee the political stability of Yugoslavia you are going to assume responsibility for a weapon called the 'death ray' being smuggled by Germans?"

Too intimidated to be insulted the young attorney stammered, "No, sir."

"Good, now you are to order the immediate capture and security of all possessions belonging to the estate of Nikola Tesla."

The OAP agent asked, "How would you suggest I go about this?"

"Are you an attorney?"

"Why, yes, I am."

"What is the only government agency with statutory power to seize enemy assets without court order? The OAP and you must understand, this is a national defense issue and during this war, you can receive forgiveness much faster than you can receive permission."

Recognizing there was no choice the young attorney called his wife. He failed to convince her he had to work. To make matters much worse, he could not tell her why. He also failed to prove he truly wanted to go to Long Island for a family dinner. He stopped trying to apologize and went for the quick hang up.

Calling Walter Gorsuch of the Office of Alien Property, he quickly organized a convoy to gather the notes and records of all experiments, formulas, and designs of machinery.

Gorsuch asked the same question, "Where is our jurisdiction in the matter?

By then the attorney had calculated his jurisdictional options. "Considering the nephew Kosanovic is probably legally entitled to his uncles' estate and he is an alien, then it is alien property we are addressing, right?"

Gorsuch smiled for the first time "Right."

***

Everything in Manhattan Warehouse and Storage Company on 52nd St and 7th Ave was impounded. On January 9th, the OAP transported two truckloads of Tesla properties from his labs and from the basement storage at the Hotel New Yorker, including: 12 locked metal boxes, one steel cabinet, 35 metal cans, five barrels, and eight trunks. These were added to thirty-odd barrels that had been in the OAP's possession since 1934. Michael King, floor supervisor for ten years guaranteed the legal owner, the foreigner Sava Kosanovic would not have access to the property. He understood there was a war.

Pulling up to the Hotel Governor Clinton six men entered the Hotel and took possession of the package Tesla had left for collateral on his unpaid bill. Dr. Trump led the team that examined the apparatus stored in its vault. His memorandum stated a one Mr. Charles McNamara, assistant manager of the Hotel Governor Clinton, permitted the OAP to seal safety deposit box number 103, which contained the "dangerous machine." Box 103 was not a specifically constructed box but definitely the largest box of the lower tiers. The team waited outside the vault. The suspect package was wrapped in brown paper and tied with a string.

There were numerous rumors around each agency that the package was lethal. In his report afterwards Dr. Trump noted he remembered how beautiful the weather was before he started. He took a deep breath and carefully cut the string. Inside was a polished wooden chest with a brass, hinged lid. Trump recognized this apparatus as a Wheatstone bridge. No one spoke a word. The team walked out carrying the harmless piece of test equipment.

That afternoon the Gorsuch team of four uniformed men from the Naval Intelligence, Army intelligence, the FBI, and Fitzgerald went on the authorized mission in two taxis. The hotel managers at the St. Regis and Waldorf-Astoria apologized. Even through Nikola Tesla had lived in their hotels he had left nothing behind except unpaid bills.

Holding Tesla's note for the confiscated box valued at $10,000. meant Tesla had been a liar or someone else had switched boxes. The documents made innumerable references to the labs. The teams searched vainly for the rest of the week, but failed to locate any of Tesla's secret laboratories, even the one he had identified as the address for receiving Amtorg funding.

The attorney's notes reflect he telephoned the Westinghouse research labs before writing up the background on the Tesla seizure. After a discussion with top management he was told; "Without Tesla there would have been no Westinghouse or maybe not even a civilization as we know it." The report was sent up the routine ladder for instructions but none came back.

321 West 46th Street, Manhattan Barbetta Restaurant

George spent another night unable to sleep. His sheets and blankets were twisted together, wrapped into long intertwining spirals. Groaning out loud and the midday light, he stumbled into the bathroom and spent over an hour in front of the mirror grooming his thinning hair, preparing for dinner.

Dressed in a three piece suit, he inspected the crate and searched around the black and white bedroom. The room was full of natural hiding spots, the painted black ceiling molding to the frame of the black-and-white print to the zigzagging rug. The black lacquer vanity desk with attached chrome lamps hid the documents and stolen package in a well-disguised hole under the desk, behind the figurine of a black panther prowling. George squatted in front of his prize. Taking a large breath, he picked up the Teleforce Accelerator and carried the box into the dining room table.

Setting up the camera was challenging him. Propping up the tripod never seemed to work on the dining room's thick carpet. After numerous futile attempts, he realized the highly polished wood motif made the lighting unusable from certain angles.

Focusing the Kodak George was obviously confused as he repeatedly moved it back and forth. It became more frequent the Reports on him have him wandering in and out of his alter ego. He was snapping pictures and reciting out loud. "The Ministry must see this information before the shaking hands ruin this print. Life is never about stealing from friends. Nobody appreciated I was trying to keep America out of the war." He was unable to find a position that made him happy. He used up dozens of film rolls.

Continuing with his loud railing against George's enemies Claudius continued shooting pictures. "Aren't journalist supposed to take pride working for Senator Lundeen of Minnesota? Wouldn't any writer would be proud of writing speeches against the war and having the speech mailed to 125,000 sympathetic voters?" Irritated he labored to move the camera around the accelerator, for three rolls of Kodak film.

Von Haak had visited and set the meeting with his superior. The real George Viereck would have contacted Dr. Hans Kiep, the charge d'affaires in Washington and master spy at the German embassy. Dr. Otto Kiep, Nazi Consul General in New York. Claudius had studied his own script well enough to know which Kiep had access to funds. There was no doubt the more powerful Hans would find the Italian when he wanted him.

This was a game of wits. Claudius liked being George. He was only happy when staying in character. He went so far as to brag in his diary what a wonderful way this is to detach one's soul from moral responsibility. There was a war. This working for a corporation and stealing for dollars required wits. He picked the accelerator up and went back to the vanity desk and struggled to shove it into the hole in the wall. The desk was set on a Moroccan rug and easily slid across the polished wood to cover the wall. George struggled to align the desk in front of the hole.

He then opened the closet and pulled out a small shipping crate addressed to the Marconi Company in London. Putting one roll of film inside a brand new shoe, he then placed the pair of shoes in the second row of neatly stacked Oxfords. He looked over the area before setting the small package outside his door and calling for the deliveryman. After putting the Kodak away George hurried down to the garage gripping tightly the two rolls of film, before putting one in each pocket.

George drove out through the garage back entrance. For his benefit A.I. let him see the brown Ford following him. Turning quickly, George sped in the opposite pattern down the alley and then to the left, and then left again and again, throwing the following car off his tail. Finally, after a casual drive around Manhattan to be sure he was no longer being followed George parked three blocks from the restaurant 'Barbetta'. He got away once; A.I. didn't falling for that trick twice. We followed him and were ready for wherever he took us. A.I. used a disguised deliveryman on a motorcycle to follow him.

George looked around for five minutes before walking up one block, backtracking down the second street until arriving at the row of four 19th century brownstone townhouses.

Donald J. had equipped the men, each team with an AN/PRC-1 suitcase radio. Each had the transmitter, receiver and rectifier hidden in a civilian-style suitcase.

They could always be safely carried in public without arousing suspicion. The drawback was that we needed to plug them into a power source. This required ad hoc setups. In this particular case we later needed to hold the manager hostage until the court orders arrived. A.I. was proud an American was never hurt, by accident.

George entered the restaurant and looked around. Kiep was seated at the far right where he could not be seen from the door, yet able to signal the maître's. The Italian was escorted back to Kiep's table. A.I. had a female agent eating in the next booth separated by grating covered with ivy.

Kiep dismissed the waiter with a dollar. After he left, the two quietly looked at each other. Hans offered, "*Guten Tag*, Heir Viereck"

George exhaled quickly. "Good day, Heir Kiep. This is a lovely garden. One would say an al fresco experience."

By all accounts Kiep had not smiled for six months, since a New York grand jury indicted twenty-six German-American Bund leaders. The Americans were now growing stronger and more focused on the European war undermining Kiep's freedom to accomplish much. Kiep was more worried than he let on while smiling with compliments. "We still call the Italians allies. We must agree you could never fault their restaurants." Laughing Kiep picked up a pack of Camels and pulled one out, tapping it three times hard against the box before lighting it.

"George, I have a wonderful vintage here. You must join me." He half-filled both wine glasses.

Feeling confident he saluted his ally. "I am most pleased you met me on such short notice, Herr Kiep.

"Why is this weapon bringing me up to New York?" Kiep patted George's outstretched hand, "And why are you not speaking with Von Haak?"

Visibly nervous George explained, "I have the most powerful weapon ever created in my possession. This is of the highest priority. Do you understand?"

Kiep asked "are you considering any option other than sending this weapon to Berlin?"

George sat back and rubbed his chin, as he always did when thinking about money. "The truth of the matter is, once Berlin realizes what they have available. I did believe there would be any other option."

Kiep glared across the dining table. It was known in certain Washington circles he hated these Italian cowards trying to profit from the war. He didn't realize Marconi Company had a far more provocative precondition inserted into their plans.

After a long drag on the fag Kiep asked, "Is not candor what you want?"

"You must understand this is complicated."

"Complicated?"

The performer enjoyed playing the role of an-other. The actor's facade freed oneself from the constraints of the church. George was quite convincing. "A dear friend recently passed away and told me the truth. He invented the greatest weapon ever devised. I have his plans and the accelerator for the weapon. Yes it is complicated."

"I assume we are talking about the death ray Nikola Tesla announced he was building before he died. Are we not?"

"He has built an accelerator. It is priceless"

George's eyes flared under his heavy brows.

"What I do not understand is what else you want. Do you?"

"Perhaps, my loyalty to Fascism is beyond dispute. I just need to know, I mean I just want..."

Kiep leaned over the table and whispered, "Why did you bring me here?"

After reaching into his pocket, George passed Kiep the roll of pictures under the table.

The film disappeared inside the Nazi's sleeve.

He leaned back and put the fork on his plate. "Is the accelerator this small?"

"These are not pictures to show you the size. I thought you would want to understand how complicated and dangerous it is for me to carry around such a weapon."

"Where is this accelerator?"

"I have stored it in a safe place."

"That is not an answer. Do you intend on keeping secrets from your allies?"

"No, I am just under tremendous pressure right now. I have a grave concern with mistakes and American spies. I moved it out of my apartment."

Kiep asked, "Let me understand, you had first chosen your apartment as a safe place?"

"That is not what I am saying. I am concerned with your contact man, Von Haak."

"Von Haak is most loyal. What concerns do you have about him?"

"I need to trust him" George sounded uncomfortable with his own words.

Dr. Kiep took a drink without removing his eyes from George "You have asked me to travel all the way from Washington just to give me the picture? I'm flattered but concerned."

He looked up and stared silently before continuing, "Very well you don't have to work with Wilhelm. I shall handle the matter personally. Now regarding practicalities George you are being followed, are you not?" The actor was perfect in feigning disbelief. "Why do you say that?"

Kiep slowed his words "Initially, you have chosen a stooge name that is a high priority case for the FBI."

"It is a stage name. They are following you too?" George asked.

Kiep stood, then pulled out a money clip and placed a five-dollar bill on the $3.48 tab. "Perhaps it is time for us to go on a walk. You do like to walk."

Reluctantly George followed Kiep out the door. After a few moments, a mousy woman in a heavy brown coat followed them.

The two walked down West 46th, among the theater crowds. After turning down 8th Avenue, Kiep pulled George into a dark overhang, fronting the blacken entrance.

The Nazi put his face directly in front of George's. "There is no doubt the FBI is following both of us. We have no time for nonsense. What is on this film and exactly what do you have?"

"You have pictures of the accelerator. I thought you might need to transmit them to Berlin for further instructions. I have already told you of its location and, yes, I am prepared to send it to Berlin at the proper price."

Kiep said, "You have done well, my friend. Do not attempt to contact me again. I need you to go to your apartment until I contact you. Do you understand?"

"What about my reward for delivering Germany's solution?"

Kiep smiled "The FBI follows me now. You head back towards the restaurant and as you near the door, turn as if you forgot something and zigzag back to your auto. I will be heading in the opposite direction."

George turned to the sidewalk and vanished into the crowds.

An emergency upstaged their priority and requisitioned our only motorcycle. A.I. lost him.

Amtorg Trading Corporation
261 Fifth Avenue

A.I. was monitoring the Russians prior to the Tesla project as staff translators. It was easy to recruit Tsarist expatriates in New York.

Amerikanskaya torgovaya was the Russian name for the Soviet's corporation developing trade in America. Amtorg had a titular leader, in President Professor Constantin Lukashev. Sitting in his office the pin stripped bureaucrat was most proud of his new

French urn. He was admiring his trophy when his two workers entered.

The awkward and lumbering one stumbled near the vase. His was one of an eternal *dumkoff* smile.

Lukashev rocked back and forth, regretting Messrs. Rostarchuk and Seldiakov attending this meeting. Every *apparatchik* must work with other *apparatchiks*; it is the Socialist path. He started the meeting by wanting to end it. "*Dah* comrades' *spahseebah*. Sit. Sit. And, you must use English, you need the practice."

Frowning, he eyed the vase. "Enough with the greetings, our comrades in the military have provided essential support leaving us to achieve greater glory. This leads to the fact the inventor Tesla just died."

Both were excessive in their mourning. Lukashev said "We must act immediately. We must have superior action this day or lose our substantial investment in his work. The Slavic particle beam generator must be secured or lost."

The massive Ukrainian struggled with impracticable furniture, built a century earlier by an effete Frenchman. He repeatedly scrapped across the floor, adjusting the effeminate chair into position behind the frilly rosewood desk. Finally settled in Rostarchuk protested, "Why are we off on such a risk filled venture when we have just secured over one billion dollars from the Americans? We could anger them and slow down our line of credit."

Looking at his protégés from behind his mahogany desk Lukashev said, "On this day, the Russian Army is fighting the Nazis. For as long as we fight, we receive American aid. It is that simple. We have no delusions about what will be after the Nazi's are defeated. *Pahneemahyu* good, this should not be hard to understand."

Rostarchuk struggled and stood, looking the other way before speaking, "What about our American comrades? They have fellow travelers. No doubt one of them had direct contact with Tesla. He is a Yugoslavian and they are allies."

Seldiakov said "His nephew is a member of the Yugoslav ambassador. His name is Sava Kosanovic. I have met him with his uncle Tesla. I told him about what glorious progress our Socialist state has achieved. I invited him to visit and work in our splendid laboratory. This Nikola Tesla admitted he was always in need of money and able to finish building a working model of the weapon. I assured him he would not have that problem in the Soviet Union. He was most gracious but would not consider moving. He told me must stay in New York and had no need for more friends. I told him the Old Russian proverb that one goes to heaven for a great view and to hell for old friends. I could tell he wanted to laugh but cared not."

Rostarchuk ordered his men "We have to exploit every contact immediately or the opening will disappear. Before 1941, I knew a German poet journalist here in New York. I remember him bragging that he personally knew Tesla. I will find him today. Perhaps our local comrades can help locate his current address."

"I should reconsider what I am saying" Seldiakov said. "I don't know about meeting the German or if he is out on bail. The FBI probably has more important agents following him than I have available. Perhaps I will get a better class of agents following me in the future if I meet him in public."

President Lukashev said "I will contact our American comrades. Was the reference to 1941 in discussion of the German invasion of our motherland?"

"*Dah*" Rostarchuk agreed to either answer? "*Spahseebah*, thank you too. What we need is to demonstrate our glorious role in securing this weapon. I want you to utilize every resource within your power and for the well being of your future. This weapon belongs to our union of Soviets." He stood.

With orders in hand, they walked out.

Sokol
71st Street

A.I. had privileges the FBI did not, given the Army was fighting a war with every breath and not bound by civilian laws. Yet, there was constant concern about exposure and Fitzgerald was often warned not to be recognized or identified by anyone. For the last year, A.I. had been listening to the Slavic meetings but had trouble keeping Serbian staff. We learned if translators eavesdrop on politics all day they are listening to true believers. It became only a matter of time before converted and inspired to action. Too many interpreters left America for the future homeland, to fight on one side or the other.

Being a diplomat with certain privileges, Kosanovic was offended the FBI followed him. There was only one safe place, the Sokol.

A.I. had a complete file on the Yugoslav social hall. One of many nationalist gymnasiums of physical-training societies where men and women perform tumbling and dance moves.

This was the place New York Yugoslav's meet privately. Seventy First Street reported sightings included the ultra-nationalist Dr. Rado Mirkovich the fellow traveler Professor Bogdan Raditsa and the activist Professor Boris Furlan.

In Yugoslavia, the king had promulgated 'The Sokol Law', dissolving Croatians, Slovene, Catholic, and Serbian Sokols. These hostilities and politics made them more than physical training societies. These independent cultures were replaced with a single Yugoslav Sokol under government control. But American Yugoslav's were independent and cabals met at the Sokol. Kosanovic called the meeting at their preferred Sokol, a place where if you were not Yugoslavian everyone in the gymnasium knew.

This day's cabal members arrived in timely fashion. Paul Radosavljevich went by the name Rado. He was sad upon meeting his compatriot, "Sava, Sava my deepest of condolences for the loss of your uncle. He was a fine man and this is a great loss to the world... Is this why you have such desperation in your voice?"

Kosanovic replied "I will explain as soon as everyone arrives."

Rado turned to see Raditsa and Professor Boris Furlan enter their sanctuary. They crossed the polished wood floor slowly and exchanged heartfelt handshakes.

Condolences were offered. Kosanovic said "Follow me, gentlemen. I have made arrangements for us to meet in the chambers." Kosanovic walked up the bleachers into the small office at the top. The old men suffered silently. They stopped numerous times. The small office housed four utilitarian chairs around a table facing the one wall of glass, opening the view to the exercise floor.

Bogdan pointed out "The women's events are there. See the vault, uneven bars, and balance beam. Over on that side are the men's events. You can see the vault, floor pommel horse, rings, parallel bars, and horizontal bar."

Rado asked "Where was everyone during the Vilija?"

Too tired to think of family dinners on Christmas, Boris answered, "At home cherishing our precious few moments."

Kosanovic said, "My uncle built a working model of the most powerful weapon ever devised. An American was collaborating on this project with him, a precocious yet quite disagreeable agent by the name of Fitzgerald. He seems to have close ties with the government men, who are unfortunately currently following me. I suspect they know I have the weapon or, at least, certain fundamental elements." He passed photographs around the table.

The air became serious. Kosanovic said "Rado believes there is a third party somewhere. When I was in my uncle's apartment yesterday, there was a box missing, one he always kept near his bed. This American, Fitzgerald acted as if he had it; in fact he seemed worried I had stolen the box. We spoke long enough for me to conclude, he did not know exactly what is missing."

Bogdan said, "Who else?" Boris said, "It has to be the Nazis."

"What about the FBI?" Kosanovic asked. Rado said "It is the Nazis. Their submarines continue up and down the Atlantic coast with impunity. They have built an efficient information network here in New York where they have a transmitter set up to send information to Berlin. They have an organization the FBI is missing."

Boris leaned forward and spoke like a veteran "The Allied invasion of French North Africa two months ago and the defeat of Rommel at EI Alamein has thrust our country into prominence. The allied invasion is aiming towards the Continent. The Italians have increased their presence to 16 divisions, adding to the German's four divisions. They intend on destroying the partisan stronghold around Bihac while denying every beachhead. Local politics no longer matter; this war will be decided by the Allied invasion across the Mediterranean. The question must be asked: can this weapon be useful in the immediate future?"

Kosanovic stared at Boris' hands. "I do not know but would not underestimate Tito. His Partisans have repeatedly proven to be adept and seasoned guerillas. They have foiled three major offensives against them. The populace wants to join them. They have won the hearts of the people with their skills and defiance. They are a magnet for the Serbs and Muslims."

The small room went quiet until all eyes begun following the line of teenagers flipping down the row of mats.

Boris was the first to speak. "It pains me greatly seeing our young men and women continue their practicing... one out of six combat deaths in our country is women. What are they dying for? If we can answer that, then we have found the answer to our problem with this weapon."

Rado said "This is wonderful poetry but let us return to the harsh reality of our country. We are all loyal to King Petar. We should give the power to him with such information. Surely the Allies would give him strong support and represent him at the next summit."

Kosanovic countered "I am not so sure. Even though he knew about it, the power of this weapon failed to help Prime Minister Chamberlain at Munich. What makes this invention more powerful now?"

Rado asked "Are you saying he continued to develop it? He did continue developing beyond his work of five years ago?"

Kosanovic said "I know this much, there has been additional work by Nikola and there are elements missing. If it is the Nazis, I do not have any information on who or how much. If it is the Americans, we need to return to Dr. Tesla's suite immediately before the FBI impounds everything."

Boris threw his hands up. "What, what are you saying? Are we travailing over nothing here or is this a viable weapon?"

Kosanovic said, "For what I understand the weapon is not working and requires significant capitalization to be implemented."

Bogdan asked "How much capitalization?"

Kosanovic promptly answered "At least two million."

"American dollars?"

"American dollars."

Everyone talked at once. "It is over." "Anything is possible." "Impossible."

"This is wartime!"

"Have you discussed this with Foreign Minister Jovanovich?"

"What we are saying here is only the three powers that can build such a weapon."

"The battle in Stalingrad will drain the resources of two of them, leaving only the American's able to afford it."

"Does the FBI know you have it?"

Holding his hand up Kosanovic said, "You and my associates are the only ones aware I have the problem. And even were I to have the money, I do not have the technical skills. I am not even sure if I have enough materials to reconstruct it."

"We have not discussed General Mikhailovich," Rado said "After all he is the leader of the Chetniks in Yugoslavia and the last hope of keeping Stalin from seizing control over our country."

Bogdan said "Stalin is busy with Stalingrad."

"If we must discuss this weapon with anyone in our exiled government I would suggest Prime Minister Trifunovic" Rado said. "I have worked with him very closely. He has greater insight on the international issues than any one."

Kosanovic explained "Gentlemen, please. The religious differences are insurmountable. If we choose any one side in the government, we are choosing the Croats over the Serbs. Does anyone think another weapon can unite them?"

From their silence Kosanovic concluded, "The military conquest and partition of the Kingdom of Yugoslavia by Germany and its Axis partners in the spring of 1941 was a tragic event for all Southern Slavs, and I for one, am not prepared to support anyone seeking a final solution against our Slavic brethren. Are any of you? Do you read the weekly *Iseljenicki Muzej*?

"The National Revolution of 1941 was genuine but at that historic moment there was no ideological program and no institutional focus" Boris said our young Petar II came into power innocent of all understanding from his immediate predecessors. What are we considering here, what are we willing to decide?"

Rado said, "Perhaps, we are sure we are not to do anything at this time. Everyone fears their enemies will possess this weapon. We need money to develop a weapon that no one can afford. Are we are loyal to our beloved Yugoslavia without a surety of who will rule our nation next? One would conclude we should do nothing."

Boris countered "That is ridiculous my friend. We must act and act now."

Bogdan stood. "I agree with Boris. This is a war and we have the ultimate weapon, perhaps the very weapon to decide the fate of the war. It would be a betrayal to our people to do nothing." Kosanovic asked "Then what? Where is the wisdom?"

Boris answered "We cannot let Tito or Mikhailovich have it. We must use this or we are giving our country to the communists or the fascists. It is impractical for us to keep it. Again, why not give it to our king?"

Kosanovic asked "What would our King say about what we stole? The Americans may stop harboring him if they feel threatened, and then what?"

The gymnasium became hushed as two men walked in and sat on the bleachers. The two removed their hats and acted like attentive fans. Everyone continued the charade. A.I. knew they knew about us. We wanted them to think they had spotted us.

That satisfied them. They never saw Donald J's well-equipped man behind the wall.

Kosanovic stood and walked toward the back door. "No one will see us leave from here.

Sunday, January 10th

Allies and Enemies

Home of Assistant Director of FBI
Private Residence, New York

While walking up to Foxworth's home, Fitzgerald wrote he feared without the FBI, the Teleforce Project would die a slow death in humid storage. Ringing the bell on Sunday morning seemed right because the cause was just.

The Field Director did not look like he agreed. Wearing only a Sunday robe and slippers Foxworth answered, "Fitzgerald what in tarnation you doing here?"

"I'm sorry for bothering you this morning. You must realize the greatest weapon ever invented is here. Why aren't we using it?"

"We can only take what belongs to us," The Director asked rhetorically "Can we?"

"May I come in?"

Foxworth stood aside and suggested his guest hang onto his coat. He set the wool coat down on the hallway chair. Foxworth led through the study. Fitzgerald asked "Are these Rockwell originals?"

Without breaking stride Foxworth answered "Not on a government salary."

Fitzgerald hurried to catch up and entered the veranda, the Director turned and asked, "And, what is this Sunday morning intrusion about?"

Fitzgerald blurted "Sir, you know all too well we are in the midst of losing the greatest invention of the war. It is imperative I be allowed to complete the development of this weapon for our government, for our war effort."

Foxworth walked around the oversized mahogany coffee table. "Are you familiar with the British death ray?"

Having regained his composure Fitzgerald explained "I know the stories about Tesla selling his ideas around England and the meeting with Prime Minister Chamberlain in 1938."

Foxworth was surprisingly knowledgeable "No, son we are talking about the Limey's indigenous designs. By 1935 R.A. Watson-Watt of the Radio Research Station at Slough investigated the practicability of the proposals. Their idea was to create a strong beam of electromagnetic waves. They would heat up anything in their path to the point where living tissue would be destroyed or bombs set off. This just was never going to be achieved in any military-acceptable scenario. Watson-Watt calculated the amount of power would be far beyond current technology. Are you familiar with their work?"

"Of course. However, my concerns are not newspaper headlines rather the very real shield Tesla invented."

Foxworth continued "They did learn from their experiments that a pulsed radio system on a wavelength of about 50 centimeters detected ships and icebergs."

Smiling he accepted the coffee his wife brought. When she turned towards Fitzgerald with a smile Foxworth said, "He won't be staying long enough."

He went on to explain "This started the serious development of radar. Fair enough. The fact that something good came out of the research keeps me interested in this 'shield' of yours but, in practical terms I see no basis for exploring anything further."

"You don't understand."

"The British Secret Intelligence Service funded the Dutchman's ray gun. All they received for their millions of dollars was a fruit preserver, a million dollar fruit preserver, for crying out loud. It's what you kids call a boffola."

Fitzgerald argued; ''the microwave search radar provided the foundation for the technology leading to locating enemy submarines far beyond the range of sight. It was able to coach in friendly craft for the sure hit. Another crucial weapon developed exclusively under the auspices of the OSRD, was the proximity fuse. This fuse was in effect a radio set in the head of the shell detonated by proximity to the target."

Foxworth did not appreciate the lesson. He turned to pace in the other direction.

Fitzgerald walked into Foxworth's pathway. "I have worked with Dr. Tesla as well as some of the finest minds in this country. I assure you this opportunity and dangers to the security of our country are both very real."

Foxworth turned left and started a new path while asking "What are your credentials to predict the future of the great weapon you aspire to build?"

Fitzgerald said "We have already discussed my credentials. Incidentally, there are more items of national interest and that is the OAP review of the potential of the materials they hold. I am the most qualified person to review the documentation the OAS has impounded and holds at Manhattan Storage."

The Director pushed his hands into his bathrobe pockets while wondering where this damn kid was learning this. "If your information is correct then why are you dropping into my home on Sunday morning?"

"It would be my honor to visit your office."

"Again, why are you here?"

Fitzgerald said "I only came here to offer my services. I would be proud to offer my technical assessments or other vital info you may need in analyzing the Teleforce. I allude to what was not found at the New Yorker Hotel and the dummy package agents picked up yesterday."

"I commend your sources, Mr. Fitzgerald. I fail to see why you are calling on me. Unless you have direct information on any sabotage you must let me have the rest of Sunday morning preparing for my trip."

"Director Foxworth, you have known someone exchanged the materials. We know Tesla had secreted them away at the Hotel. If stealing weapons is not foreign espionage then... hell, we have already lost."

It might have been his imagination but Fitzgerald was sure the Director snarled at the conclusion. Fitzgerald asked, "All I'm asking is that you recommend that the OAP put my office over the investigation of Tesla's property. I will provide you with first-rate assessments and progress on all materials found. You will still have the OAP report. Isn't two better than one?"

The director stared intently while asking "Tell me exactly what you are talking about."

"We are talking about four separate yet integrated concepts" Fitzgerald watched him carefully as he explained "Number one is a new high vacuum tube that opens to the atmosphere. And Number two is provisions for imparting to a minute particle an extremely high charge. The number three is a new terminal of relatively small dimensions and enormous potential. And number four is an electrostatic generator of very great power. These elements in concert could form a hundred or two hundred mile protective shield around a city. This is a highly controllable force field offering absolute security."

The Director nodded in approval "You seem to know what you are talking about and, yes, I'm aware of these discussions. Now will you allow me the rest of my morning to finish packing?"

"Can we afford to wait until tomorrow?" Foxworth turned and explained his choice clearly

"Listen I will not be late for President Roosevelt's departure today, given I'm going to be on the airplane following him. Understand?"

"May I call on your office tomorrow morning to present action items?"

"Call my secretary."

"I will only call you when it is important, some-times too hot to sit on."

Irritated, Foxworth agreed, "Call my secretary. She will have instructions."

Fitzgerald was oblivious of adversity, "Today?"

"Tomorrow," the Director concluded. "Very good, yes sir. See you tomorrow."

New York Harbor

In every report Fitzgerald entered personal notes regarding his disapproval against going. The harbor each time seemed colder than the last. Walking to the dock's end Fitzgerald recognized British Agent Sandy Griffith working on the side of his 35-foot sailboat. He was tanned and wearing khakis. There was little Fitzgerald could do about spit shined shoes, slacks and pale skin.

The weather at the North Cove Marina blew through the jacket. Sandy was wearing an open shirt and broken smile. He waved back before returning to the sailboat's lines. Sandy's English accent was pronounced. "Hello, hello, hello. I do love her. What do you think of my lady here? She most definitely cost me all my, as you yanks say, moola." Looking down he pointed at my feet, "Are those the only shoes you have?" Sandy was not about to compromise. "You can't wear black soled shoes aboard. They are most assuredly a real pain to clean off. How about taking off your shoes?" Sandy continued pulling the cover off the mast. "Get comfortable and we will cast off in a minute." Obviously at home with his rig, the boat was readied and made seaworthy. He swung around and sat down next to the rudder. Sandy pushed the boat off with one hand while steering with the other. The sloop sailed away from the marina. He had a sailor's eye, staying focused on the horizon while asking "How are you Yanks handling Tesla's estate?"

"We impounded it." Fitzgerald said with mixed pride.

"Jolly good. That's what I like about you Yanks; you attend to matters. Do you have the weapon secured?" Still holding onto the side of the boat Fitzgerald answered slowly, "I know where the materials are kept and they are safe."

"Is this your first time on a boat?"

"Does it show?" "Don't worry, mate."

"Did I tell you I never swam before?"

"Mate, I never sank before." Fitzgerald laughed. "Fair enough?"

Sandy opened the lid under the seat and pulled out a bulky, military life jacket and handed it over. "You better put this on."

While fumbling with the bulky vest Fitzgerald asked, "When Tesla had discussions with Chamberlain's people about building the weapon, did he leave any documentation?"

"He was an American," Fitzgerald said.

"All very well, old chap but the problem comes about in a most inconvenient time. We have information the Nazi's decided an atomic bomb is not feasible. I have it on good authority your government has decided an atomic bomb is feasible."

Fitzgerald remained silent while the sloop turned sharply into a large wave.

Sandy laughed in glee as the boat left the surface and bounced down hard. "The Nazis are about to either crush Stalingrad or Stalingrad will turn the war back onto them. The war at sea is far more costly for the Nazis than they had planned. Our fate is on far away fields between great forces." Fitzgerald's color was rapidly changing from alabaster to coral green. Sandy stopped smiling, "Are you all right mate? You look none too well."

Fitzgerald stood and announced "Enough, I'm going to resolve this once and for all" then turned, bent over the side and deposited breakfast and lunch into the ocean. He spent the rest of the journey munching graham crackers.

Once beyond the harbor heavy freighters were pulling in and out of the shipping lanes. Pointing at the horizon Sandy's sharp eyes saw a periscope on the horizon and lamented, "The U-boats descend with impunity with their 'wolf-pack' attacks. The city glare gives off the background light making sitting ducks out of your merchant ships approaching the Ambrose Channel entrance to New York Harbor. You Yanks throw up six miles of glowing lights to silhouette against the southbound shipping. Ships are being sunk and seamen drowned for the convenience of enjoying the cinema." The Englishman explained with disdain.

He said, "At least the fuel shortages have put a crimp on your tourist boats filling up the harbor to make fat targets."

Fitzgerald blurted "We need your help on a project."

Sandy said "I was beginning to worry old chap, if you were ever going to get around to the reason for our visit not that it is not good to see you and all."

Fitzgerald was well aware of the immediate problem and beyond "The wolf packs may be able to operate off our coast but here in the city we know what the Nazis are doing every minute. They are going to do everything to steal Dr. Tesla's weapon. The reason I'm telling you this is we have information one of your old friends is directly involved."

Sandy's smile returned easily "Really? Fancy that, who?"

"George Sylvester Viereck."

"Georgie. I thought you chaps had locked him up. I must confess I presumed Georgie was far too busy dealing with his pesky legal problems. He should know we are going to be in control of Nadya Gardner's testimony before the Supreme Court. Viereck is trumped prior to the cards being dealt."

A.I. had not expected this twist. He wanted the real George and A.I. wanted the actor. This created a real problem. A.I. wasn't sure how much he knew and where he was going with it. Fitzgerald had to pursue this by first finding out what he knew. "We locked him up and he is still in prison. It seems there's an Italian who looks vaguely like him who has taken on his identity. That's all we know at this time."

"Why do you need us British for an Italian? Surely you Yanks hardly feel threaten by the Italians. Good god, man, what a shock."

Ignoring the dig Fitzgerald said "All we know is that he is receiving funds from a private London address."

"What else do you know about him?"

"What we have concluded is he's adopted Viereck's identity to exploit the relationship with Tesla. He might have somehow connected with the local Nazis. I'm not surprised in the least."

"Actually old boy, we do know a little about the matter."

"Why tell us now?" Fitzgerald asked.

"However, we do know a bit" Sandy said. "We believe his name is Claudius. He repeatedly contacts the Marconi Company in London. His home is in Rome. We believe he is a commercial spy, most likely does corporate contract work. And he's a thief."

Private company espionage created more problems than an outsider could understand during a war. Certain rules change against national conglomerates. Fitzgerald graduated at the top of his A.I. class and had never discussed such an option.

Fitzgerald said "A corporate spy stealing weapons in the middle of the world war for money?"

"It might be for money. Perhaps it has to do with Tesla's case against Marconi."

"Who do you know is involved with this?" Fitzgerald asked "Or you suggesting what would you would have us British to do on your soil?"

Sandy explained "You were doing such an excellent job outmaneuvering George in court I presumed you would have certain information and resources you would are willing to share with us."

"Perhaps we can work together to crush this bloody fascist. What would you suggest?"

"I will be in charge" Fitzgerald said. "I have the resources of the FBI and the Army. We are looking for his Achilles heel. I want to throw his Fascist ass into jail."

"I will be too happy to provide information on his shall we say, Achilles heel. What are you offering us?"

"What do you need?"

Sandy grinned. "Did you know Dr. Tesla had also created a torpedo?"

Surprised Fitzgerald answered, "Where did you learn about…?"

"The question becomes: are we going to work together?"

"Are you suggesting... what?"

"We appreciate your lend-lease program and all the ships you Yanks have sent over. We also had in mind receiving the newer items such as this torpedo."

"This torpedo is not an active project."

"So you say. This means you have it."

The only thing he knew was the answer was about ten levels above his pay grade. Turning to the wind Fitzgerald answered, "We know where the plans are. Let's get back to Viereck's weak point. I'm not going to let that Nazi keep us be-hind the eight ball. I want to give him a kick to force him to talk."

Sandy said, "What was it you said?"

The sun was beginning to set. Some time passed without either speaking. Pulling his jacket tightly Fitzgerald sat down. "It's not my project. I believe we are only at the early stage on the torpedo. This torpedo would require a major retrofit of every submarine, an impossible task, especially at this stage of the war. My God, man, who has years to set our fleet aside on an untested principle? I can see developing this after the war. It will be impossible to have the military rethink everything at this critical juncture. There will not be any funding for this project. It's not feasible."

"How do you American's say it? Oh, yes: are you wangling?"

"You're a smooth article you know that, Sandy?"

"You're no Willie boy yourself, Fitzgerald." The moment was now; we could choose to never trust or to trust absolutely.

After a long pause Sandy asked "Do you know what Viereck has in common with this Claudius fellow?

They both have an affinity for opium tinctures."

"Opium? I would have never guessed."

Being young then Fitzgerald put out my hand to Sandy. "Really, it may very well be your chance to join this American circus. Would you have interest in such a venture?"

The Frank E. Campbell Mortuary
Madison & 81st

Knowing foreigners would attend, Donald J. had hidden eight microphones. Kosanovic entered the funeral home first thing in the morning, hoping for a private meeting. It was ordained for this never to happen. King Petar II was enjoying his exile in England. The King preferred not being disturbed by the war destroying his country. Even though he was highly regarded within his government's circles, Sava Kosanovic was allowed to speak with King Petar's emissary. Only his leadership within the Eastern European Planning Board made this possible. Given the weakness of the king's reign, Kosanovic worked for Yugoslavia in New York, not Washington. A man of Kosanovic's talent wisely stayed away from the embassy crowd where sophisticated ears detect subtleties and suspect loyalties. He also knew the only unforgivable sin for a diplomat in the U.S. was communism.

Kosanovic feared his knowledge and experience within the volatile nature of leadership in Yugoslavia. Even though Petar was no longer the de facto leader; his majesty remained the *de jure* leader. A national leader without power and young and horny or it could be said a nobility who was always very satisfied with the delights of England, most every night.

Although Kosanovic never met the King, he closely followed his every step. Petar II had succeeded under the regency of his cousin, Prince Paul, after his father, King Alexander was assassinated in Marseilles. Paul's government signed an agreement with the fascist in March 1941 when the populist army overthrew the regent. Petar's personal rule began with the German invasion and was exercised from the security and luxury of England where royalty was treated with deference.

Unable to raise an army in Yugoslavia, the king was granted the facade of a militia in England, the Order of St John of Jerusalem. Lieutenant Grand Master William Sohier Bryant was the most devoted of all. His loyalty was measured by his numerous large and colorful medals. The aged master stood as straight as a cadet.

When he shook Kosanovic's hand Bryant snapped his movements with rigid efficiency, wincing from arthritis. The full regalia of gold buttons, honorariums and three gold braids couldn't cover up his pain.

Only direct questions were accepted protocol, answers were a different practice. Following procedure Kosanovic asked, "What is his majesty's position with the local Serb and Croat factions quarreling over arrangements for the funeral?"

It seemed he was born stiff in body and speech. Grand Master Bryant stared unblinkingly at Kosanovic. "We agree with the consulate office position of dividing the church seats. Put the Croatians on one side and the Serbians on the other. Keep the Montenegrins in the rear."

Kosanovic asked, "Would you ask the church if this is the place to formalize our country's divisions?"

The king's bootlicker could only answer as instructed; unable to function on his own. He became confused crossing the aims of his two revered institutions. "It is not the place for the regent to address the political actions of the church. No, that is not exactly what I meant. The regent does not have to do anything. No, you are confusing my words out of context." Exhausted, his eyes dropped.

"What I need is how I can put forth a matter of great secrecy and urgency before the king."

Straightening his thick ornate uniform, the doddering grand master said "The king is open to his people. Being emissary-at-large in New York, I must remind you of the chain of command. You are not entitled to speak directly to the king. The very chain of command recognizes the king chooses his advisors. Certainly you are capable of understanding the necessity of protocol."

Kosanovic was experienced in the ways of emissaries representing royalty. "Given that the Jovanovich government resigned and reformed in the last two weeks it was my considered belief and hope the King would be interested in direct communications in matters of serious national concern. Our country has state interest in the recent demise of the king's dear friend Dr., Nikola Tesla. Would you not agree?"

The grand master showed expression for the first time. "Yes, yes, the king has great fondness for Yugoslavia's favorite son."

Kosanovic wrote this was the moment he concluded there were no wise men in this government to entrust such a weapon. This created yet another inner dilemma. Without the government the weapon would be useless. Yet with this archaic government thinking the weapon could hurt them. Kosanovic said "I appreciate your role serving the king," with regal grace. "How-ever, you are also functioning in a role that dictates Yugoslavian foreign policy, a matter that is of grave and complex national interest. Perhaps it would be best for me to convey this critical issue to the king. I must speak to him immediately."

The grand master dictated, "I will convey your message to his highness. Now speak to me is this matter? And do not burden your brief message with foolish details."

"Grand Master this matter is of national interest, Yugoslavian national interest."

"My integrity is beyond reproach. I am a loyal soldier to the king. I have no interest in your personal issues beyond whether or not they endanger or better serve the king. You must respect me the same here in America."

"If you please, not all of our concerns are the business of the United States."

Bryant became indignant and said "My role supersedes any national interest beyond my complete and utter loyalty to the king. I am unable to understand your hostility towards the Order of St John of Jerusalem or the Americans. President Roosevelt declared he was deeply interested in the young king since the tragic death of his father, King Alexander I. And Roosevelt offered his personal invitation for the young King to visit the United States with his mother, Dowager Queen Mary." He punctuated with a blink.

With a bow Kosanovic left.

FBI Field Office
West Broadway

The university never prepared Fitzgerald for military efficiency. A.I. was kept apprised of all events related to the project. The report on Foxworth escalated the war for Fitzgerald. After receiving orders to support Roosevelt's meeting with Churchill, Foxworth received permission to bring his wife and her three sisters. A week or two in Casablanca with all fifty passengers were looking forward to the trip as a working vacation. Foxworth was to be joined by Special Agent Harold D. Haberfeld who worked in Algiers. His teams of thirty-five specialists arrived on the military transport in time and were surprised to find fighter escorts waiting.

Rumors of a bomb on board caused the pilot, Benjamin Dally, to land in Trinidad and search the plane. No bomb was found.

The C-54, flown by a proven crew under contract to the Air Transport Command, crashed in the jungle 30 miles from Paramaribo, Dutch Guiana, killing everyone on board. There was a failure to determine the cause of the crash. Deputy Director Percy Foxworth's body and those of his extended family have not been recovered.

Fitzgerald received notice of the explosion that afternoon and called the FBI office. Agent Allen answered. "I heard about Foxworth," Fitzgerald said. "I was just at his house just before he took off. Were you able to speak to him over the weekend?"

That an outsider was ahead of the bureau on his own turf was not going to happen with Allen. "I didn't speak to Agent Foxworth." His voice faded as he added "My last instructions were to monitor your leads."

Fitzgerald made his play and explained. "Hoover will send us some special ops guys and we will scour every place Tesla has been and find that weapon. Hoover realizes Foxworth was working on the case of the missing weapon and, now his airplane is mysteriously shot out of the sky. We have to find out where the weapon is hidden. Once they see we are out there in force they will react and we can get them then, right?"

"I'm sure the bureau will uncover the answer." Allen's words carried the emotion of a training manual.

"Listen Allen, I know you as Jake. Foxworth trusted you because you did what needed to be done. What will it take for someone to warn you about the most powerful weapon ever created? Look, if I get on the horn to Hoover and you see what resources you can produce in the next 24 hours. I will meet you in your office in two hours. This will be our chance to take control of this weapon. All right I have to run and get through to J. Edger." Fitzgerald heard the beginnings of confused agreement so he grabbed it "Great, see you then." and hung up.

Allen called department heads to see who was going to be the 'chalk eaters'. There were none. Every department offered support in pursuit of Foxworth's killers.

Focused on one goal Fitzgerald showed up early and walked straight into Allen's new office unannounced. "Agent Allen you know I am the only one who saw the weapon or understands the magnitude of its power. I figured you wanted our original team in on it, too."

"How are you sure it will work?" He asked.

Fitzgerald explained "When Robert Peary was making his second attempt to reach the North Pole, Tesla notified the expedition that he would be trying to contact them. They were to report to him the details of anything unusual they might witness on the open tundra. Accompanied by his associate George Scherff, they aimed Tesla's Wardenclyffe tower pure energy signals under the Atlantic towards the Arctic, to a spot he calculated was west of the Peary expedition.

On June 30th, 1908 a massive explosion devastated Tunguska, a remote area in the Siberian wilderness. Five hundred thousand acres of land was instantly destroyed. Equivalent to ten to fifteen megatons of TNT, the Tunguska explosion is the most powerful to have occurred in human history. The explosion was audible 600 miles away.

"Nikola apologized that his ray was too powerful and had overshot its intended target and destroyed Tunguska. Tesla dismantled this ray gun at once, deeming it too dangerous to remain in existence. Six years later at the onset of the First World War, Tesla wrote to President Wilson and revealed his secret test. He offered to rebuild the weapon for the War Department, with the caveat that it must only be used purely as a deterrent. Wilson's aides decided Tesla's preconditions were unacceptable to the military and they never showed the President the letter."

Allen looked at the other agents in the office. The six agents on leave from the various departments were impatient. Allen stepped forward and announced "Gentlemen, a highly lethal weapon developed by the late Nikola Tesla is lost. This is Special Agent Fitzgerald."

Fitzgerald stepped into the center of the agents distributed lists of Tesla's last known residences, laboratories and offices. "The Office of Alien Property has secured Nikola Tesla's materials and documents. Our focus today will be his laboratories. Here are the addresses,

- o   89 liberty St, at Temple
- o   175 Grand Street, at Baxter
- o   33-35 South Fifth Ave
- o   46-48 East Houston St.
- o   Wardenclyffe, Shoreham Long Island.

Fitzgerald explained to the team "We are going to break up into teams. A Team will be Agent Allen and you will investigate the four addresses in Manhattan. I will head up B Team and we will investigate the Wardenclyffe Lab in Long Island."

Stepping in Allen said, "The FBI only takes direction from FBI. Understood? Agent Harless will head up B Team. I will have Fitzgerald wait here for the special ops teams he is going to have Hoover send us. Fitzgerald, given we have been understaffed since the war started and I need to see these guys actually show up. Otherwise I think you had better get back to your engineering and let Hoover run the FBI. What do you say?"

"Do you think we should wait for them," Fitzgerald asked "They have to come all the way up from Washington?"

Allen waved to Harless for the teams to head out. Fitzgerald said "I will wait for Hoover's men.

Where shall we rendezvous?"

It was unlikely Foxworth had ever seen this side of Allen, who snarled. "When we need your help we will let you know and let me explain Director Hoover is definitely not going to send you a team from special ops. We need you to vacate our offices. Understood?"

Abruptly the door opened and four Special agents marched in. The first said, "We were told to meet Fitzgerald here. Where can we find him?"

George Viereck's Suite
1001 Madison Avenue

Lying on his bed exhausted, George always kept a bed light on. He was staring at the ceiling when he heard a banging on the front door. He struggled out of bed, groggy as he staggered. The banging continued until he opened the door.

The huge stranger walked inside and stopped. "George Viereck, it is so good to meet you. I am Comrade Rostarchuk of Amtorg. This is good this has brought us together. Should I come in?"

Without waiting for an answer and being well over a hundred pounds heavier than George, Rostarchuk walked over to the sitting room. George stumbled backwards accidentally banging into the door.

Walking around the room, as if he was searching for a secret, Rostarchuk turned on the radio. As George started to protest, the Russian's fat finger quickly went to his lips. Rostarchuk whispered, "Security, the walls have ears. George, I knew you were such good friends with my friend Nickola. Yes, on the radio they announce Mayor La Guardia is going to read a eulogy over WYNC. I was most sure you wanted to hear it."

Walking over to the large Zenith he turned the radio on. The mayors' speech about Tesla couldn't have included one more accolade without sinking from the weight of the praise.

George become nervous, wondering how much the Russian knew. Walking towards the kitchen, the bewildered host asked, "I am going to have coffee. Can I suggest something to drink?"

"Vodka, do you have any Russian vodka?" George asked "Is Stolichnaya satisfactory? Presuming the answer George turned towards the well-stocked sidebar.

Laughing loudly Rostarchuk proclaimed, "You are too good I knew you were special."

"Can I offer you something to eat?"

"No, no. I need to watch my weight" Amused, Rostarchuk lumbered up next to George, "Heir Viereck, let me make you bright with some good Russian humor, sound good? Good. A lieutenant, fresh from a military academy, reports for duty to his commanding officer.

The C.O. invites him to have a drink. He pours two glasses of vodka, drinks his vodka and takes a bite on a cucumber. The lieutenant drinks without eating. The C.O. refills the glasses, drinks his vodka and takes another bite of a cucumber. The lieutenant drinks his glass without eating anything. The C.O. says, 'Have some cucumbers. Do not be too shy.' The lieutenant showed surprise and answered, 'so, was it a lunch you invited me to?"

Roaring at his joke Rostarchuk wrapped his huge hand around the drink. George set the jigger down. The Russian picked it up and poured another drink. With his left paw smacking across George's entire back Rostarchuk bellowed, "Salute!"

After the stinging back slap subsided George remembered. "I need to eat."

"Do you like my jokes, George?"

George replied "I remember now, you were the funny Russian."

Rostarchuk tilted his head slightly and smiled, "You remind me of a very funny story. I tell you about the three young Russians who went out hunting. One of them was drunk and started shooting at his companions. When the shooting was over, the third one climbs out of the bush asking: 'What got into you, man? Why did you start shooting at Kol'ka?' 'Well, I thought he was a kind of a dear.'

'Okay. When did you guess it was not Kol'ka?' 'When that crazy man began shooting back'"

George smiled knowing there was deep Russian meaning somewhere in this humor. He walked over to the radio and turned to WYNC.

"Do you want me to drink *a la ruse*?" Rostarchuk changed the station to the opera.

George was well aware of the Russian custom of drinking: No ice, no mix, no food, no occasion and always a toast. "I am going to eat, enjoy your *la ruse*."

Rostarchuk poured himself another shot. "Salute to your friend, Dr. Tesla was a great man, was he not?" Retreating into the kitchen, George jumped seeing Rostarchuk at his shoulder. The Russians vodka breath nearly made George gag.

"Let me tell another of my very funny jokes. They make you laugh, no? Without waiting for an answer Rostarchuk continued on "A doctor asked to his patient 'Do you smoke?' 'No I do not' 'Do you drink?' 'No I do not' 'You need to start drinking and smoking' 'What for?' 'It will be a lot easier for me to make the right diagnosis.'"

George headed for the icebox and opened the door between them. He turned the radio dial back to listen to Tesla's Eulogy.

George put his finger over his lips for silence,

"Mayor La Guardia is starting to speak. I read he is using Louis Adamic to write for him." Seeing Rostarchuk blank stare he explained, "He wrote the best seller *The Natives Return*. Are you familiar with the work? Never mind"

Rostarchuk asked, "Do you know the meaning of vodka?"

"No."

"Rejuvenating potion, isn't that funny?" His laughter rattled the cabinet's glass door.

George gave a long hard look at this huge Russian, who had barged into his home and was trying far too much to be his friend. For George, there was no doubt what would happen if this crazy bear knew what was in the nearby cabinet: George would be dead.

George turned up the radio's volume. Mayor La Guardia's voice boomed, a natural. The hero 'Fiorello', who without telling the kids he was the Mayor, read the comics to the children during a citywide newspaper strike.

"George" Rostarchuk yelled in his ear.

Startled, George turned to find himself tête-à-tête with this huge head exhaling a lungful of vodka.

"George, you probably wonder why I am here. I want you to know that no matter what exists between our two countries, we had nothing to do with the Drew Pearson article causing the grand jury to investigate you."

George knew full well the British were behind it. This Russian had to be an idiot for not knowing the real George was in prison."

Rostarchuk looked at the picture of Adolph Hitler and headed back to the vodka. He poured himself another drink, toasting George "Salute."

The huge Russian lumbered back to George "We have proof the British have violated the same charges that convicted you. Nadya Gardner's damaging evidence is falsified. Did you know she was employed as a British censor in Bermuda? You did not know that did you?"

George shook his head no.

The Russian continued "My sources say at the next trial they will bring back Nadya Gardner and Sandy Griffith to testify. Sandy Griffith is also an agent of the British. They will commit perjury. It is in their interest to destroy you. You are the symbol of the peace movement and you will be tied to subversion."

"Why are you telling me this?"

"George, you are a brilliant man who has no sense of what is happening in the world. The British are broke and have been since before the war. Without the Americans, they would fall. That is in the interest of both of us, yes?"

George feared being set up by some secret Russian gambit but, agreed anyway. "I also know our countries are at war with each other. If Stalin knew you were helping a German while Stalingrad is in the midst of its greatest battle you would be purged, would you not?"

Rostarchuk moved about "We are not here to worry about the war; we must focus on the future. You know and I know you will not be so fortunate before the Supreme Court next time. You will lose everything if you return to prison."

"And again, why are you here?" George asked.

"We can eliminate your problem. Without witnesses they have no case. Is this not correct? This Tesla has many documents, ones we paid for. We want what is ours before the Americans steal them."

George played along "The FBI has already impounded all of his possessions."

"They have, but what have you secured?" George challenged in a mock tone "Am I not a journalist? Why do you think I am a spy?"

Rostarchuk pointed his thick finger at George.

"You are too humble. You stayed close to this Tesla for a reason, no? I respect your loyalty but you must realize the Nazis will let you go to prison. You will lose your family and everything you own. Do you want this to happen?"

"How do you know what the Nazis will do?"

"I know you will be in prison by this summer. You will be there for a very long time, will you not?"

George knew the real George's handlers failed to offer any help. They had only demanded more, with no concern about his future. "How can you help me trust you?"

Rostarchuk wrinkled his heavy brows then walked over to pour another drink. "I do not expect you to trust me but I do expect you to work with me for your freedom and to destroy the British who have targeted you. Who else is helping you?"

"How do you know my countrymen have not already started?"

"How?"

"I am out on bail," George lied.

"I know they have not eliminated your accusers. You know you are being railroaded. As our American hosts say, it is in your interest to play ball, is it not?"

George asked, "What do you think I have?"

"You want to stay out of prison. Think about this, and do so quickly for there is no time to lose."

George guided his massive guest to the door. "I will give your visit great thought but for now I must have my privacy."

Laughing and slapping George on the back Rostarchuk said, "Then we have a deal, no?"

Reaching over his own shoulder to rub his neck George opened the front door for the Russian to promise "I will call." And the moment he left, closed it. Returning to his bedroom, no sooner had George fell asleep. He heard a different, hard knock. Mumbling incoherent Italian curses, he got up, expecting the Russian. Opening the door, a delivery boy handed him a shipping tare receipt. Grabbing it, George slammed the door and tore the sheet in two, leaving one half on the table before crawling back into bed.

Gypsy Bistro 52nd

The wily Russian knew his contact could set up the urgent meeting with Kosanovic without raising questions. The small Gypsy Bistro proved the point of contact best suited on short notice. A.I. had monitored them here before. Seldiakov was a stern man who kept his Lenin beard trimmed to perfection. His eyebrows were thick as sickles, as any cosmopolitan from Russia should. His eyes were determined yet his style was grace. The diplomat Kosanovic walked unnoticed past the tables of self-absorbed diners.

Seldiakov stood and extended his long arm. "Good of you to meet me on such short notice, Comrade."

It was hard for Kosanovic not to contain himself knowing were it not for his uncle's death the Russians would never meet him. They would not bother with a Yugoslav. Kosanovic offered his hand, "It is always interesting when an official of the Soviet Union's commercial heart invites me for pasta."

Their large right hands wrapped around the others. Smiling, they sat down.

With a nod, Seldiakov beckoned the waiter who quickly stepped up to their tableside. The Russian offered, "Sava may I select our wine?"

"I would be honored."

The communist said "I admire their fine selection. They take great pride in their Georgian wines. Many people do not know Georgia is the cradle of wine civilization. We have produced wine since 3000 BC. In Georgia, wine is not just a drink; it is part of our traditional culture." Pausing to look over the server he ordered, "We will have some Khvanchkara."

The waiter dutifully answered "Sorry sir, we are out of Khvanchkara."

"Very well then, give me a bottle of your oldest Akhasheni."

The waiter apologized "Sorry sir, we are out of Akhasheni."

Sitting back and looking at the waiter "Odjalesh?"

"Sorry."

"What do you have?

The waiter offered, "Tvishi?"

"Tvishi?" Seldiakov paused to look over at Kosanovic and shook his head in disappointment. "It's good. A bit acidic, perhaps. You might enjoy the only white wine they have."

Kosanovic suggested, "It's a bit fruity. Let me recommend Pirosmani."

The waiter quickly chimed, 'excellent choice and we have both premier vintages." Surprised by Kosanovic's choice, Seldiakov tipped his head in deference. "1927?"

"1927 it is, sir."

Kosanovic was bemused by the waiter who rushed away and quickly returned to offer the first sip to Kosanovic who commended "Excellent."

After the Yugoslav's approval the waiter poured the first full glass for the Russian, who knew he had lost the first hand of the unspoken game they were playing.

After the waiter left, Kosanovic offered a toast, "For fine food and interesting conversation."

Seldiakov lifted his glass, "To wine, food and the Slavic peoples."

Kosanovic leaned forward and offered a mock whisper, "Someday the world will appreciate the vineyards of Georgia. They are situated at the same longitude as many of the finest producers of France."

"For now, it shall be our secret."

They took a polite drink and then a second sip and a third.

Kosanovic savored the drink "Excellent."

"Yes, yes I commend your selection most highly." They both laughed.

It was not the Russian's nature to laugh for long. Seldiakov instantly became serious and looked quizzically at Kosanovic.

Kosanovic's laughed only half of a note longer than the Russian before reverting to his stately expression. Taking a cue from the mood change led Kosanovic to ask "To what do I owe this honor?"

Seldiakov answered, "Sava, you know how to bring truth to the table. I want you to know my messages can go directly to Secretary General Stalin."

The fact this was an obvious lie is not what puzzled Kosanovic. It was that this low level Russian bureaucrat had the courage to use Stalin's name without fear. If he were caught saying such a lie out loud he would surely spend the rest of his days in Siberia or follow the path of predecessors and die during a reroute.

The Russian offered the macabre humor from the hard fought Urals. Leaning next to Kosanovic, Seldiakov whispered, "The shadow of Josef Stalin darkens Yugoslavia's future. I heard this story from a Yugoslavian general; when Josef Stalin went to his deathbed he called in two likely successors, to test which one of the two had a better knack for ruling the country. He ordered two birds to be brought in and presented one bird to each of the two candidates. The first one, Molotov grabbed the bird, but was so afraid that the bird could free himself from his grip and flyaway, he squeezed his hand very hard. When he opened his palm, the bird was dead."

He paused for a drink and to note the effect on Kosanovic. There was none, so he continued his story, "Seeing the disapproving look on Stalin's face and being afraid to repeat his rival's mistake the second candidate Khrushchev loosened his grip so much that the bird freed himself and flew away.

Stalin looked at both of them scornfully. 'Bring me a bird,' he ordered. They did. Stalin took the bird by its legs and slowly, one by one; he plucked all the feathers from the birds little body. Then he opened his palm. The bird was lying there naked trembling, helpless and hugged his hand for warmth. Stalin looked at them, smiled gently and explained, 'You see, he is even thankful for the human warmth coming out of my palm." The Russian sat back and waited for a reaction.

Kosanovic baited him. "How long will it take you to get action from the Secretary General?"

Pretending to be jovial the Russian was nervous and said "I would not suggest I control the Secretary General's schedule."

"You do have his ear" Kosanovic asked.

The Russian repeated "what is important is we put you on the Secretary General's good side."

Having never spent a personal moment in fear of Stalin, Kosanovic paused before repeating out loud, "good side?"

Smiling at the supposed confirmation, Seldiakov asked, "And, I must ask you how you became such an authority on Georgian wines?"

"I thought you knew" Kosanovic baited.

"Knew what, comrade?" Underplaying Kosanovic softened his delivery, "I drank with him. You knew Stalin was from Georgia. You knew that did you not?"

"*Dah*" Sounded like comrade's last breath.

Kosanovic chose to play this game through "I have not been in contact with Stalin for quite some time. I am most pleased you have maintained your contact."

Looking down at his wine, the color seemed to flow out of the Russian's face. "*Dah*."

After a long silence Seldiakov spoke with renewed vigor; "we Slavs are proud and loyal, right comrade?"

Kosanovic said "I remain curious why you wanted to meet me and why it is so urgent?"

Lowering his voice Seldiakov punctuated each word with individual emphasis, "I can keep you on Stalin's good side."

Kosanovic repeated the words "Stalin's good side."

"Stalin's good side" The Russian echoed without guile.

"How and why are you going to do this?"

"You are a Slavic brother in an enemy country."

"And?"

"And, you are the nephew of Nikola Tesla." They both laughed at the obvious.

Kosanovic pointed out "Both of these facts have been true for a very long time."

"Yes comrade but, there is one other fact is there not? Your uncle recently died. Is that true?"

"Yes it is."

Putting his hand on his heart Seldiakov explained, "My heart goes out to you at this time." "Thank you."

Seldiakov seemed so sincere, "As a Slavic brother during this time of war we must work together. No?"

The Yugoslav explained "My country is in turmoil. Forces from other countries are in the fields attacking us."

"Comrade, we are both under attack from the Germans. It is a racial desire of theirs to destroy the Slavic peoples and you, the southern brothers. They despise all Slavs."

Kosanovic drank the last sip of his wine before asking "How would Russian rule improve our 'southern' lives?"

Reaching for the bottle and refilling both glasses, the Russian declared, "To the Union of Soviet Socialist Republics and Uncle Joe."

With a long hard look Kosanovic asked "You invited me to lunch to speak about our current or postwar relations."

Smiling the best he could, Seldiakov shook his head. "I am here to talk about today and what we need to do to stop the Nazis and

Americans. We must take action immediately to secure Dr. Tesla's inventions for our people."

"Our people?" the Yugoslavian raised his eye brows.

The Russian changed the subject. "Have you taken possession of Tesla's private papers?"

"It's a matter best handled by the courts," Kosanovic explained.

"You cannot be serious. You are going to trust your uncle's inventions, his ray gun be handled by the American courts. Tell me this is not true? This is not true."

"The Americans have already impounded all of my uncle's papers. They have done so illegally. It will take years to unravel the courts from his work."

The Russian stroked his beard "You have nothing?"

The southern Slav Kosanovic distrusted the Northern Slav Russian. His hate was only greater for the Teutonic Germans who have attacked his country for centuries. If he must choose the lesser evil, at least the Russians are against the Germans. "I have not heard why I want to have this discussion."

The Russian drank the rest of his glass and poured himself another. "I thought we discussed the advantages of being on Stalin's good side."

"The last time we were together, I was on his good side. Is there any reason to believe otherwise?" Kosanovic decided it was necessary to continue the deceit.

"Perhaps Amtorg can provide assistance to your concerns."

"I am not sure what you believe I can do to be on Stalin's good side." Kosanovic needed to know how much the Russians knew.

The Russian's forefinger punctuated each word on the table. "I have it on good authority that the OAP has acknowledged there are missing papers. You know you have secured his papers; I know you have secured his inventions. I know you are far too intelligent for it to be otherwise. Is this not true?

"I'm not at liberty to discuss this matter."

"I knew it was true. This is very good comrade. We can work together as comrades should. What are your needs?"

Unprepared for the opportunity the dilemma of desperately needed resources going to his homeland was one offer he was not prepared to turn down. How could a serious member of the Eastern European Planning Board think for a moment there was any choice but to accept supplies to keep his countrymen alive. "As you know, Yugoslavia is in need of everything. The Germans, Italians and rebels in the mountains are attacking us from all sides. What are you offering?"

The Russian sat back and returned to stroking his beard, and looking at the wine. "Tito is unstoppable, if he survives the current Fascist onslaught. Everyone knows Tito was Moscow trained." Seldiakov asked "Where do you have the papers?"

"I have secured necessary materials here in the city."

"We can secure them today?" Seldiakov looked up.

"They are secure." Kosanovic looked over to pick up the wine and fill the glasses, "They are too valuable and must receive immediate assessment. No?" Without a rhetorical answer Kosanovic was facing a devil's bargain. The Yugoslav government-in-exile did not have the resources or even a safe haven to develop the weapon. The Nazis were out of the question, leaving the Russians as the only alternative to America. He looked at the Russian across the table, who was pouring a glass from the second bottle. Kosanovic remained the diplomat. "What are you offering?"

"The importance of these papers should be seen by top Soviet scientists immediately. You will receive their report when I do."

Kosanovic asked, "Then what?"

"We must build it and destroy Hitler. There is no other choice." He looked at Kosanovic like he was a fool for considering any other thought. Again, Kosanovic found himself in a corner. "I understand what you are saying. We need to further these discussions very soon but not tonight."

"What do you mean? What could be more important than the immediate destruction of fascism? A.I. file notes on the Russian clearly stated he was not a dramatic person, but he slapped his own head before ranting on, "We are at a critical juncture in history and you, you, my friend, are able to provide the decisive nail for Hitler's casket. You should be proud."

With that yet another toast was raised to Kosanovic, who responded, as a diplomat should, "Our dedication to ending Fascism."

They tapped their glasses in agreement.

Ritz Theatre
219 W. 48th Street

The sidewalks were filled with a Sunday evening theater crowd walking slowly, each trying to be noticed by others. The two men did not want to be noticed. The German emissary Dr. Kiep walked down West 48th Street with an undocumented alien, Wilhelm Von Haak. Ignoring the team of agents, the Germans knew there was one agent following 500 steps behind them and another the same distance back, across the street.

Von Haak asked quietly, "We have brought two agents together to follow us. How are we going to talk?"

Kiep took hold of Wilhelm's left shoulder, and guided him into the Ritz Theatre. Kiep asked, "The question is how are they are going to get good tickets minutes before show time?"

Kiep picked up the two tickets in his name to the sold out show, "New Faces". They entered the Ritz and Von Haak followed Kiep quickly upstairs to the private balcony seats.

After they sat Kiep gave the usher five dollars then asked, "Do you enjoy the cabaret?"

"It has been far too long since I have indulged myself."

"You will find this show has, shall we say, its bright spots. I understand Orson Welles is satirized quite well. The reviewer mentioned clown Irwin Corey with his too-long lecture on Hamlet. Did you study Hamlet?"

Von Haak pointed his finger at the nearest aisle on the main floor "Yes of course. Look, there are the clumsy Americans looking for us. We have the most visible seat in the theatre and they cannot find us."

What the Nazi's failed to realize was Donald J. knew about the tickets and had visited their seats beforehand.

"Give them time they will look up."

Von Haak said "Our U-boats continue to operate off this very coast and they act as if they are unaware of their fate. The Americans have drafted 900,000 men from New York alone and at Christmas time the city is gay with holiday decorations. The newspapers wrote the season had the most reckless spending on Christmas ever."

Kiep remained focus on the agents walking the aisles below ignoring his subordinate's assessments. "After the fall of the Philippines, these American's acted as if it were a holiday for people who don't care. They rushed madly about, in a Coney-Island dim-out. They spent foolish as in the midst of a carnival."

Kiep said nothing.

"I have always wanted to ask you about the honor in delivering the Fuehrer's declaration of war to the Americans."

"I read a speech and signed the declaration? I am proud of that moment, for it is history serving notice to whomever stands in the path of the Fatherland." Von Haak sat back and watched the cabaret.

After a moment listening to Orson's monologue he whispered, "We need to discuss George Viereck."

"When the show starts I will show you the best seat in the theatre. For now, we must be realistic in our assessments. The Russian front will change our tactics in America. Our eastern front is collapsing. Rumors are the 6th Army in Stalingrad is about to surrender. The Slavs would murder us before sharing food. We are withdrawing from the Caucasus, between the Black and Caspian Seas. The US Fifth Army has begun an offensive against the German forces in Italy. The British 8th Army has taken 45,000 Italian prisoners."

The relationship with officers was markedly different in America. It seemed more permissive. "Can I know what direction we will be following?"

Kiep said, "On our Western front the *Kriegs marine* begins Operation Drum Beat, the first coordinated attack by five U-boats against US shipping along the east coast. You understand our greatest victory is in New York. Here, where we have sunk their tankers."

Von Haak pointed down at the agents walking the aisles "The FBI thinks they are following us. No, we are leading them where we want them to go. Look at them, they have taken seats. Look at the fool, the one on the far side of the aisle is pointing at us, informing the others."

Kiep looked at the wandering agents, who one by one looked up at the box seats in the balcony? "Within five minutes, they will be lurking in the hallway outside our door." Kiep held up his forefinger to cover his mouth. "Of course, they will. Wait for them to stand then follow my lead."

When the first agent nonchalantly walked to the back, the second followed. The curtain slowly lifted. The orchestra opened with an original tune, followed by a troupe of young entertainer's performing a medley of medieval songs, dances, and sketches for openers.

"Now" Kiep quickly stood and stepped out the door, exiting the box seats into the balcony outer aisle. Four doors down, two men wearing brown suits and brown shoes, left their box seats and hastily walked past. Kiep and Von Haak walked over to the far box seat. Pulling their new chairs to the rear of the box seats, the spies sat in the back, little more than dark shadows. They pulled this last time and A.I. was ready this time.

Quietly, Kiep said. "It is important for you to understand George Viereck. He is a romantic and one who may have the key to the war. This accelerator he holds, yes, the one he failed to mention the night you visited him. I have seen pictures of this accelerator. It appears authentic. I have read enough about this Nikola Tesla to tell you his genius is capable of anything.

"With that being said, we have no delusions about the counter efforts set about by the FBI. We know they are more efficient than the G-men wandering down the hall standing around wondering what we are talking about. The FBI is working very hard to attack our organization and hinder its growth."

"What should I do?" Von Haak asked.

"We need to get this film to Berlin for assessment and then secure this accelerator from the Italian. You must remain available for the next four days. I intend on resolving both of these problems. You shall return as his prime handler. Understood?"

Von Haak nodded Kiep stood and motioned for him to follow ignoring the comedian Professor Irwin Corey making a mockery of *Hamlet*. The audience's laughter created a commotion. Following the servants' stairs down to the side alley provided the opportunity for Kiep and Von Haak to walk in opposite directions.

Monday, January 11th

Foreign Contacts

South of Montauk Point, Long Island

George crawled deep into his oversized bed. Unable to close his eyes he stared at the statue, in front of the accelerator. His prospects were Nazis first Russians and allies were a distant last.

Sitting up before speaking out loud to himself, he recited the only poem Tesla ever wrote for solace, "While listening to my cosmic phone, I caught words from the Olympus blown."

It had been ten years since Nikola wrote his *Fragments of Olympian Gossip* a heartfelt attempt at true friendship. Startled by the ringing, George grabbed wildly at the telephone. Whoever it was, hung up. George jumped out of bed and ran over to look through the curtains. He pulled his slacks on and suspenders over his undershirt.

The front door was rapped on three times. George hurried to the door. He found a slip of paper shoved under the crack with instructions, "Walk around the block at exactly five a.m. You will be met by a gray Plymouth. Bring pictures for transmission." The message was unsigned leaving George flipping the paper. His goal was simple; one payment and then the president's suite on the next boat to Italy.

After he finished dressing George put 40 photos into his pocket. He carefully moved the accelerator in the attic to outside the apartment. His self-styled notes written in his appointment book referred to a hiding place, in one of Tesla's old labs. However, there was no address. He planned on hiding the accelerator there soon.

Checking the room one last time George walked out the door, around to the servant quarters and down the side stairs. He put his head down against the biting wind coming through the alley. He came out the opposite side of his building to see the gray Plymouth. George walked up to the car. Von Haak started the engine. Following Wilhelm's wave, the Italian obediently climbed inside and the Plymouth entered the morning traffic.

Von Haak spoke first "How many photos are there?"

"I have them." George snapped his answer.

Von Haak wrapped his thick hand behind George's spindly neck and spoke slowly. "I want you to think of me as your friend. Is that what allies should do?"

George answered, "I have forty pictures. Do you want to see?"

"Hold them next to the dashboard so I can get a quick look?"

George pulled out the top eight pictures and fanned them out.

Von Haak dropped his hand onto George's wrist, just to show he could. "Hold still." He studied the photos. "We have a long drive ahead of us."

An hour later they arrived at a private dock, south of Montauk Point, Long Island. It was cold, wet and dark. Tugging his coat collar tight, George followed his Nazi handler over to the old work shed.

The FBI agreed to postpone a raid, after A.I. confirmed how much information could be collected by monitoring.

Von Haak rapped on the door three times. After being unlocked from the inside, George was surprised by the sophisticated radio controls for numerous transmitters. The short-range FM sets gave voice communication capabilities free from interference. The gadfly of an operator, Koedel turned a dial down before grabbing his cigarette and lit it, while scrutinizing George up and down.

Von Haak put his large hand over George's shoulder "I want you to meet George. He has pictures. These top secret images will be carried to Berlin by submarine. You must interview Heir Viereck and transmit the answers to Berlin for evaluation. We must await further instructions."

The radioman looked at the deliverable. "Let me see these."

Viereck pulled them out and handed them to Koedel. He was a mushy man, slouched over in a permanent position. His agility was surprising when Viereck dropped the package of pictures, Koedel caught it.

Von Haak picked up Koedel's pack of cigarettes, pulled out one and tapped it on his fingernail three times. The old man studied the pictures, humming single notes of approval. He asked "Is this the weapon that could end all wars?" Without waiting for an answer he asked, "The weapon's range is the horizon?"

"Beyond," George answered not caring if he was correct.

Everyone was startled when the door swung open. Followed by his two aides, Kiep marched in. "This security breach will end your mission. This will cause a failure we cannot afford." Von Haak stood at attention.

Pointing to the Magnetophon Kiep ordered, "George, you need to pay attention. Martin is going to record your voice." He proudly added, "This is the only machine of the war capable of providing sound with no background noise."

George looked for Kiep's direction.

Kiep pulled up a chair opposite George's. Kiep grabbed it by the mount and spoke clearly "Testing, testing, 1, 2, 3."

After reading the meters the frog of an operator nodded. "Tell us how you came about this accelerator known as Nikola Tesla's force field weapon?"

George lied, "I was to visit Dr. Tesla on a legal matter. He was in need of money and the poor soul was unable to even pay his hotel bills. Being a life-long friend, I was willing to advance him some funds." He stopped and drank some coffee. It made him choke before continuing "He gave me the invention as collateral. Recently I have realized the power of this weapon."

Martin was skeptical. "Do you know why no country sponsored this project?"

"He revealed the project to the U.S. Military and they insisted taking control over further development without him. Tesla later went to England and spoke to Neville Chamberlain's military. The army demanded the weapon without the inventor. His reputation had been tarnished by then. You have to understand, J.P. Morgan blackballed Tesla for decades."

Von Haak asked "Why would the great Morgan blackball an inventor?"

"Tesla used Morgan's money to make electricity free for everyone and he took offense."

"It is understandable why a capitalist investor would have a problem with the absurd notion of giving power for free.' Kiep said. "Why would Morgan black-ball a weapon that works?"

"I have known this genius for years. Dr. Tesla was told he could not invent light, he did. He was told he could not light a city. He lit Buffalo from his generators in the Niagara Falls with one switch. He created lightning. My god, he created an earthquake." The only time George was not afraid of them was when he was defending Tesla. "He is a true genius with impeccable integrity."

Kiep asked, "This is true, is it not?"

Smiling George acknowledged his handler. "I also have his notes."

"What notes?"

"He did extensive work on this project and he kept notes.

This is the first time we recorded Kiep when he was angry. The German spewed his words *Why are you telling me now about these notes after we had one of our submarines risk everything? You have only given us a small part of the plans. Tell me heir Viereck is this not true?"*

George repeated a rumor "The accelerator can bounce beams off the moon. I may not know where all the notes are but suspect Tesla's nephew has them."

When the red light in the corner started to blink Martin announced "The sub landed we must hurry to take advantage of the predawn light."

Soviet Consulate
Sixteenth Street

The lieutenant colonel could blend into a crowd or dominate any conversation in the room. The sly Russian, Akhmarhov was the chief of the NKGB in the United States. He soon heard about Amtorg's spy network. The Colonel called the meeting with Rostarchuk and Seldiakov as well as the Amtorg president, Dr. Constantin Lukashev.

The Colonel had a well-earned reputation for vindictiveness and intolerance of unauthorized activities. Akhmarhov stared intently at the three civilians who had violated his territory, without receiving his authorization.

Walking in one by one, Seldiakov attempted a good-natured, *"Dobrahye ootrah."*

The Colonel glared at the *apparatchik*. The head of Security was known to prefer bureaucrats be purged. The military solution was to send his enemies to the German front. Akhmarhov's iron jaw aimed directly at President Lukashev, who sat down and then turned to the two. Rostarchuk stumbled and almost fell, trying to grab the furthest chair.

The Colonel's thick voice was frightening "President Lukashev, I understand you instructed these two civilians to perform espionage without receiving authorization or discussing the matter with me. Is this correct?"

The President of Amtorg explained, "I had every intention of bringing you up to date at our weekly briefings. We only learned of Dr. Tesla's death after Friday and you were unavailable."

When angry the Colonel syncopated his words. "Do you have a contact number?"

President Lukashev explained "And you specifically instructed me to only use that in the event of an emergency. We were attempting to take advantage of the very limited time and our existing contacts for the glory of Soviet Russia,"

The NKGB chief spoke slowly "If I hear of espionage by civilians without authorization then I assure everyone they will return to Siberia for reeducation. Am I clear?"

Unable to withhold his exuberance in spite of the overt threat Seldiakov bumbled out, "Did you hear what we achieved?"

The Colonel sat back. "What is that?"

Seldiakov offered "I made contact with George Viereck. He has knowledge of Tesla's death weapon. I think he knows secrets."

"Are you civilians?" the Colonel asked.

Rostarchuk said, "I too, made a significant contact, Dr. Tesla's nephew. Sava Kosanovic had knowledge of the force field weapon and is interested in Yugoslavia receiving our favors."

Looking at Lukashev the Colonel asked sarcastically, "Who did you meet, Hoover?"

Lukashev answered "No sir Gus Hall, the President of the U.S. Communist Party."

The Colonel said, "Let us understand what has happen here, yesterday you three civilians engaged in top secret affairs and highly sensitive relations with three major military targets and you did this all in one day. Is this what each of you want-me-to-understand?" The Colonel looked at each man, one at a time, as they each replied, *"Dah."*

After a prolonged silence, Seldiakov blurted out to the Colonel "Should we call you Michael Green?"

"What?" the Colonel demanded.

Cowering, Seldiakov nearly lost self-control to tears. "No sir. Please I just wanted to be cordial and I thought you wanted us to use your alias. Forgive me what shall I call you?"

The Colonel pulled out and placed his TT33 pistol on top of the table "Gentlemen allow me to explain this service weapon.

It chambers the 7.62 x 25 cartridge. The ammunition is loaded to higher pressures. The barrel and slide are temporarily locked together for a fraction of an inch during rearward travel. This allows the bullet to exit the barrel and reduce pressure before the casing is ejected. Also, the Tokarev is fed by an eight round single stack magazine."

He looked at the three bureaucrats and the Colonel deferred to the immediacy of the problem "Are you under my jurisdiction Comrade. Do you understand me?"

Seldiakov said "Yes comrade, I always have been and am honored to be."

The Colonel asked "What happened to George Viereck?"

Seldiakov struggled for a breath. "Yes, it was who I knew where his apartment is and I visited him."

"Visited him?"

Seldiakov had no reason to believe he could speak freely yet did so, "I called to his apartment in the middle of the night when I was sure to find him. We talked, drank and told jokes, spoke as we were allies and then we drank and told more stories. He is really quite a charming man. I explained we can help him with his trial expenses and he was most interested. He really does not want to go to jail. I am sure of that. We drank together, meaning good things. Does it not? He was the last one to see Dr. Tesla alive and he has secured his valuables."

Stopping for a breath Seldiakov pounded his fist.

"We can get ahead of the Nazis who are not giving him enough money for his legal defense, I am sure."

The Colonel yelled, "You are a fool and an idiot. George Viereck has been in jail for months."

"He told me he was George." He then looked down to avoid the Colonel's glare. The Colonel turned to Rostarchuk "and Tesla's nephew?"

Looking forward to the opportunity to receive his due and recognition, Rostarchuk said, "I spoke to Comrade Kosanovic yesterday. I have gained his confidence and found he had a long affinity General Secretary Stalin. He gave me complete assurances he has secured his uncle's documents on the weapon. After hearing Seldiakov's ridiculous story it will be an honor to transfer directly to your command." President Lukashev silently bristled at the suggestion.

Colonel Akhmarhov asked "Lukashev who did you visit?"

"I used my contacts with the American communist Gus Hal to secure Tesla's addresses. My men verified their status."

"Their status?"

Lukashev explained his suspicion. "My concern was to act quickly during an emergency. At this point, we defer to your expertise. I hereby assign you this project. Do let me know how your work progresses, will you?"

The Colonel picked up his TT-33 pistol. "You will not assign anything. Do I make myself clear?"

Lukashev knew now was the time to blink. It was wartime and the Colonel was threatening retribution, final retribution. "I only meant this in terms of comrades working together."

"Incorrect comrade" the Colonel explained, Dialectics dictates you listen to me." Wisely Lukashev agreed with a slight bow. "Yes sir"

The Colonel turned to the others and snapped, "You will take all further orders from me, do you understand?" He handed Lukashev a typed decree and while studying his weapon, he motioned for Lukashev to read.

"Our prime directive is to watch Churchill and Roosevelt and to learn whether they are going to reach a separate peace agreement with Hitler and then go to war against the Soviet Union together. We are to obtain Hitler's plans of war against the USSR which the Allies might possess; to learn any secret goals and plans of the Allies related to the war; to find out when exactly the Allies are going to open the second front in Europe; to obtain information on the newest secret military equipment designed and produced in the USA, England and Canada."

I am assigning Lt. Colonel Abel as your project chief; whenever any of you have any news or contacts you must report to Abel. He has a cover as a photographer. Am I clear?" After checking each face for obedience, the Colonel drank a glass of water before he returned to his normal voice, "We have 2,500 personal working here. That number changes daily. Am I clear?"

Long Island Private Dock

The U-123 was waiting in shallow water and commissioned under Operation *Paukenschlag*. The Roll of the Drums was designed to blockade America's Atlantic ports while serving as high priority weapons couriers. On the way home, they were free to smuggle. Contraband is as old as seafaring and U-boats needing to refuel continued the tradition. In fact, it was encouraged on their way home to the Fatherland.

Kiep ordered Von Haak and George to stand watch. "George, you stand next to the front door." Looking out the window, the short spy fidgeted. Von Haak watched out the back door. Kiep and Martin walked down the wooden steps to the pier.

Feeling left out, he asked Von Haak, "Tell me what you see?" Von Haak glared until George turned back to the front door.

The Nazi stood a little taller. He was willing to brag about the submarine's rise along the coastline, "I can see the U-123 now. The captain sunk the *Norness* sixty miles off Montauk Point on Long Island. Those are the true heroes. See, the crew is wearing their *Arbeitspackchen*, their work suits."

Turning back the killer pointed his finger out the window like a schoolboy, "The crew is putting on bowler hats. I believe, yes, it is Captain Hardegan wearing his service suit and the white cap. He is the commander. How can you appreciate he has sunk over 50,000 tons of allied shipping? Fortunately for the Americans, he ran out of supplies and must return to the continent. He is very disappointed, I am sure."

His laughter echoed. George realized the submarine was here, now, part of the pack that killed thousands of American's, within sight of the military up and down this coast. If anyone comes, he will never get out of jail.

Von Haak snorted again before boasting, "Our submarines use the American buoys as guides around their nets. We continually prove our superiority. Here comes Martin. He seems in a hurry.

Martin rushed back to the neat set of files piled next to the transmitter. He continued to examine a nautical chart of the coast while bringing Wilhelm up to date. "They're following a parallel course westward along the south shore of Long Island, toward New York City. They almost beached on the Rockaway shore. The crew did not have detailed charts of the area and failed to anticipate the Rockaway's southward curve."

"Unsatisfactory," Von Haak concluded.

Martin explained, "From the reports of the area including the description of a hotel, shore lights, and sand dunes backed by low, dark woods, they probably came close to beaching on the shores of Fort Tilden or Jacob Riis Beach. Captain Hardegan reported viewing the lights of New York at 330 degrees and the Parachute Jump and Wonder Wheel of Coney Island."

"That was quite a view" George added.

"He bragged he could see the men of Fort Tilden posted as lookouts in the tall towers where neither Fort Tilden nor Arverne could spot them. Even with the lights dimmed out, our patrol boats were able see the glow of New York from a distance of 25 miles off shore."

Martin placed three coastal maps under his arm and hurried down to the mooring.

Von Haak continued "It was hazardous last November when our U-608 submarine laid ten mines in the New York Harbor. They have radio direction finding stations at Jones Beach and Montauk in Long Island as well as Sea Isle City in New Jersey. They were no match for German engineering and expertise."

George pointed out, "These stations can now home in on enigma-coded transmissions. They have started using new technology such as sonobouys, magnetic loops, hydro-phones, surface and B-17 aircraft mounted radar and sightings by patrol aircraft, Civil Air Patrol volunteers, blimps, Pan Am Clippers, Eastern Airliners, and merchant vessels."

"Even with all that, today, we witnessed our U-123 come dock on their shores to meet us."

Frightened George watched a man walking down the path and nervously called out "Will, come here quickly."

With surprising speed the German agent was by George's side. Drawing his pistol, he studied the slowly approaching man. Von Haak whispered, "You quietly walk down the hill and tell Kiep an intruder has seen the sub. I am going to resolve the problem. Now, go quietly."

George's legs wobbled across the small room, to the back door. He turned to watch the Nazi dart quietly out the door towards the incoming man. This frightened him even more, "uhhaa" and, he rushed out.

Stepping rapidly down the hillside stairs, the captain pointed at him. Kiep and Martin turned to watch George stumble, barely avoiding a fall.

Nearing the waiting Germans George blurted, "There's someone coming."

Kiep put his forefinger over his lips, signaling him to shut up. George didn't say another word until he was next to the threesome. Kiep snapped at him. "Now, what more bad news do you have?"

"Wilhelm sent me down here to tell you a man was coming down the road to the cabin."

Martin interrupted. "Is he short and bald?"

"Yes I eliminated our exposure." George proudly said.

"It must be Franz. He's my neighbor and a supporter. He was not supposed to be here." Martin wisely realized he could be next.

Kiep asked "Is everything clear?"

"Yes it's almost daylight. I must submerge now and celebrate in Germany next week." "Heil Hitler,"

Kiep gave him a salute. The accompanying SS officer returned the salute. The captain waved and sat in the raft while being rowed to the submarine. The three men walked half way up the hill. They turned with Kiep to watch the Captain drop in followed by a seaman pulling the hatch down.

Looking over at George, Kiep asked, "What exactly did Wilhelm say?"

"He said he was going to resolve the problem and I was to go quickly to tell you."

Kiep ran up the hill, two steps at a time, into the cabin. By the time George and Martin reached the cabin, they knew enough to stand still. They watched. Kiep listened to Wilhelm whisper in his ear. Kiep's right hand clenched. Turning, Kiep whispered a few indecipherable, abrasive words directly into Von Haak's ear.

Kiep motioned Martin to come over. When George started to follow, Kiep ordered, "Not you. You stay there."

George froze.

While the old ham operator walked up to Kiep, the Nazi put his hand on Martin's shoulder and whispered a few words.

Martin snapped, "He was my best friend for forty years you bastard."

The recording extended our priority for resources and the FBI had enough evidence for a raid.

Manhattan Warehouse and Storage Company 52ⁿᵈ St and 7ᵗʰ Ave

The floor man was a frumpy sneak. Michael King guided the inspection team down the aisles and extensive aisles and catacombs of storage lockers. Fitzgerald was the head of this group. Colonel Ralph Doty from Military Intelligence; FBI Agent T. J. Donegan and two brutes dressed like agents followed each carrying two cases of photographic equipment. King stopped to point out the secured locker.

Fitzgerald ordered, "Open it up."

King muttered a final, weak protest, "You guys look like the real McCoy but don't turn this into a circus, okay?"

Instructed to avoid conflict Fitzgerald joked with his best John Wayne impression "Listen Pilgrim open the door. Let us deal with the war."

Smiling King unlocked the lock key and stepped back.

"We will call you when we need you, alright Pilgrim?"

The King left.

Fitzgerald announced, "We want the safe and those contents first. We need to take pictures of everything."

Donegan protested, "I'll follow the orders I was given from Washington."

"All well and good," Fitzgerald agreed. "However I am the only qualified physicist and Washington wants me to lead this investigation. Correct, Colonel Doty?" The Colonel's narrow eyes looked like war weathered slits that never missed anything. He was smart as hell. Doty was career military and one of the liaisons to A.I. "Gentlemen, our job here is to make sure we are not sending weapons to our enemies of today or tomorrow. No one here is our enemy. We are all Americans Right? Right!"

"Of course we are" Donegan explained. "But my job here is to investigate the handling of materials that may affect our national defense."

Fitzgerald walked over to the safe. "This is where we start. Be careful, we can get challenged for tampering with potential evidence, we are going to take pictures of every document."

While turning the dial of the combination lock Fitzgerald lowered his voice. "I know who set the new combination before they impounded the equipment."

The FBI were professionals, some were bureaucrats. Agent Donegan was the latter. "I recommended to the New York District Attorney that Kosanovic and Swezey be picked up on burglary charges."

"You what?" Fitzgerald snapped

"You heard me" Donegan fired back. "We know someone is stealing documents. I say grab them all while we still have the opportunity."

Fitzgerald said, "You need to withdraw that absurd charge."

"Why should I?" The Special agent protested. Fitzgerald was disgusted by this toy soldier, "Because Kosanovic enjoys diplomatic privilege. And the only qualified relative of Tesla."

"What about Swezey?"

"You mean the writer and publisher?" Fitzgerald asked. "What makes you think ridicule in scientific journals will help?"

Donegan said, "Just what are you looking for and what do you expect to gather from this excursion… that may not even be legal?"

Fitzgerald said "we cannot futz around. You just focus on gathering copies of any and all information to do with the Wardenclyffe project."

Donegan asked, "What is the Wardenclyffe project?"

Fitzgerald stopped turning the dial and signaled Doty to continue with the overview. Picking up on the cue Doty began explaining, "After Tesla secured financing to communicate across the ocean without wires he leased a remote wooded parcel adjacent to the Jemima Randall and George Hegeman farms at Shoreham, Long Island, 65 miles from Brooklyn. The site was named Wardenclyffe."

Fitzgerald signaled Doty that someone was listening and climbed over the back wall of the storage room to the next aisle. Picking up on the cue Doty continued lecturing "The contact tower was constructed entirely of large wood beams assembled on the ground and hoisted into position. It would rise to a height of 187 feet. Below the tower a well had been dug 120 feet deep and twelve feet square, lined with eight-inch timbers. A spiral stairway encircled a vertical steel shaft to the surface."

King's yell was quickly muffled.

Smiling Doty went on to explain, "Owing to a variety of unforeseen causes, there were delays in the delivery of electrical equipment. Then in 1901, it was announced that Marconi had signaled the letter "S" across the Atlantic from Cornwall, England to Newfoundland all accomplished with devices in no manner approaching the magnitude of Wardenclyffe. The plant was not to be solely used for the transmission of signals across the Atlantic, but more ambitiously, the transmission of electric power to any point on the globe without wires."

The aide asked, "Why are we focusing on his failure?"

Doty said, "Tesla found it desirable to move his laboratory from the city to Wardenclyffe. While experimenting with the weapon and keeping with his desire for secrecy about the investigation, he remained in seclusion. Early in 1903 the 55-ton, 68-foot spherical rib-cage dome on top of the tower was nearing completion. The large dome enclosed the cage with copper plates to form an insulated metal ball. The completed tower had the appearance of a huge mushroom rising above the trees along the North Shore. It could easily be seen from New Haven across the Sound."

Suddenly all eyes turned to the doorway. Fitzgerald was escorting King with a pistol held to his right ear. "This man here is spying on a government investigation."

The two FBI agents stopped snapping pictures. The larger agent stepped over and grabbed King away from Fitzgerald. He spun the sneaky manager around and slammed him against the wall.

"What do you want?"

"I was just keeping my eyes open."

"Do you want them closed forever?" Fitzgerald always wanted to say that even though his profile concluded he could not shoot anyone.

The floor man stuttered, "No. no, please."

"Then go downstairs fast and we won't report you, okay?"

"Yes sir. I'll stay downstairs."

The angry agent shoved the frightened caretaker toward the hallway. He stumbled awkwardly down the hall.

Fitzgerald looked at him, "Continue." Doty carried on, "The papers were full of the death of Wardenclyffe designer Stanford White, who was murdered on the roof of Madison Square Garden by Harry K. Thaw, a Pittsburgh financier. White was shot three times in clear view of New York's prominent socialites, the victim of a fictionalized triangle involving Thaw's wife before they all vanished in the night. Tesla and his staff quietly de-parted from Wardenclyffe."

Doty was frightening. He had a number of combat medals and the look to assure everyone was paying attention. He went on

"The Waldorf-Astoria attempted to convert Tesla's property to cash in various ways. The War Department was approached without success in connection with the activities at Camp Upton near Yaphank.

Tesla was not in New York when the tower finally came down. For this reason Tesla removed critical information and kept it with his personal possessions. And that is what we are looking for, with your assistance."

Donegan agreed reluctantly "All right, where do we start?"

Nodding, Fitzgerald directed everyone "take out every box and we need pictures of each one."

The agents opened the boxes.

Returning to the safe, Fitzgerald smiled at Cody "Watch me crack this box."

Spinning the dial back and forth, Fitzgerald entered a series of memorized numbers and the four foot floor safe opened easily. After looking through a number of drawers, in the upper right-hand corner a compartment with a square door left unlocked. Fitzgerald opened the compartment and then the inner drawer. On the bottom was the Edison Medal awarded to Tesla in 1917 by the American Institute of Electrical Engineers.

Fitzgerald dropped the Medal into his pocket and when Cody looked at him, "Not to worry. I will not keep it. But I am sure as hell not going to let Edison's medal end up in 'Slavland'."

Cody asked, "Where should it go?"

New York Public Library
Ottendorfer Branch, East Village

The mission was gaining heat and that meant additional resources. Now A.I. had personal on George to prepare for his normal routes, assuring Donald J's work would be in place. It was the third time he visited the small library in the East Village, full of German books and magazines. George searched the periodicals. He took down and read the article on local internment camps and detention centers used for German civilians. A.I. had to understand was he thinking as Claudius or George? The camps located in Fort Meade and Camp Forrest incarcerated both 'foreign' civilian and military prisoners. For convenience German's were called 'prisoners of war'. Everyone knew the Viereck case had been handled by a kangaroo court to avoid political embarrassment. Claudius wasn't sure what they were going to do with his alter ego. He knew the real George was a political hot potato who would be railroaded through the court system.

A.I. concluded the visit was nothing more than Claudius surveying the library's Queen Anne and neo-Italian Renaissance styles. The artisan walked around feeling the exterior ornamented by innovative *terracot-ta putti*. Looking up while turning made him dizzy. He grabbed a chair to sit down before he fell. A sweet looking woman, who could have been the librarian sat next to him.

The voice whispered, "Excuse me."

George looked over, into her brown eyes. Smiling ever so gently as a Tuscan hillside she whispered "I would like to use the periodical guide and you are resting on it."

The short man struggled to pull out the guide he was sitting on. Grinning nervously, her face opened up to take his heart across a bridge in Pisa, *cha cha de Amor*. George was in love and wanted to sing while coming to her. She offered a wisp of a smile. Rubbing his eyes, feeling as if he had woken in a Parish painting where the Greek Gods offer the maiden's face, George apologized, "I'm so sorry. My mind was, ah, in thought."

The lady was not overly beautiful or well-endowed but, dear-Mary-mother-of-god; she sure was sexy with the soft pink sweater covering her enchanting breast. There was a natural pout to her full lips. Her hair was amber. He dared not look again to see if she had a bra on. The cold made her breasts firm. She seemed to whisper her words "Silly, deep in thought? Tell me all about this deep thought you were having."

George smiled. "I am a poet, among other activities."

She put her hand on his, "Oh, please tell me a poem. I need so very badly to hear one right now." The lady leaned in ever so slightly.

He wanted to parlay the question into a conversation and perhaps more. She was maybe 30 something and all too alluring. He took her hand with a nobleman's grace. "And, why do you need a poem so very badly right now?"

She smiled before looking painfully serious de-scribing her dreams, "I decided to leave my job in the smallest library in Phoenix after my mother passed away last month. I have degrees in library science and engineering. I want to work in a grand library. Should I be able to do that?"

He said, "I am of the same mind. Why you are starting off just at the right place and the right time. My name is George, may I ask yours?"

"Betty. You know what, I've been in New York for over two weeks and I cannot get one interview or find one person who will be nice to me. Nothing is going right."

"Is there anything I can do?"

She leaned forward a bit more, "Recite one of your poems?" Betty was oblivious of her breast touching the top of his hand.

Close enough to leave their hands touching George recited, "A haunted place when I did yield to passion's swift demand one of your lovers touched me with his hand. And in the pang of amorous delight I hear strange voices calling through the night."

Betty looked deeply into his eyes and cooed, "That is the most beautiful poem I have ever heard. Did you write it?"

Puffing up his puny chest George boasted, "Of course I was composing when you arrived. Looking at you revived my muse. I have prayed to the gods for such an inspiration. I'm so very much in need of an inspiration this moment. You have given me an experience poets dream about."

Pulling her hand back slowly Betty asked, "What is your name?"

"George and what is yours sweet princes?" George recognized her southwestern accent.

"Betty Gardner. Do you think it is foolish for an experienced librarian to come to New York?"

"No, no, not at all" George reassured her. She whispered "Would you help me?"

George stood up too quickly and realized his lips were two inches away from hers. "Oh, excuse me; I hardly meant to." And he offered a quick smile.

The approaching heels of the bespectacled librarian pounded on the next aisle, prompting them to sit straight up. She walked by and gave them the 'look'.

Putting a finger over the other's mouth, George and Betty looked at each other and giggled. While twirling her strawberry blond hair, Betty suggested, "Maybe you did mean to and maybe, just maybe, that was what you should mean to do."

George looked into her eyes. She lowered her head, brushing her soft hair into his face. George closed his eyes to take delight in the smell and savor the touch of this alluring creature next to him. Instinctively, he put his right hand around her waist.

Her voice softly posed the seductive question, "Why do you feel so good?"

Whispering into her ear George suggested, "Because we feel good together."

Both looked down the empty aisles before softly kissing. After an ever more passionate kiss, they each pull back for a moment. Then in heat they ravenously push their lips deep into each other's hungry mouth.

After his embarrassingly loud moan he muffled his laughter.

Grabbing each other's hand they walked down the end of the aisle, around the far corner. Turning around at the end, with her back to the stacks, Betty pulled him by the zipper towards her. George dropped his hands down to his side for a moment and took a deep breath.

He skillfully pulled her skirt up to find her without underwear and he gasped. Passion was hot, breathtaking and quick.

The two stood with George resting, leaning on her panting, wanting the feeling to never end. After a few moments they managed to separate. He bent over and somehow pulled his pants up. Betty dropped her skirt back down. Smiling, she kissed him again.

Betty was the first to speak "God, I have no idea what came over me. I am embarrassed. I have never done anything like that before. Have you?"

Shaking off his afterglow George mumbled something like, "Not in a library."

Softly Betty confessed, "I hardly know what happen. Maybe it was poetry or maybe you."

"Maybe it was us," he agreed.

"Can we get something to eat?" Betty asked, smiling.

They quickly straightened out their clothing and fussed over each other for a few seconds. Walking outside into the cold the two leaned into each other. George put his hand around her waist while they walked out and down the street.

Betty was the first to speak. "Where exactly are we?"

"We are in *Kleine Deutschland.*" "What does that mean?"

"Little Germany."

"You sound German?"

"There are 150,000 Germans here, in this neighborhood alone. Over 200,000 Germans have moved through New York since Hitler took over."

Betty asked "Does the government leave you alone, you know with the war and all"

"What do you know about the war and our government?"

Pulling back Betty cooed "I really know little about politics and certainly don't want to be involved in their sorted affairs." After a few more steps she leans over and asks, "I do know, maybe if you think it is all right can have some real fun."

George smiled for the first time in weeks. "Great, there is nothing I would like better than more enjoyment today, what do have in mind?"

Her face scrunched. "Can I trust you?"

With a sweeping arm gesture George asked "How can I promise enough to win your trust?"

Betty opened her purse and showed George a dozen pharmacy grade opium tinctures. He stared at them. Looking around uncomfortably she could barely be heard. "Do you know what these are?" The pain in her face was obvious.

George held her purse open while carefully fingering the tinctures, "Indeed, I do. Where in the name of good times did you obtain these?"

Betty confessed, "My mother was very ill and had a prescription. She passed away two weeks ago. I kept her medicine. Did I do OK?"

Putting his left arm around her shoulder and neck, he pulled her close. The street was busy with pedestrians and the noise was distracting. George closed the purse and turned Betty towards his two-tone, tan and charcoal Cord. He held her walking down the street.

She whispered in his ear "Can we practice some-thing foreign?"

The Museum of the City of New York 1220 Fifth Avenue at 103rd Street

Kosanovic stepped along the staircase's gentle curve. He saw Seldiakov on the other side of the elegant French column, walking toward the Fire and Police Collection. They met in the middle and shook hands, next to the Americus 'Big 6' double-decker fire engine. Each was being tailed. The two A.I. agents recognized each other and trained to switch assignments and move in close, on each side.

The Russian looked up towards his taller contact "Sava, my friend, good of you to meet with me so soon." His tempered baritone voice echoed across the hallway.

The Slavs voice carried "During these times I must be available for our allies," Kosanovic asked "I trust you spoke with your superiors about this matter." Seldiakov looked across the aisle and pointed,

"See the police paddy wagon?"

Kosanovic realized his Russian solicitor was nervous and was in need to gain his confidence. "I certainly hope that is not your expertise."

"*Nyet,* I have no such types of experience or training. Do you?"

"Let us walk around. I understand there are many interesting, what the Americans call urban artists."

"I reserve judgment for important matters." They turned into the wall art portrayals of New York street life, where Kosanovic stopped, "And what are our Russian brethren offering us for this weapon developed by Dr. Tesla?" With no answer he continued, "The necessity for frank and open debate amongst comrades is what makes dialectical discourses superior. Do you agree?"

"That is fine." Kosanovic didn't flinch "let us pursue this further. Is Marxism prepared to invest millions of dollars into development?" With a dismissive wave he answered his own question, "Not while the Nazi's control the Ukraine."

The Russian had a habit of starting each sentence with a slight jutting of his jaw. "Are you worried about arming the Russians with the ultimate weapon? Of course not Russia has always been able to crush Yugoslavia but instead has always supported their southern cousins."

"Smaller neighbors must live by their wits not their power. Shall we move forward or not?"

Grabbing the taller Yugoslav with a slap on each sleeve the hefty Seldiakov looked directly into his eyes and proclaimed, "The Russian bear has never and will never become more fearful than the dreaded neighbor you already face. You have to ask the first question, what could be accomplished with this weapon by the Prince?"

The lanky diplomat gave a shrug to signal the Russian to release his arms.

Letting go Seldiakov said, "If we are to move for-ward I need you to provide me with solid evidence this weapon exists and is capable of advancing the Soviet effort to defeat the fascists."

Kosanovic said "When Tesla tested the weapon Robert Peary was making his second attempt to reach the North Pole. As you may know the inventor had notified the expedition he would be contact them. The group promised to report details of anything unusual they witnessed on the open tundra."

Seldiakov fidgeted uncomfortably, unsure of the conversation's purpose.

Kosanovic said, "On the evening of June 30th accompanied by his associate George Scherff atop the Wardenclyffe tower, Tesla aimed his directed ray across the Atlantic towards the arctic to a spot he calculated was west of the Peary expedition. Tesla switched on the device. At first, it was hard to tell if it was even working. It emitted a dim light that was barely visible. Then an owl flew from its perch on the tower's pinnacle, soaring into the path of the beam. The bird disintegrated instantly.

"On June 30th, 1908 a massive explosion devastated Tunguska. The explosion was audible 600 miles away. Your frightened scientists believe either a meteorite or a fragment of a comet caused it, even though no obvious impact site or mineral remnants of such an object were ever found. Dr. Tesla explained it was plain that his 'ray' had overshot its intended target and destroyed Tunguska. He was thankful beyond measure the explosion had miraculously killed no one. Six years later, at the onset of the First World War, Tesla wrote President Wilson and revealed his secret high powered transmission test."

The sharper tone indicated a deeper anger, "Tesla offered to rebuild the weapon for the War Department as a deterrent. The military would not accept any limitations on their control over it. Tesla demanded he remain in charge of the weapon or it would not be developed any further."

Kosanovic stopped, awaiting a response. Seldiakov turned and walked over to the Military Collection. He stopped in front of the displays of history of military uniforms ranging from fatigues to officer's full-dress. There were associated regalia, weapons and souvenirs linked to New Yorkers who fought in the American Revolution. Kosanovic walked up next to him.

Finally the Russian spoke, "We know all to well about Tunguska, the great hole of Siberia."

Kosanovic pressed his position, "And you question Tesla?"

Seldiakov pointed at the group of steel-engraved portraits of New York military figures and World War I posters. "We never heard about this weapon during the Great War. We do not want to overstate its potential."

Kosanovic suggested, "Perhaps we should discuss this on a different day, when you have more authority to negotiate."

Clearly offended, the Russian official turned towards Kosanovic. "I have authority. What I need is proof."

"Were you not aware of Amtorg's subsidies and did you not work with Tesla five years ago?"

"Of course I am part of the high command." Seldiakov was a poor liar.

The Yugoslav diplomat turned and left the Russian staring at paintings of wooden ships. He stopped to offer, "When you have the authority to negotiate I look forward to working with you."

Bryant Park
Sixth Ave and West Forty Second

Fitzgerald looked around for monthly contact with NKGB Chief Akhmarhov. Sometimes common interests are best explored outside diplomatic channels. They both came from academia, not the military. Opinions did not matter other than respecting his intellect. The scheduled meeting was at the American Radiator and Standard Sanitary Company building across the street to discuss technical issues, off line. The building stood out from all the rest, clad in polished black brick with gilded details. The pigeons were overwhelming, with piles of droppings everywhere.

Fitzgerald was insulted to see a communist stroll freely out of the Carrere and Hastings Library. Akhmarhov walked through rows of trees. It was a warm day yet the Russian was dressed for a Moscow winter. There was little Fitzgerald liked about these meetings or this Red, nothing personal.

Akhmarhov's gloved finger pointed at the neat rows of trees. "Mr. Fitzgerald, good to see you again. I welcome meeting in a park that has 'order' about it." He was older and enjoyed taunting the kid. "Is there hope here?

The comment seemed offensive. Fitzgerald walked over a few steps to meet him and chided "Beats a Bronx cheer."

Without shaking hands Akhmarhov asked, "What does this mean? What is this Bronx cheer?"

Enjoying the moment Fitzgerald answered, "A local custom."

"I trust it is not at anyone's expense." He nod-ded with a belated understanding.

Impatiently Fitzgerald demanded, "Let's get on with business."

"You mean the business of Tesla's weapon and our alliance?"

"I only know about the weapon and that you hired Tesla before we were allies." He explained, "There were others and there was the problem producing a weapon able to achieve accurate distance."

"Ah, the distance problem," Fitzgerald said. "Did he tell you about the Grindell-Matthews device that used a powerful ultraviolet beam to make the air conduct? With this, high energy current would be directed at the target."

Akhmarhov speculated "The range of a ultra-violet searchlight would be much less than what Tesla was claiming. It took one of our scientists to point out that all the energy of New York City, and we are talking about one and a half billion watts, transformed into rays and then projected twenty miles. All of this power would still not kill a human being."

Fitzgerald walked down the row of trees with Akhmarhov alongside. Fitzgerald needed to identify what the NKGB really knew. "The apparatus projects particles may be relatively large or of microscopic dimensions conveying a small area at a great distance trillions of times more energy than is possible with rays of any kind It is a stream thinner than a hair can transmit many thousands of horsepower. Nothing can resist its power." Pausing to look him over Fitzgerald asked, "Did he explain this to you?" The one thing Fitzgerald liked about him was in his heart, he was a scholar.

Akhmarhov raised his voice. "What Tesla had in mind with this defensive system was a large-scale, completed version of his Colorado Springs lightning bolt machine. When enemy airplanes or ships entered the electric field of his charged tower, they would set up a conducting path for a stream of high-energy particles. These would eradicate the intruder's electrical system, much like the early electromagnetic invention by a Rus-sian engineer named *Grammachikoff*. It is used for destroying airplanes."

"Do you really expect me to believe you have already developed such a weapon and have chosen not to use it?" Fitzgerald asked.

"We already knew and Tesla agreed that distance involved problems capable of tearing the very framework of the universe."

"Then why did you test it?"

"You Americans know very well that with the aid of German technical experts, a large-scale demonstration at Podosinsky Aerodrome near Moscow was a success. The revolutionary Military Council and the Politburo decided to fund a shell of electronic anti-aircraft stations to protect sensitive areas of Russia."

Fitzgerald asked, "Are you going to share with your allies?"

"By challenging every law of physics, we ignore the problem of distance and tear at the very fabric of nature."

Raising his head back he looked down his nose at the American "What have we gained? Is your thirst for power so out of control you are willing to destroy the universe?"

"Your commander of the Air Services, Rosenholtz was very impressed by the weapons demonstration. He proposed to curtail the activity of the air fleet because the invention rendered a large air fleet un-necessary for defense."

The Russian countered "Perhaps if you had an elemental understanding of dialectics then you could understand the complexities of the world."

"American's have rejected dialectics in favor of our proven Constitution wouldn't you agree?"

Akhmarhov pointed at Forty-First Street. "I find it amazing you Americans have created this well-ordered park in the midst of the surrounding irrational streets. The dingy urban architecture creates absurdity. Perhaps that is why you struggle to understand the warp and wolf of the universal set of laws."

Ignoring him Fitzgerald asserted "I understand Tesla's work."

The crafty bear played the game well "We Russians remember a remote area in the Siberian wilderness. Five hundred thousand square acres of land were destroyed by the equivalent to ten to fifteen megatons of TNT. The Tunguska was the most powerful explosion to have ever occurred in human history. Had Dr. Tesla's accident been just a few degrees to the West he would have *accidentally* obliterated Moscow."

Fitzgerald nodded toward the southwest corner of the park, behind the library. "That was Tesla's favorite place to feed pigeons."

"We know. We were watching him, too."

"How are you Russians getting along with your cousins, the Southern Slavs?"

"I presume that is your meager attempt to describe Yugoslavia?" he said.

Fitzgerald proposed "Then let's stop futzing around and discuss Tesla's nephew, Sava Kosanovic".

"Tesla did not trust him"

That was true although the reason was Tesla did not trust any politician. "A most serious problem but Kosanovic has legal priority in all property claims."

"Not in Russia." The NKGB chief added, "Kosanovic has become a proper and permanent sight around New York. Have you adopted him?"

"He is here on a diplomatic Visa."

Akhmarhov pointed out, "He shall stay long after the young King Petar has abdicated."

"Do you really think he would turn his loyalty away from the King and follow Tito?" Fitzgerald asked.

"I have no doubt he would follow any Yugoslavian leader allowing him to stay in America, regardless of their color."

"Will Tito survive the Nazi campaign?" Looking off at the distance as if he could see his homeland, Akhmarhov's words become deeper. "Comrade Tito is as tough a rebel and guerilla leader as this war will produce. Not even Mao can lead or fight alone.

You watch, Tito will bait the mighty German divisions into chasing him through the mountains and lead them into hell. Their armies will be picked apart and Tito's feats will inspire a new army. History is on his side. Dialectical history dictates that kingdoms will pass. This war will make Yugoslavia a fine example of historical dialectics dictating the inevitably of socialism."

The Russian's right arm started hammering the air. "Mark my word; Tito will rule Yugoslavia by year's end and Kosanovic will follow the inevitable path of all history."

Knowing the NKVD agent assessments could be perversely correct Fitzgerald realized this wartime ally wanted Kosanovic to hide whatever parts he had of the weapon. He believed the International Federation of the Communist Party will be taking over Yugoslavia. The possibility Stalin could get control the weapon terrified everyone. All Fitzgerald could write about was the war had created an American ally, who was diametrically opposed to our future. Fitzgerald walked over to a vendor and bought a bag of pigeon food. The old bear in his heavy fur coat grunted, trudged away, frightening the pigeons to flight. A.I. informed Fitzgerald the Russians were tailing him.

Tuesday, January 12th

The Funeral

Frank I. Campbell Funeral Home
Madison Ave and 81st St

Those unable to attend Tesla's funeral kept their radios tuned to Mayor LaGuardia's broadcast. A.I. predicted everyone who ever wished to know Tesla or ever wanted to pick over his bones, would be there. They were on the level.

The assigned seats were coveted at Tesla's memorial services. Arrangements were made through the Yugoslav Information Center and its public relation firm. Thousands of the city leaders and intellectuals along with tens of thousands Tesla countrymen and fans scrambled to secure their reserved seats.

All sides of Yugoslavia's civil wars viewed Nikola Tesla as a hero. Nikola Tesla was born a Serb and his fatherland was Croatia. There were numerous dimensions to this bitter war. The Serbs and Croats killed each other. The fascists and the communists killed each other. The nationalist and war lords killed each other. Every side killed civilians. Nationalities ill with loathing offered ideology as a path to redemption. It seemed every single Yugoslav had a need to kill another except for Tesla, a hero for every side.

At church that cold day the masses came in peace – in homage – to worship. The overwhelming number of incoming cars caused traffic jams. The groups or gangs of Serbs and Croats stayed apart and remained reverential. The thousands of well-dressed attendees remained humble.

A.I. knew the memorial would be attended by most every major scientist and foreign agent in the country. The live wire, Donald J. built New York's largest ever, hidden microphone system utilizing more stenographers and translators than was ever built inside the U.S. during the War. A.I. was allowed to watch and wait proactively. Fitzgerald told Donald J. we had to undermine the agents working in the middle of crowds. The gadget man promised a practical weapon to neutralize foreign agents conversing with any American scientist.

Evidently, George thought he could sneak in early and not be seen. After indulging himself with a tincture, he was blissful and obvious in his wrinkled suit. His sloppy appearance was a sight with a dream doll fresh drugs flowing through his veins. When he walked in wearing yesterday's clothes, George looked down at himself with mock disgust. Struggling not to laugh, he struggled to pull his suit straight by yanking on each side of his jacket. Taking hold of Betty's arm, he walked stiff legged into the room.

It was unlikely she had indulged in a tincture last night. She always had such bearing and was wearing a black cashmere sweater over a black pleated dress. She was looking no worse for the wear. George on the other hand looked like concurrent hangovers and Betty described an evening with this actor as one great first act who never shows up for the third. She held George's arm to guide him. They walked onto the street-level access to the first floor.

Betty whispered "The arrangement office is across the lobby. Can you walk that far?"

George needed her guidance. The lobby was large and crowded. She struggled to steer her stoned companion. By the time he reached the receptionist, George told Betty his legs no longer needed to touch the floor.

Betty laughed. Looking in through the doorway, George stopped, looked around at the fireplace and comfortable sofas. This private suite created a warm, home-like atmosphere for arrangement conferences. George was slurring. "Where may I *paaay* respect for my close friend Nicola Tesla?

Pointing toward the hall, the woman wearing an off blue hair piece glared at George. Addressing Betty the guide explained "There is a large reposing room with an adjoining sitting room down the hall."

George looked at Betty and purposefully rolled his eyes. She gently guided him. Walking arm in arm, the pair stumbled up the magnificent staircase. "I do not like this place," George pouted. When they entered, the only person in the great hall was the Russian. From his chair the outsized, loud man stood and waved "George, George" he called, lumbering towards them ignoring the falling chair, swaying like a bear in heat.

Before they could turn and walk away the Russian put his huge arm around George's thin shoulders. With one motion the Russian replaced Betty's grip. "George, I knew you would make it. You are too good of a man not to be here for your friend's funeral."

"What are you doing here?" George was not ready to focus much less become involved in a conversation with anyone not stoned on opium. He tried to answer anyway, "No one is supposed to be here. It's early, you know?"

He laughed loud enough to cause an echo "I have been waiting for my friend, you George; I need to talk to you." He leaned closer to whisper into George's left ear, pulling him off balance.

Miffed, Betty hooked George's right arm and turned him the opposite way, hoping the dazed Italian would go along. He did and became slightly green and dizzy, alarming the Russian to release him. She pointed George towards the chairs. He welcomed the lead and followed. The room was quiet were it not for the Russian grunting, trying to keep up. They all stopped, hearing the steps coming down the hall.

Halting at the entrance the only relative in attendance, Kosanovic looked at them, surveyed the room, turned and left.

George froze, staring at the doorway. The Russian Agent and Betty looked at each other

The Russian asked George "Did you see who that was?"

Murmuring something incoherently in Italian and then German, George snapped out of his stupor and answered clearly "Yes I did. Have you any dealings with him?"

Betty asked, "Who was that anyway?" The men ignored her.

Rostarchuk answered George "He is quite the dandy at the parties. He is usually quiet yet always manages to have ugly escorts following him into the shadows."

"Well he looks quite alone now," George gloated.

They stopped when they heard a dull echo of men marching out of step. Three dozen rugged men dressed awkwardly in suits strutted in. They walked around the room before standing together on one side. The one with the long scar across his cheek looked at George. He asked, "Which side is for the Croatians?"

Not having a clue George pointed to the opposite side. Quietly all the men gathered over in the seating section on the other side, to kneel and pray before sitting.

A few minutes later another group pounded down the hall. The moment they came through the doorway, the 40-odd Serbs bristled. The Croats sat on the opposite side. Both sides watched each other. One by one, each of the second group sat on George's side. The scarred man from the other side sneered at the disheveled Italian who feigned innocence.

Betty asked, "George, dear, don't you think we should go back to the house and change into clothing for the services this afternoon?"

He agreed "That would be the right thing to do wouldn't it?"

Rostarchuk started to protest "I think I will go too. It will be a long day. I already miss my old friend, Nikola."

The three stood together and tried to ignore the glares. It was as if both sides were angry the only neutral party was leaving. George could hardly focus and Betty struggled to hold a smile.

Another small army of men from one side or the other marched towards them.

When they walked outside the doorway, the three took refuge next to the wall. Rostarchuk shoved his way next to Betty. "Did you see the newspapers this morning?" The Russian bellowed "They found the body of the anarchist Carlo Trescalying in the gutter at the northwest corner of 15th St. and Fifth Ave. They say he was an advocate of Syndicalism. Have you ever heard of such a movement? Don't suppose you English women know of such things do you?"

"I'm American" Betty snapped. "My mother was English."

The Russian pulled out the article and read "As Tresca rounded the corner of Fifth Avenue, which was dimmed due to recent wartime regulations, a man came up from behind him and fired a shot into his back, spinning him around to face his assailant, who then fired a second shot, which entered under his left eye and killed him. Police theorized Tresca's murder was political, but a professional weapons man fled in a waiting auto."

Looking directly at Betty he pressed, "Can you imagine this happening?"

"I have no interest in politics if you please." Betty hugged George's arm as they continued walking, leaning against each other.

The Russian followed "I was only trying to have a interesting conversation talking about today's news. I can tell by your accent you look like you have lived in England, have you?"

George turned quickly and looked at her anew. Betty pulled George close and waved goodbye to the Russian.

In the lobby Rostarchuk found a telephone and immediately called Seldiakov "Whatever are you doing, no matter what it is you must come at once. I am at the Campbell Funeral Home on Madison Ave and 81st St. they are both here. Kosanovic is too. Yes, now." He watched Kosanovic walk across the lobby.

Stepping in front of an employee, the nephew asked with great concern, "Are you sure we can keep the two sides apart?"

The mortician answered "No. They are all in one room now and, so far everyone has stayed on their own side. There needs to be a third party there to keep them apart. Could you please go down and speak to them?"

Looking at the room down the Renaissance hall Kosanovic promised "I will look into it." The diplomat sent the nervous mortician on his way.

Kosanovic walked into the reposing room. From both sides, all eyes followed him. He walked to the front of the lectern crowned by an enormous King James Bible. He tipped it upright for all to see. After a tense moment Kosanovic announced "On behalf of the Tesla family we want to thank you all for coming here to honor the national hero that belongs to every one of us. As his nephew, I assure you… he is humbled by your attentions and honored by your respect. I trust you are here to revere this day of mourning." And with a respectful nod toward each side Kosanovic walked out the door.

In the foyer Kosanovic met the Russian from Amtorg, Seldiakov bowed in a small way while extending his hand. Kosanovic smiled with a proper shake.

"Mr. Seldiakov, I must confess I am surprised to find you here."

"Comrade Kosanovic, on behalf of my countrymen and our common Slavic heritage I came here to express condolences for your uncle. I know how close you two were."

Even at this early hour Kosanovic looked tired.

He shuffled over to the nearby wooden bench. Seldiakov followed and sat next to him. They sat quietly.

The *apparatchik's* words were clumsy. "Rest assured comrade, I am not concerned about criticizing anyone's mythologies. When our two countries are joined under the international banner such meaningless differences will fade away. Good, no?"

Kosanovic had little in the way of Christian loyalties but had not come to his uncle's funeral to renounce the church. Kosanovic answered abruptly, "We believe in God."

The Russian put his pudgy palm over his eyes. "If I could disprove god to you and could share the proletariat dream, I could put you on Stalin's good side. And you know what that could mean?"

Kosanovic said "Quite a feat."

Seldiakov did not care to acknowledge his blunder and continued on "I attended the same school in Moscow as your Tito. I have an unfair advantage. I have studied dialectics. You should take note of that before I start. Are you prepared?"

Kosanovic nodded coolly.

"Let me ask you one question disproving your god 'did god take a risk creating the universe?" Seldiakov leaned back gloating with Marxist fervor and satisfaction before proudly concluding "*Because if* god did not take a risk then his act is not creation *and if* god did take a risk he is not god, your thesis demands god is dead. Does it not?"

Kosanovic kept his own counsel for a weighty moment before answering, "Dividing the question is a game of man, not god. God is absolute; man is sinful and confused without the churches guidance."

Did you know...," the Russian interrupted himself "never mind. What we need to discuss is the fact our country and this war is at a nexus and the turning point is Stalingrad. You know as well as I do, the German assault is about to collapse. When they crumble, Hitler will never regain his momentum. Tito will also rout the Germans and rule Yugoslavia by next year. Our international unity is dictated by dialectics. That is your reality, your future. The question you must ask is: are you going to stay loyal after your country becomes a member of international communist movement?"

Kosanovic abruptly stood "Will you excuse me? I must attend to my uncle's affairs" and quickly walked away.

Watching him Rostarchuk remained sitting, stroking his beard.

Kosanovic had long kept a journal. This meeting was important enough for him to write down both his experiences and his interpretation of them. Donald J. knew where it was hidden. Later with a Gilhooley, the size of an ordinary briefcase he was able to enter the Slav's office and reproduce documents, charts and half-tone illustrations.

Kosanovic walked across the vestibule and looked through the open window to recognize the Nazi 'diplomat' Dr. Kurt Kiep, speaking with the same couple he saw in the reposing room. Across the way, standing near the intersection Kiep demanded "George, you cannot keep operating this way."

Betty struggled to hold George steady. He would have been insulted had he been sober enough for public conversation. Instead he slurred "My friend Nikola is dead. Why can't you people see that? Where is your compassion?"

The doctor turned sharply to Betty "Would you mind leaving me with my patient for a moment?"

Betty forced a smile and slowly let go of George's arm and he teetered. Shrinking under Kiep's glare she slowly walked away while watching over her shoulder to see if George was able to remain standing.

Kiep waited until she was halfway down the block before turning to George. "What are you doing with her?"

"She's helping me through my grieving."

The Nazi stared in contempt "She is helping with drugs. Does the American know about us?"

George challenged "Us? There is an 'us'? I await your report from Berlin. Who is, the 'us' you are referring to?"

Kiep shot back "Who is this, this... babe of yours? Have you known her for a while or was this sexy woman just accidentally become attracted to a much older man?"

"Leave Betty out of this" George demanded.

Changing tones the doctor asked "Have you considered what is happening? We are at a critical point in the war. The FBI has doubled its size in the last two years, primarily to chase, imprison and destroy every loyal German in this country. Our submarines used to operate with impunity in the harbor. Now they have to hide from the Americans. And you know what is happening in Stalingrad? This is not the time to collapse." He stopped as his head cocked, "You are using opium, are you not?

George had sobered up to the point of realizing questions could not be answered well. He countered "Why are you attacking me?"

Kiep grabbed George by the arm "You must give me the accelerator. You understand I retain diplomatic protection, do you?"

"I understand what you are saying. Have you heard any response from Berlin?"

Kiep stepped closer. "George, I want you to go with me and get the accelerator before that bimbo, that hussy of yours, cons you out of it."

George agreed "Okay I will get it for you later. Today I must attend my friend's funeral. Don't worry about Betty. She is not interested in this war or politics. That is why I like her."

Spinning him around Kiep grabbed both of George's arms with a vice grip. "Everyone is involved in what you are doing now. Are you off your nut? You cannot be taking up with a strange woman."

George was unable to pull free. "I will get it for you. Now I need to attend to more immediate affairs." Kiep let him go to turn towards Betty who was waiting down the street, watching. George started to walk and looked back to say, "I will meet you tomorrow and we can discuss the transfer of funds."

The Cathedral of St. John the Divine
1047 Amsterdam Avenue at 112th

Reporters from across Europe and America stood outside, filming the crowds pouring into the thirteen acres surrounding the Gothic cathedral. Early that afternoon, the bronze doors opened for Dr. Nikola Tesla's funeral services. On the West Front the great rose window glimmered for yards. The crowds commented how the ten thousand pieces of sparkling stained glass gave off a heavenly message. The eight granite columns stood 55-feet high behind the altar with the nave interior arched 124 feet. Barbedienne had cast each of the seven chapels, one for each immigrant force. By four o'clock the magnificent house of worship was filled with well over two thousand mourners.

The ritual followed the Serbian Orthodox Church, an autocephalous or ecclesiastically independent member of the

Orthodox communion A.I. was everywhere and prepared background on most notables. Honorary pallbearers included Dr. E. F. W. Alexander-son of General Electric, Dr. Harvey Rentschler of Westinghouse (missed his train from Chicago), W. H. Barton, curator of the Hayden Planetarium of the American Museum of Natural History and Professor Edwin H. Armstrong. Three U.S. Nobel prizewinners in physics, Robert Millikan, Arthur Compton, and James Franck participated in the eulogy, declaring Tesla "one of the outstanding intellects of the world who paved the way for many of the most important technological developments of modern times." It was a time of awe for more than anyone could appreciate.

Author Louis Adamic's eulogy included "Tesla lives in his achievement which is great, almost beyond calculation, and an integral part of our civilization, our daily lives, our current war effort. His life will always be a triumph."

After the eulogies the mourners quietly shuffled down the aisles.

Kiep extended his hand in condolence to Dr. Alexanderson "My deepest regrets I remember him fondly speaking of you.

"Weakly offering his hand the doctor's sadness gave way to confusion over what recognized him. "You are so kind. Forgive me, I believe I should remember you and my mind fails me at this moment." "Please call me Kurt. All my friends do. I have the great privilege of writing a biography about Dr. Tesla."

"Is that Kurt with a *K* or a *C*?

"A. *C*." and with a smirk "forgive the pun." Alexanderson gave a hint of a smile. "How far along was, excuse me is your work with Tesla?"

"I am near the end of the research. I spoke many times with Dr. Tesla. He was particularly keen on his work financed by John Jacob Astor."

Dr. Alexanderson asked, "Would you forgive me? Nikola was a trusted colleague and friend whom I admired greatly. Quite honestly I knew little of his current work or sponsors."

Kiep said "After Dr. Tesla upstaged Edison by proving he was the only man capable of repairing the generator of Astor's yacht, he received a grant to develop the potential of electricity. He moved to Colorado Springs for open access to the atmosphere. Tesla built a 200-foot pole topped by a large copper sphere rising above his laboratory. He generated lightning bolts up to 135 feet long. Thunder from the released energy could be heard 15 miles away in Cripple Creek. People walking along the streets were amazed to see sparks jumping between their feet and the ground, and flames of electricity would spring from a tap when anyone turned them on for a drink of water. Light bulbs within 100 feet of the experimental tower glowed even when they were off. Horses at the livery stable received shocks through their metal shoes, and bolted from their stalls. A surge of Butterflies became electrified and "helplessly swirled in circles - their wings spouting blue halos of 'St. Elmo's Fire'."

The doctor was hooked "What a fascinating story. I never knew that about him or his illustrious investor. I look forward to reading your work."

Kiep nodded "I would be honored. Perhaps I can bring you an early copy. Of course you would be interested in contributing insights?"

"Well, I'm quite busy. Surely you can imagine my schedule at GE is one of overtime, the war and all. And necessarily so, I might add."

"Dr. Tesla's benefactors are going to need a new project for funding." Kiep offered.

Dr. Alexanderson nibbled "Perhaps we can have lunch later next week."

Kiep held his left hand bracing up his chin. "Did he share his work with you on particle beam generator?"

"What exactly was that work?"

"It is far too complex to explain here" Kiep said. "I do not know about you but, I can explain anything over a hot meal." The new found friend smiled with the toss of the bait.

Alexanderson continued to nibble "Please do. Perhaps we can meet earlier, you know, get together over a cup of tea on a Saturday afternoon."

"Shall we say next Saturday?"

"I really should not but this is far too interesting. Yes, yes we must."

Kiep saw George Viereck stumbling across the street cavorting with an American agent. Turning back to Alexanderson he offered, "The Cathedral's performing arts program features a number of dance, theater and music companies in residence. Perhaps I can secure some excellent seats and you might enjoy the brighter side of this cathedral?"

The GE scientist agreed. "Perhaps, do give me a call."

Kiep asked, "At what number?"

"The office is fine. I can hardly let the wife know. I should not even think about other projects." He enjoyed his own humor.

Alexanderson asked "Are you all right?"

"It is mad what goes through one's mind at such an affair. Dr. Kiep you say your name is very good. Give my office a call. We have an historian on staff. She will be happy to assist you."

"I was hoping to call you at home when you could afford a full conversation. And, with all due respect to your staff, you knew the master. Perhaps I can introduce you to others who funded Nikola."

"Allow me a bit of time to shuffle some dates.

Leave your number with my secretary."

"Very well" Kiep bowed American style, with a nod.

George and Betty were slowly pushing their way through the crowd when George saw Kiep, who picked out George, who was turning Betty away. While he adjusted the hat brim Kiep gestured Wilhelm to secure George. Kiep stared intently at them before they were lost in the crowd.

From across the street Fitzgerald pointed out both Dr. Rentschler and Dr. Alexanderson to the FBI agent who was to debrief them.

He signaled back with quick thumbs up. Fitzgerald turned back in time to see George disappearing into the crowd. "I'm going to follow that couple Kiep was staring at."

Donald J. acknowledged with a simple look. While wading through the crowds Fitzgerald lost sight of the couple. The masses continued pouring out of the cathedral, blocking Fitzgerald's path who was about to give up and consider an alternative route when the back of their heads appeared. They had gone in the direction of the crowds who parked in the streets. Zig-zagging through the masses Fitzgerald could depend on the FBI tail.

George and Betty had stopped in front of Von Haak. They held each other while looking up. Ten feet from them, Fitzgerald hid behind a hefty Croatian wearing a broad brimmed hat who was vainly attempting to console his mother.

Von Haak looked at George, who was peering to one side avoiding Wilhelm's gaze. "George, we need to talk."

George could not stop his hands from shaking. He leaned over to Betty and whispered "Go home. I will call you later."

"I came in your car George" She protested. Von Haak grabbed George's arm. "It is time to talk now." He started walking leading George, who glanced back helplessly at Betty.

The two marched down Amsterdam to 113th with Fitzgerald following across the street.

With an iron grip around George's left bicep the German looked straight forward. "Surely you know your compromises put everything, our very victory in jeopardy."

George was being forced to walk too fast and strained to watch forward while attempting to look at his iron escort. "I don't know what you are talking about. What the hell are you doing here anyway?"

Increasing the pace Von Haak explained, "You are to take me to all materials you have collected from Dr. Tesla. Am I making myself clear?"

Meekly George challenged, "Who put you in charge of me or the project? I want to speak with Dr. Kiep immediately!"

Von Haak said "I believe you have been in America too long. Perhaps it is time you visit your family. Won't that be wonderful George?

"Are you mad? Do you know who I am?"

"Your problem is you underestimate the Nazi crusade. I work with impunity in New York. You are safe with me."

"I have no intention of going underground. I have no reason to go underground or leave this country."

"You will follow orders. If you do not follow orders then you will be committing treason."

George surprised himself "I want to hear these orders from Dr. Kiep. You are making this up for some insane reason. This is your problem, not mine. Do you understand anything?"

Von Haak insisted "We must pick up the accelerator and we must pick it up now."

"Why, why now?"

The discussion changed when the military spy shook George into silence. "You are to follow orders. Do you understand? Do not insist that force be used." Von Haak pulled George's lapel close, to stare straight into his eyes. "I am an obedient soldier who will do whatever he is instructed to do. Our fatherland is in danger. I do not understand why you have not come to understand your duty."

Trembling before taking a second breath, George agreed from necessity, "I understand my duty. Why must I go to Germany now?"

"Dr. Kiep explained you were quite worried about the foolish use of the identity of someone going before the Supreme Court. He wanted to offer you his assistance."

This act of concern by Von Haak frightened George more than the earlier threat. His arm was going numb "Could you please let go of my arm?"

"Of course George, we must learn to work together for the common good of our Fuehrer. Is that correct George?" He gave a parting squeeze

After wincing George offered, "Let us return to the Funeral and meet after the procession into the graveyard."

"Very well" Von Haak agreed. "We will meet tonight. Where is the graveyard?"

"Ferncliff Cemetery, are you familiar with Hudson?"

Offended by the question Von Haak looked over his shoulder and watched Kiep walking towards them. Holding George by the arm, they walked back until they met Kiep. The three headed south and walked into the throngs of mourners continuing to mill around the Cathedral.

Fitzgerald took a short cut to get ahead of them. In route Fitzgerald saw Agent Harless and extended his hand. There seemed to be a hint of recognition.

"How is Agent Harless treating you?" Alexanderson looked at the young FBI agent and complimented him, "He has a recent interest in Nikola Tesla and has warned us the Germans do too."

Fitzgerald pointed at the three men walking up to the grey Plymouth. "You mean them?

Alexanderson said "Yes that one told me he was writing a biography about Tesla."

Rentschler leaned across until he was directly behind Alexanderson and patted him on the back. "That's him."

Fitzgerald put my hand on Rentschler and then Alexanderson before commenting, "We don't want to be too obvious."

The two gentlemen quickly turned away. Harless asked "And you were going to explain to me how a world class inventor ended up in poverty." Rentschler half prayed "Dear God life was not fair to my friend. It was never fair. I'm not sure if it was the events of 1904 or the ones in 1914. After Nikola gave power to Westinghouse and – in a convoluted way—to General Electric, he built generators for Niagara Falls.

He made the first city in history light up with one flick of the switch. He was rich and famous.

Rentschler continued "The nightmare began when he accepted money from J.P. Morgan and John Astor. They gave him whatever he wanted because his inventions were worth a million times whatever they invested. Then, when they disagreed with Tesla, they destroyed his reputation, work and access to corporate money.

I see where you are going," Alexanderson said, "You are talking about the letters. "Nikola trusted too much. His heart was bigger than any scientist I have ever met. He was not only smarter than everybody else he also cared more for life than anyone I knew."

Agent Harless repeated, "But what about the letters?"

Alexanderson replied "Tesla was about inventing and helping humanity? J.P. Morgan was about money period. Right after the turn of the century Tesla had been financed by Morgan to develop greater and more powerful ways to deliver energy. Tesla built a tower at Wardenclyffe to that end. He wrote Morgan a modest proposal, explaining the planet earth was operating on one frequency, one to connect into, just as Nikola had harnessed the Niagara Falls. Taking this to its' logical end Tesla proposed a global power plant giving everyone free electricity. He suggested Morgan could make his money back selling appliances and clocks." Everyone immediately understood how the greatest capitalist the world has ever known would react. We all looked sad.

"Dr. Tesla wanted to develop electricity and deliver power without wires. Just as he had developed critical early work on the radio, he not only wanted to send messages through the air, he wanted to send power itself freely through the atmosphere. He recognized the earth has a definable frequency, which renders issues such as distance academic. It would be possible to light the entire U.S. The current would pass into the air and spread in all directions, producing the effect of a strong aurora borealis. It would be a soft light, but, sufficient to distinguish objects."

Harless blurted, "That's crazy!"

Fitzgerald interjected "What you mean to say is no one else could see how this works."

Harless asked, "How is this possible?"

"It hardly mattered how. After Morgan read the words "free to everyone" nothing else mattered. He was not about to allow Tesla to develop his capitalistic sacrilege any further. Morgan not only cut off funding for all research, he made sure everyone else on Wall Street knew such heresy would never be allowed inside the sacred halls of the stock market."

Alexanderson added "to make the insult worse poor dear Nikola kept writing, letter after pleading letter. Striving against the unforgivable sin, Nikola sent ingratiating letters, logical letters, practical suggestions and he tried all other approaches known to man but the monopolist would never listen again. Morgan never forgave and he made sure nobody else did either."

"It was horrible" the Doctor added "All of the great work at Wardenclyffe collapsed around Tesla and there was nothing he could do. He wrote letters for six months and not one of them was ever answered. He wrote until all funding for all projects dried up and disappeared. It was very sad, indeed."

Harless said, "I read the manifesto he wrote in 1904 Tesla knew it was the Edison, Pupin and Marconi in combination who robbed him of his funding and reputation."

"Those inventors who robbed from Tesla, they were all guilty just as they were all successful in their nefarious dealings."

"The thieving three were in worse financial shape." Fitzgerald ridiculed them.

Harless asked "Then why did you say it might have been 1914?"

"It was his work with the Germans." Dr. Alexanderson shook his head "It was never simple. I'm not sure to this day just how much work he did beyond fixing the Kaiser's generator. I think it was more of a case of him trying to get a reaction from Morgan, who had working trips to Europe every year."

The Doctor disagreed, "I think timing was his enemy."

Alexanderson admonished him, "You know very well that Tesla's plant at Sayville tripled its output by erecting two more pyramid-shaped transmission towers, five hundred feet tall, boosting output from 35 to 100 kilowatts, giving Germany the world's most powerful transatlantic communicating stations."

Rentschler went on to explain "His benefactor George Westinghouse died in 1914. The following year his other benefactor John Astor died on the Titanic."

"Just as J.P. Morgan died about the same time" Anderson added without emotion. "Does that offset Westinghouse, who had long since stopped supporting Tesla's projects? The superrich Astor kept Tesla around for amusement more than serious investment. Tesla was blackballed. Can you believe that? After giving the world light, power and the ability to transmit it, Tesla could not raise a dime."

Harless looked up. On the rooftop Sandy and Fitzgerald watched George walking away from Kiep. Next to them Donald J's baritone demanded attention "I call this the, 'Who, me?' He showed the soft metal tube with a screw cap on a projecting tip before continuing, "When the cap is removed and the tube squeezed, it squirts a liquid chemical of violent, repulsive and lasting odor. Each tube is covered by a cardboard sleeve for protection. A.I.'s first version was a repulsive tube of treated English feces, which is extremely offensive to the Orientals." I remember his being so proud of his latest modification "I made Teutonic and Slavic versions. For German targets, I used chemically treated Slavic feces and for the Russians I use Teutonic feces."

Fitzgerald sarcastically asked;"Crap?".

Donald J. explained "It was not simply racial genes; it was racial diets. Once a target is sprayed by the "Who, me?" they must avoid everyone." He looked proud of his modifications. Fitzgerald was worried about him.

The scary gadget man headed downstairs and everyone watched over the ledge as he walked up behind Kiep. This was the first of four other foreign diplomats that day. An agent came in and bumped an unsuspecting Kiep, while Donald J. expertly squirted on the German. The cream immediately soaked in and the agents disappeared into the crowds.

Being struck with the overwhelming stench, Kiep turned and looked up to see Fitzgerald.

Ferncliff Cemetery
Ardsley on Hudson, N.Y.

Leading the 25-mile long procession of autos, Kosanovic rode in the mortuary's sedan along with Tesla' cremated ashes. Hundreds of cars drove slowly north on the motorcade. The convoy pulled into the cemetery on a balmy afternoon. Kosanovic stared at the well-kept landscaping. The motorcade drove straight toward the Ferncliff Mausoleum, a medieval labyrinthine with gray marble walls, eternally barred windows and innumerable private alcoves. The caravan of automobiles pulled up in front of the mausoleum. Kosanovic remained sitting, continuing to write in his notes.

Donald J.'s translated records show the diplomat was plagued by questions; Trust the Russians? Do I have a choice? Will Germany fall at Stalingrad? Can the Nazi's twenty-five divisions catch Tito in the mountains? Is King Petar politically impotent? How can we ever forgive Mikhailovich's force of Chetniks treaty with the Nazis is designed to destroy his opponents and thousands of innocents? Do the British interpret Allied policy towards Yugoslavia? What will we look like after the war? Should I go home after the war? Will the Soviet shadow fall over Yugoslavia? Will the people follow the king in England or Tito at home? Is communism is inevitable? And, perhaps the most troubling of all was that Tesla never wished to be cremated yet the nephew decided he be burnt to ashes and put inside a urn.

A discrete knock on the window brought Kosanovic back to the moment outside. The crowds were walking into the mausoleum. He placed his notebook inside his jacket and stepped out of the limousine. A reflection struck the tall Slav's eyes. Searching across the horizon, he saw two men with binoculars. Kiep and Von Haak were both watching the procession from behind the row of shrubbery, next to the tallest tombstone.

Kiep did not have time to change clothes. He spied from an angry distance "Wilhelm, after the ceremony is over I want you to find this Italian, Claudius.

He is not to be trusted. I never accepted this, this using George Viereck's identity. I cannot accept his story he wanted to find us by having us find him. I cannot accept his continued use of Viereck's identity. He is up to something more. I want to know what and why. But I want that weapon under any conditions. Do you understand?"

They never saw the A.I. man in the foliage. Von Haak had taken a few steps to the side because his eyes watered. He attempted to remain oblivious to the sickening odor. Once Kiep turned toward the tree, Von Haak turned away to talk "I would suggest we bring him into a safe house and interrogate him there."

The diplomat used his souvenir dagger to stab the nearby tree, repeatedly. Grabbing the black metal scabbard and composition handle and after sticking the polished cast metal blade too deep, Kiep struggled to pull it out and stared intently at the engraving 'Allies for Deutschland'. He stared at the ground. "Keep me apprised."

Von Haak announced "Look, there he is. Where is the woman? I'm sure she works for the Americans or maybe just maybe the British. Have you seen her any-where before?"

"*Nein, Heir Kemp. Eich bien...*"

"Speak English. Your American accent is pathetic."

"Yes sir."

"The Italians shame Fascism. They make their professors wear their gaudy uniforms while their solders bring dishonor on the battlefield. It is no wonder they attacked Ethiopia. It is the only country they dare." Dr. Kemp added, "I should not laugh at our allies. At least their Navy has some dignity. The Italians will patrol our Mediterranean bases after the war."

"Yes sir. I doubt they will have an army after the war. Their army was humiliated in our attack on Stalingrad."

"I believe so. That actor or spy or whoever he fantasies himself to be is not from the military. Their military has neither the will nor the resources for such a weapon. The blustering Mussolini's declaration of war on America was a vain hope the Japanese would somehow glorify him at Pearl Harbor. He is an ally seeking to claim victory on the accomplishments of others. A friend in the SS told me Mussolini is being treated for an ulcer. He certainly deserves one but, that too is no doubt a figment of his imagination."

Von Haak laughed, sounding like a chortle.

Kiep pointed to the dark brown Desoto Betty was exiting. "I knew she would show up. See how she is dressed in a plain black hat with the veil draped over her face. Women do have an advantage in our game. She's a predator that one is, yes, she is.

Watch her. I will give her thirty more seconds looking innocently down to mask her entrance into the crowd before her eyes prowl across the pack looking for her prey."

Von Haak looked at his wristwatch.

Kemp glanced over to realize his underling took him literally. "Very well."

Focusing his binoculars the doctor watched Betty enter the crowd, walking three rows deep and stopping. She raised her head high and scanned the mourners to spot George.

Von Haak read out loud "Twenty-nine seconds."

"Fascism power is the imprecision of our enemies," Kemp murmured.

Quick to impress his superior Von Haak declared, "The future is inevitable; the Third Reich will give it precision."

Searching familiar faces Dr. Kemp's jaw tightened. "This will no longer be tolerated. It is time we secure possession of this weapon. We must once again come to the Italian's rescue. They are such a pathetic race. No, this Italian is not from the military. He is corporate espionage. Now, the question is; what corporation?"

"We confirmed he is from the Marconi Company."

Von Haak reported.

Kemp looked over at Von Haak. "I take this was determined during this morning's search of his residence?"

With his eyes watering, Von Haak stepped back before answering. "The complete report will be waiting for you when we return to the city."

"What else do we know?"

"He is receiving his funds from a London bank account and he has a private mail box in Manhattan" he explained, looking to take a few steps back.

Kemp asked "Did you find any evidence of the weapon?"

"Only the pictures."

"I think the woman is close. She is still stalking him." Kiep focused his binoculars on Betty taking hold of George's arm.

Watching Tesla's urn being carried, George jumped when Betty wrapped her arm around his. "I expected to find you here. Sorry about what happen back there business, important business."

Betty squeezed his arm. "Shall we go into the mausoleum?"

George shook his head "Perhaps another day." He turned around with Betty arm-in-arm, skipping to keep up and headed for the autos.

She whispered, "Could you give me a ride back?"

George pulled her close and kissed her until he noticed people staring at him. He grabbed Betty by the hand to walk quickly to his Cord.

Down the road with the motor running, Von Haak and Kiep waited to follow.

Wednesday, January 13th

Forces and Eulogies

Coenties Slip
Pier 5, East River

Dozens of ship-to-shore lights were flashing back and forth across the piers. At the Coenties Slip, one of the few without freight in transit, four ragged day workers huddled around the fire spewing from the metal drum inside the open-sided shed. They stared blankly at Sandy and Fitzgerald walking past them.

The morning was hazy. Fitzgerald pulled down his heavy fur hat far over his ears. The harbor wind blew through his trench coat. Skinny guys hate the cold.

Sandy seemed oblivious to the chilling weather. Beyond the immediate problem the Brit wanted to manage the whole damn war. "Your entire Atlantic seaboard relaxed its dim-outs and air raid precautions."

Shivering Fitzgerald reacted "After we discovered those ten German mines in the harbor last November, the port authority woke up to what is happening on your side of the ocean. We are securing the area."

"Not fast enough." The Limey said as looked around the port.

Fitzgerald remembered feeling compelled to argue "Have you read about the YNG-39's we installed? The technology enabling their power generators was invented by Tesla."

The YNG-39 was equipped with hydrophones for underwater listening, ASDIC gear, and magneto telephone to Hoffman Island. This was connected in turn to the Harbor Entrance Command Post (HECP) at Fort Wadsworth and to Swinburne Island, the site of the Degaussing Section. The YNG-39 was also equipped with one .50 caliber and two .30 caliber machine guns, as well as a 1-pounder."

"It's a start." He continued looking down his nose at most everything. The Europeans were never tired of complaining.

"And we will finish it, just like we did last time." Fitzgerald thought the dig about WWI would shut him up but was wrong.

Sandy ranted on "Americans fail to take civil defense seriously enough," he complained. "I was sailing last night and your bloody civilian lights silhouetted merchant ships from fifteen miles out." His Tory accent carried a pitch of imperialism. The English considered Americans like the youngster promoted over them. "The civilians are still in denial and have failed to take this war seriously".

"Of course, Americans were distressed," Fitzgerald explained

"Just how do you intend on searching all these ports for one box?" Sandy was both a good ally and a wet blanket.

Fitzgerald explained "Given we never fought this new war our countermeasures are developing. The Nazi sympathizers are getting used to moving freely around the docks. They don't seem to realize we have focused on the port issue." Fitzgerald pointed to strategic places around the port. "We have their operatives under surveillance. They misdirect shipping orders and we correct them after they leave. We will continue this game until we are sure how they transmit the information to Berlin. The Nazis have enjoyed their time but our day is in sight. Those bastards will regret the day they picked this damn fight."

Sandy stood quietly for a long minute. He offered a gentlemen's bow. "It is an honor to serve with you and I shall never question your competency again. Now, how can I help you get that bloody Italian operative, the one pretending to be Viereck?" He had an ability to smile through every conversation and Fitzgerald the ability to ignore his comment.

Walking cautiously into the warehouse Fitzgerald said to Sandy "He thinks this is some damn white collar game stealing trade secrets."

Sandy was sounding like the streets of New York. "He's going to be one unhappy grease ball when he learns Roosevelt proposed imprisoning every foreign agent in civilian clothes for life."

Fitzgerald asked like it was personal, "I need your help exposing this bastard."

"What are you proposing?"

The Englishman had the dream assignment, being a foreign agent in a friendly country. He simply provided free support and confirmed sources. Ostensibly there was only his report. Realistically he was to advance Britain's interest. His assignment was working with Americans whenever possible.

Fitzgerald explained "The box he sent to London might be the part of Tesla's weapon Claudius stole. We searched his apartment during the funeral yesterday and came up with some interesting clues. Our men confirmed he is being paid by Marconi Company out of London."

"We have a top cryptologist working on a crude poem Claudius had written on the back of one half of a tare sheet. He is evidently shipping a small crate to London."

"There are 1,100 bloody warehouses down here.

Once I gave this a go, I was shocked to find forty million feet of storage in this port. Without the other half of the bloody shipping doc, you cannot very well search through six hundred ship anchorages?" Fitzgerald complained.

Sandy bragged "Was not planning on it."

"Then just what did you plan on?"

"We'll drive the snake from his hole. A rookie agent was following him and lost sight of him when he was down here. He will come back here if our ploy works."

"I find it more than a bit of interest Claudius chose bad poetry, given he is pretending to be a poet of Viereck's caliber." Fitzgerald explained, "Our background profiles put his poetry in the same class as Hitler's drawings. They are insights into their sick minds."

"You are ahead of us on that front."

Fitzgerald explained "What we are going to decide is, whether this crate has been shipped out or not."

"A bit of nuisance we do not know where it is, don't you think?"

"Sure, but given our recent experiences following German bastards in their campaign against our docks, we have learned enough on how things work down here to have a running start."

Sandy stopped walking. "Are you saying you brought me down here for an unauthorized search?"

"We know from Mussolini's daughter that Marconi built a death ray and demonstrated it a few years ago."

"You cannot be serious?"

"I sure and hell can," Fitzgerald was so sure of sources he was surprised they needed defending.

Sandy had a snide tone most of the time "You Yanks know Marconi died years ago?"

After looking at him Fitzgerald felt obligated to answer his insinuation "Sure we do."

It was surprising to see him upset without ever losing his English composure. "Let us hope you did not drag me down here to waste my day on some ridiculous rumor you could not get authorized. What am I doing down in this bloody dock beyond tolerating this insufferable New York wind?"

Fitzgerald put his hand on Sandy's shoulder. "I know Marconi died in 1937, okay? Our problem is that the Marconi Company works freely in London." For the first time he appeared on the defensive, "Are you suggesting...?"

"Not at all or we would not be having this discussion."

"Half of Mussolini's' armies in Russia were lost," he pointed out. "Their navy is immobilized for lack of fuel. They lost half their soldiers in their aborted attack on Greece. The Italians are losing every ship they send supporting the African campaign. Claudius is most definitely not pursuing a military goal."

"Exactly, he is from some corporation."

Sandy said "Listen to this scenario, the only piece of Tesla's weapon I know he had was the Accelerator. This becomes critical considering the only problem reported with Marconi's demonstration was a lack of power."

"You really believe Claudius has the prototype?" he asked.

"It is a serious possibility. We must never let anyone find out if the two parts fit."

Sandy explained "Marconi has stolen ideas from Tesla, fair enough. What have you learned?"

"The experiment took place in 1934 and Marconi killed sheep and stopped car motors at a distance."

Sandy shook his head. "We heard the same story. Nothing more came from that story beyond rumors. We concluded it was the radio transmitter technology Marconi demonstrated for ship navigation."

"Radio's cannot kill motors or sheep."

At times it was most difficult to differentiate between British snobbery and Sandy's skepticism. He challenged Fitzgerald "Do you have evidence that Marconi stole the weapon from Tesla or that his company now has control of this weapon?" Fitzgerald pulled his coat tighter and walked toward the loading crates.

Sandy followed "I know that oily bastard stole recognition for inventing the radio." Sandy looked over at Fitzgerald. "This 'lead' of yours is a bit thin, is it not, old boy?"

Fitzgerald said "I read all about your contest awarding a hundred pounds to anyone who could kill a sheep at one hundred meters. Is it true nobody claimed your prize?"

The British would never be outdone that easily "Actually the contest was quite the success. The British Committee for Air Defense compiled a report on such scientific possibilities. One of our scientists, Richard Watson-Watt by name used the report to conclude that with electromagnetic waves the speed and distance of an airplane could be measured from the ground."

I knew the required reading for every Eaton trained engineer: the 26 February 1935 experiment built by Marconi at Daventry in the Midlands. They detected a bomber's approach from eight miles out. The Italian army did not care and the RAF did. Impatiently adding, "I know the story of radar but that's not my concern. This is far more serious and you seem to miss my point. If Marconi extrapolated his project from Tesla's work prematurely, he failed to create the final piece required to give the weapon force and distance."

"With all of his faults Marconi was pursuing the development of frequency not power. Your issue is one of electrical power without wires." Sandy argued,

"Fair enough," Fitzgerald countered. "That is exactly the purpose of the prototype. And, we both know that the Marconi Company is the only ones in Italy with the resources to put the two pieces together."

"If they fit" Sandy added dryly.

"I want to know that answer before they do. Don't you?"

Given his first acknowledgement of the day, Fitzgerald knew he would go along with bigger plans. "We must find out before that crate is shipped to London."

By then the two had walked back to their autos. Fitzgerald got into the 1938 Ford and offered, "Do you care to join me set the trap? I assure you we will end up back here to pick up your beautiful Pontiac this evening." Sandy opened the door and sat down and they drove to Claudius' building. Fitzgerald parked around the corner, facing the Harbor before showing him the copy of the tare sheet. "See, Claudius' crate was broken and could not be shipped in its present condition. The broken crate would be held for 72 hours before being forwarded to claims storage."

Fitzgerald explained while getting out of the car, "This will be fast." Fitzgerald put the note in the envelope and gave it to him.

Sandy walked across the street and met the uniformed deliveryman. Fitzgerald could see him show the notice. Sandy watched the cyclist ride up with the letter for the doorman. Returning to his auto, Fitzgerald sat behind the steering wheel "Now hurry up and wait."

Less than twenty minutes passed before Claudius' white and brown Cord pulled onto the street. He drove slowly and then accelerated around the corner, straight for the harbor.

Fitzgerald slowly pulled out and remained two lanes over for the entire drive towards the pier. The Cord zigzagged several times. Fitzgerald remained in the original lane to end up back where the Italian started. Claudius pulled up to Pier Five, parked, got out and looked directly at Fitzgerald sitting behind two rows of parked cars. The foreigner continued to search the parking lot for several minutes and finally turned around to walk away. He entered the nearby warehouse. Sandy and Fitzgerald got out and followed him.

Claudius was waiting, standing next to a crate and dusting off his Woolf Brothers tux. "Good morning, gentlemen."

Fitzgerald hated this guy and let Sandy answer. "A good day to you, I gather you were expecting us?"

Claudius looked us up and down, "Who do you work for General Electric or Westinghouse? No, let me tell you. Neither of you are 30, so it must be Westinghouse."

Fitzgerald looked at Sandy, who quickly answered, "You're right. Why do you ask?" Claudius complimented himself. "I thought so. They warned me to watch for Westinghouse operatives."

"Operatives!" Laughing, Fitzgerald blurted out "What's your game?"

With a smirk Claudius looked around the warehouse. "I don't see a net, is there one?"

Fitzgerald had no delusion about this actor who could care less about the war. The Italian used his hands to accentuate every word, "This is no game gentlemen. May I suggest it is in our mutual interest to have a simple business transaction?"

There was nothing easy about this encounter. He wanted to be someone else and believe we were someone else.

"Is there a mutual interest?" Fitzgerald asked. "Of course we do" he answered with a wave of the hand. "You follow me for the same reason. No?" Stepping forward Sandy asked, "And what is our reason?"

Claudius walked the ten meters towards us until he lowered his voice "I am a businessman. I have long since found it useful to meet my competition and perhaps my customers."

Fitzgerald was taken aback "Do we look like palookas?"

"Now gentlemen, you must appreciate I attended university here and have visited your fine country many times. I admire your free market. I seriously doubt either of you has not exploited a moment or two for your own benefit. What are we competing for? The very question troubles us all. You must agree?"

"My name is Fitzgerald and this is Sandy. And yours?"

"George." He looked for a response and without one continued, "I am most happy you have calmed down and listened to reason. I announce my return to New York to alert your men in suits. And, most certainly you would sneak in and nibble on my lure."

"Before we as you say, nibble, perhaps you could give us a better idea of what exactly we can catch and bring home?" Sandy asked.

Claudius feigned incredulity, "Come, come, gentlemen. We are businessmen here not street vendors. Why did you follow me?"

"Actually, we want more of an international relationship between our company and yours" Sandy continued "We exchange information, ideas and market ourselves in more of a cooperative relationship." The Englishman was enjoying this encounter "Would you say?"

As he did often Claudius lifted his chin. "I would say you are attempting to play me for one of your fools. I cannot negotiate with underlings. You return to your superiors empty handed, and see what they offer you."

Without hesitation Sandy fired back "If you have any insights regarding General Electric, we have the authority to disburse upwards of five figures but only if the information is useful."

"Now we understand each other." Claudius nodded. "This is what may interest your company. I am aware of the military contracts Westinghouse has with your military. I can offer you a weapon to advance your war efforts, a weapon beyond your hopes. You two gentlemen will also have the opportunity to become very wealthy."

Sandy asked, "Where does that leave you and the Marconi Company?"

"That is hardly your concern." Claudius snapped

"The price is seven figures. Do you need to consult your superiors?"

Maintaining his smile Sandy offered, "Fair enough. Perhaps we can set up a time for a demonstration."

Rocking his finger back and forth as if we needed to be corrected "It must be said though; this weapon will require development capital, as with all weapons."

Fitzgerald asked "How do we know it works?" "I will show you why you followed me." His large nose protruded with his head slightly back. After pulling the informative half of the invoice out of his pocket, he turned and summoned a nearby worker. "Bring this to me."

Claudius included a five dollar bill with the Tare sheet.

After grinning widely the stout worker walked quickly to retrieve the crate.

Sandy asked "What in the bloody hell brought you to New York?"

"I came here to negotiate with Dr. Tesla." Making no effort to cover his conceit, Claudius answered "Alas the visit proved to be providential and the old man died just before I arrived."

Fitzgerald blurted "What did you have to do with it?"

"Nothing that crude" Amused Claudius explained with some disdain "He was very old and not advancing his ideas convincingly anymore. It was only natural he died and providential I was there. I merely exploited an opportunity."

Fitzgerald did not care how his challenge sounded; "you stole from his grave?"

Claudius turned towards Sandy. "You must speak reason to your crude friend. The old man was still alive when he gave me this collateral for a substantial loan. If you continue with your insults then we have nothing more to discuss." The Italian was indignant.

"Calm down" Sandy reassured him. "We prefer to know who we work with."

"I care not to be your friend." Claudius challenged him with an indignant sense of security. "I will give you a roll of film and it is for you to make me an offer. It is that simple. Before you see this prize I will need a telephone contact number."

Sandy looked at Fitzgerald. "I will give my number at the dock." He handed him the five digit telephone number.

The worker carried the 3x4 crate and set it next to Claudius.

The Italian instructed the warehouseman to open the wooden box. Claudius leaned over and warily removed the film. He flipped it towards Sandy, who easily caught it. "I look forward to your offer gentlemen and bidding starts at $1,000,000."

He started to leave and the worker asked, "What do you want me to do with all of these shoes?"

Without turning back Claudius called "Wear them with the knowledge they have been in the presence of greatness."

Hotel Ambassador, Park Avenue
East Fifty-first and East Fifty-second

Each time the German dignitary, Kiep drove up from Washington he stayed at the Ambassador. Ironic name aside, the Hotel was the last word in refined elegance.

He never visited German town when there was Park Avenue.

The hotel was designed for accessibility, not security, making it easy for Donald J. to wire Kiep's room. A. I. would have insulted the German agent by not listening in on his New York visits. Everybody he met was of concern. All of this made more difficult by the fact, unlike the 200,000 recent German immigrants coming through Ellis Island, Kiep was on a diplomatic visa. A.I. was under strict orders to respect his status as an envoy and was not allowed to even consider invading the privacy of an attaché without express permission from the court. The concern was not to get caught. Donald J. never missed a word Kiep uttered or failed to identify a visitor to his apartment.

A.I. was careful to never embarrass their diplomats. Every visitor had his picture taken. Donald J. changed the light bulbs in the hallway. Over Kiep's door, he switched the 40 watt bulb to 75 watt. Visitors welcomed the 75 watt bulb hanging directly over Kiep's door, considering the neighbor's lights were out.

Kiep's first visitor heals dug in with each step as a military walk. Without speaking Kiep waved him in. The visitor carried a suitcase over to the mahogany table, sat down and lit up a English fag.

The visitor told Kiep, "We have brought field gear you should find useful."

"I shall decide what is of use" Kiep snapped, "What else do you have?"

The man pulled open his full length jacket, exposing his Nazi Infantry Man's WWII leggings. "See the double thickness, green canvas with leather reinforcements and straps. Notice the roller buckles on the leggings."

Pacing back and forth Kiep was visibly upset. He replied "They should be very useful the next time *I attack Stalingrad.*"

Yelling was not Kiep's nature. He remained temperamental ever since Donald J's trick at Tesla's funeral. He seemed insulted, with the permanent stench on his $300 dress suit. The diplomat cussed after he threw away the clothes worn at the funeral.

Three raps came from the door. Kiep let Von Haak in and led him over to the table, on the far side of his suite. Kiep motioned the visitor to open his suitcase. The solder carefully laid out the blanket on the table. He unrolled a large weapons belt, with three weapons in holsters.

A.I. watched but under orders to wait until receiving further instructions or being directly threatened. This meant the foreign agent had created an imminent threat. They had crossed that point by distributing weapons for the intent of sabotaging the American war effort and killing Fitzgerald. This was one of many sobering realizations about war. Fitzgerald was not trained to be brave when someone wanted to kill him. At the beginning a couple of guys thought debriefing Fitzgerald about the plot to kill the brain boy was funny. After Fitzgerald failed to laugh his handlers became serious. Response tactics were defined.

Kiep bragged, "These are the weapons we stole from the OSS." He reached down and picked up the 6" pistol, "and this weighs less than one point eight metric pound. It is a single shot .45 caliber hand gun. Use it well because it requires a full minute to reload." He set it back down.

Kiep picked up the 15" pistol, "This is a weapon we will use. the Welrod silencer is detachable and quite accurate from one half of an inch to fifty yards." Kiep handed it back.

"We will never be humiliated again. What will they say when we shoot them with their own weapons?" It was the first time Kiep had shown emotion. "I attended the funeral out of respect for our neighbor and these Americans insult me in the most offensive fashion. How dare they? I want Fitzgerald dead."

Strutting like an Teutonic knight in a three piece suit, Von Haak stepped up to the table, "Heir Kiep will you give me the honor of choosing the weapon?"

"What do you prefer?"

Picking up the two weapons, they were different except both sported a metal tipped dart. Von Haak asked, "These came from where?"

"The Americans call the modified .45 automatic pistol a Bigot; accurate up to 15 feet. The other is the Little Joe, a hand-held crossbow made from aluminum. It has twice the distance." Kiep's eyes turned steel blue as he leaned into the weapons. "If you choose one of these, you will call it your best friend."

The men laughed.

Von Haak chose the Bigot and swore to the weapon "I want to be close."

Serbian Orthodox Cathedral of St. Sava
20 W 26th

There was the international funeral and the national services. Even though Yugoslavia was suffering through devastating loses and divided loyalties, each and every expatriate was deeply saddened by the death of their favorite son, Tesla. The Slav Bishop William T. Manning presented the afternoon eulogy for the Serbs, with local Croats and Montenegrins being allowed to sit in the back. They entered separately and left too demoralized to hate each other, for the remainder of the day. The nephew sat in a place of honor, quiet unto himself. His notes recounted the burden of choosing to cremate his uncle, for the sanctity of the body in a land of jackals and scavengers.

There was one refuge left in the sanctuary. The Serbian cathedral had neither great ceilings nor walls of sparkling glass. It was a humble, pious building filled with miserable faces and sad hearts. The Orthodox Church was the national church. When the government attempted a pact with the Vatican in 1937, the

Yugoslavian Church exercised excommunications and forced the government to rescind judgments on many of the same expatriates in attendance this very day.

In preparation for the unique congregation, the FBI had provided A.I. invaluable assistance in monitoring the targets and remaining respectful as the somber services drew to an end. Everyone left except Kosanovic who remained alone on the far side of the chamber. Dr. Rado Mirkovich, Jevtic' and Prof. Boris Furlan quietly joined him. They realized each other was following the news and there was no need to recount the daily deaths in their homeland. The day by day reminder had worn heavily on these aging expatriates. Yugoslavia had no national army. Across the country, the Nazis were attacking communists who were killing domestic fascists, who were slaughtering everyone else. Serbs and Croats killed each other daily. For every one soldier who died, two civilians paid the price. The civilians had no choice. The men that remain knew this to be true. No one was at church for small talk. They were there alone, except for Donald J. who was well hidden.

Kosanovic apologized, "I had so hoped last week I would be bringing my friends better news. We are old men and we must discuss harsh reality with great candor. I want to be clear that every question shall be construed as an open discussion. My thoughts are meant to initiate debate. Quite simply my friends, I seek your counsel."

One by one the men gave him grunted assurances he could speak freely.

"This matter of Tesla's weapon has weighed deeply on me every moment. I have spoken to friends at our embassy as well as to King Petar's representative. Our small country has neither the resources nor the ability to finish building this weapon. I have been approached by the Russians, who have made substantial overtures for my releasing this weapon to them."

Rado was the first to speak, "How do they know you have this weapon?"

"They only suspect" Kosanovic answered.

Unable to contain his hate for the Russians, Bogdan said, "What for one mad moment could lead anyone to believe in their dialectical shroud of self-serving deceit and contradictions? If they want us to follow Dialectics they must first explain contradictions of the German Jew, Karl Marx."

Rado suggested "Before we begin a discussion of Russian morality, it is important to understand their source and extent of information they have about this weapon. We must remain practical. We lost four and half million men in the last war. That's 60 percent of our fighters and we still fight. We can no longer pursue this insanity. We must use this weapon. We must stop our people from killing each other."

Bogdan explained, "It is practically certain their spies attended today's eulogy. The agents from many countries are waiting outside and recording our names."

"Do you know this as a certainty?" Rado asked, shaking his head in disbelief.

"I certainly know they are capable. I know if they believe Kosanovic has the weapon, and they will be following him and... as of this moment, us. Our diplomatic protection and American police mean little now."

"The burden is mine gentlemen" Kosanovic apologized, never showing emotion but unable to conceal the fatigue in his voice. "I did not choose but am living with the increased awareness of this war and this weapon. I apologize to my friends if I have brought Russian agents into your lives."

"And, no doubt the American FBI", Bogdan added. He pulled out his handkerchief and rubbed his eyes before roaring, "War has its' moment when the stark truth of one's personal death engulfs the mind of each and every collaborator. One cannot question its power, for the pervasive truth is war." Becoming excited he could not help but to stand. "War is the time when a man first realizes he can die, no, that he will necessarily die, it is just a matter of when. The only question remaining is will his death be during the war or will God allow death to be after? All warriors know he will see friends and all innocence die during war. War is not a question of heroics, cowardice or ego; it is the ultimate awareness of one's own death." The others waved their hands downward and Bogdan lowered his voice. "War is sheer mortality. How pathetically shallow are those men who go through life without such a life altering experience. This is not a moment to study, no the revelation of war must be experienced. War is the one time when humans realize the clarity and stark truth they will necessarily die. War is the time when a man prays to cross the abyss over death's alluring temptation. War brings joy to the heart in hope God will allow life, after the war before they die. Comprehending one's death offers more for when war becomes personal the acceptance of personal death makes a man free, free to die, free to live, free to fight and then die, years later." The room was quiet in appreciation.

Rado stood as he said, "We are already in this war. I will not shame my country with fear of whether the Americans either hide us or pursue us. This is a war we must contend with. I am proud of who I am and what I choose... my brothers who sit here with me. I refuse to give one inch to those roaches choosing the shadows for their knowledge. Let them follow us, they cannot ever see inside our minds."

Clenching both of his fists, Boris broke his silence. "Nor can they understand the resilience of our people." The room's silence resonated.

Kosanovic continued "To answer your earlier question, I do not know if they know for sure but given they have contacted me on two occasions in the last few days, we would be foolish to conclude anything other than the Russians know for sure."

Bogdan's quaking bass voice forced our receiver to regularly adjust the squelch control. He said "We cannot separate this from Tito. If Tito had such a weapon, the future of our country would be predetermined, not even god would do that to us."

"We are not prepared to become a puppet of the Russians," Rado protested.

Boris countered "Surely you would not support Mikhailovich and his Chetniks who make peace with the Nazis." He raised both hands in surrender "So he can turn around and slaughter his own people."

Rado pointed out "Our country is teetering. We will collapse and never recover from the Nazis."

The fatigue in his voice changed the tone of his words. Kosanovic pleaded "Gentlemen, the bitter truth is our nation only stands because we have so many enemies holding us up from so many directions. We all recognize the slaughter of our people is unrelenting. No nation in this war suffers greater losses than Yugoslavia. This must be our only focus."

"Then should we not discuss the shortest route to peace? What is the most this weapon can contribute to that one end?" Rado asked.

Bogdan repeated himself, "The slaughter of our people is unrelenting."

"We agree why we are here," the diplomat beseeched his friends. "How can we produce solutions, not emotions?"

Clasping his hands Boris challenged his countrymen, "What we have not discussed is the very nature of this weapon. When Nikola Tesla invented this weapon he believed no one would use it. Are you prepared for the consequences?"

"Consequences?" Bogdan bellowed his challenge.

Leaning over the pew until his girth prevented his coming any closer, Boris pointed out "Consider what happens with any army holding such a weapon. When Tesla conceived this weapon, did he understand the maniacal Stalin or Hitler threatening to pursue their form of evil over our borders? The world is a far, far different one today. Who in this room wants to be responsible for the death of a country? Imagine what those sadistic tyrants, who have already killed millions, would do with a weapon that would make them a hundred times more efficient murderers? Put this damnable weapon on a swivel and they could kill everyone for hundreds of miles."

Rado sagged "That is not of our concern. Our duty ends at the Yugoslavian border."

Reddening Boris declared, "This war started over this provincial morality entitling one race to rationalize killing another. How can we sit in this temple of god and seriously discuss empowering armies to kill millions?"

Looking at the Holy Cross on the wall Kosanovic became nervous, unsure of what to say. "We are not talking about mass murder. We are talking about protecting Yugoslavia."

Sitting back to look at each member of the cabal, moving from one set of intent stares to another, Boris posed the question, "Then how do we put such a weapon in the hands of any government without giving them the power to use it as they choose? I knew your Uncle would never let this out of his control. He turned down the every offer that excluded him. They needed him but, he refused. Why? Military powers do not want any of us. If it suits their purpose we are dead. After they dispose of us, they will do whatever they choose."

Rado offered "Then, we agree the weapon will not go to those ideologues or any of the madmen. Let me suggest anyone of the many leaders in Europe who only seek peace. We have to ask the question, why not the Americans?"

"Why would you ask?" Because of his loyalty to the Prince, Bogdan was uncomfortable with any references towards democracy. "We would lose all control, they would take all control, and no one would have any idea what would happen next year. With their resources the Americans could become a world power. They could depose any kingdom. What is to prevent them from attacking a country their corporations want to exploit?"

Pausing for an answer and not receiving any Bogdan continued, "Capitalism is but one step away from plutocracy, a form of imperialism beyond any horror written in the past. Look at the Italian *corporativist* sup-porting Mussolini. Give them this power and they could easily overthrow a reluctant prince who refuses trade. They are a power capable of rewriting European history."

Boris interjected, "This war will change the world balance. It is naive to suggest we can predict what will happen. We cannot offer such a power to any country without endangering our home. We cannot expect such a weapon to do anything other than be used to eradicate an entire race. We cannot release this weapon to anyone."

"My friends," Rado pleaded "we are not here to plan world history. It is presumptuous to suggest anything different. If Tesla invented this weapon, in time so shall someone else. We cannot protect humanity. We can protect our homeland. There is no other way to use this power."

"We do not know how long it would take before the holders of this weapon will be able to deploy it. We don't know how much money would be required to prepare for its use. There is too much we do not know."

Adjusting his glasses Kosanovic pondered out loud, "We can only hope the lure of this power can leverage an increasing security for our people. No gentlemen, we must agree doing nothing is not an option."

"What do you know?" Rado challenged "Is not the underlying issue. How is this certain and why did your Uncle dislike his own nephew?"

"I live in the world of politics" Kosanovic answered. "I know Nikola was naive and offended by my suggestions of releasing his work to the American military. Our problem is not one of trust or guarantees because such dreams do not exist in this world. If the Germans take Stalingrad and defeat the English in Africa the war could be in New York next year. If the Germans are frozen in by the Russian blizzards and Hitler ignores his generals then the war will cave in upon Berlin. We cannot affect either outcome. We can only affect Yugoslavia. This is what we should discuss and nothing else. How can we solve the world's problems with this weapon or any weapon?" His voice trailed off as he dropped his chin onto his hand.

"The problems" Boris blurted, "is that we are in God's temple mourning a death. Are we here to discuss the morality of what we do? Are we not obligated to honor the words and intentions of the very soul that created this weapon?"

"I respect your concerns," Rado answered. "The crisis is we are in the middle of a war destroying our homeland. We can save the metaphysical discussions until after the war."

"Metaphysical?" Boris asked. "Today is not metaphysical. Our people are being slaughtered! If Hitler has the weapon tomorrow, he will massacre us. For as long as this weapon exists, Stalin can steal it and will create a bloodbath beyond our wildest nightmares. It is evil and beyond redemption. We must destroy such a horrible device."

The back door opened and an older altar boy walked up to the front row of pews. He kneeled at the Alter.

All four watched the teenager praying.

Boris whispered "I ask which of you is willing to put a weapon into this world to kill that young man?"

Bogdan explained "You have failed to under-stand Tesla's intentions. The weapon is designed to render war obsolete not to shoot and not to allow anyone else to be shot."

"Has there ever been a weapon not used?" Rado asked.

Boris said "How long shall we pursue such speculation? Good, so we shall. Has anyone ever created a weapon of such power its' existence rewrites history? Is this in our future?"

Rado argued "History will not agree with you and without respecting history, surely will we repeat those errors. The first weapon meant nothing until it was used. We are talking about human nature. People conquer others and take what they choose. Any country, at any time is vulnerable to a dictator. What do you think will happen if Tito succeeds? Do you think, for one moment, he will be better than Stalin?" Extending his hands, he sarcastically asks. "Did not Tito volunteer to study in Moscow?"

Kosanovic suggested, "We have agreed certain countries cannot have such power. It is not realistic to expect our prince has either the resources or the ability to make use of this weapon. Even if Tito becomes all you suggest, we must consider selling the weapon for the reconstruction of Yugoslavia."

"Sell the weapon to the highest bidder? How much do you think any government would give for such a weapon?" Bogdan challenged. "Have not the British and the American armies already refused to invest in such a weapon?"

"This is a different world" Rado explained with obvious reluctance, "Britain and America are now in total war. Tesla is not here with his... preconditions. His condition was to manage the completion, was it not?" The wrinkles above his glasses deepened.

Kosanovic answered "No one knows if it was an issue of completion or production."

Glancing over at the praying teenager, Boris asked "Why are we not answering the fundamental question? Shall we unleash upon him and his generation a weapon of mass destruction? The destruction will no longer be measured by the death of one soldier, rather by the destruction of cities."

Bogdan tried a new tack "Airplanes are weapons of mass destruction and they have never destroyed a city. Germany has missiles and they do not destroy cities. Dictators can destroy entire cities as you suggest. No, you are speculating and we can no longer waste time on this alarmist argument."

"You misunderstand the real nature," Kosanovic explained "This weapon is not designed to attack cities nor shoot down missiles. This weapon is the pure defensive weapon, rendering all other weapons obsolete."

They stopped talking when the young man stood up. He walked over to ask, "Excuse me sirs, did any of you know Doctor Tesla?"

"We all did." Kosanovic answered before asking "What is your name?"

"Daniel. Forgive me; I came here to listen to his services." He had short black hair and a dark complexion. He was an intense lad who looked at each man in the eye.

"What did you think of him?" Bogdan asked.

Daniel said "Oh I am sorry I certainly didn't mean any disrespect. I am studying to become a priest and wanted to hear final services." He bowed dutifully.

Kosanovic wondered, "How old are you?"

"Nineteen."

"What does the priesthood teach us about the war and our involvement?" Bogdan asked before stopping to control his labored breathing. He angrily refused any attention from his friends.

The aspiring priest waited until receiving a wave from Bogdan before answering "We pray and send our families what we can. Beyond that, I know very little. The patron saint, *Krsna Slava* protects and encourages us to look past the war."

"What about our Prince?" Bogdan looked pleadingly to his travel companions. "I heard the priest say the Prince will never return. In our history we have endless wars and far away kings but in our homes, the candle of our patron saint never has been extinguished."

Rado asked, "What do you know of our homeland?"

"Where the Serb lives our home is where Slava is also. He was here today and gives us a connection to this Dr. Tesla through our prayers. That is actually what I wanted to ask."

The old men found his lack of guile covered a multitude of his blind declarations.

Rado encouraged him "Go ahead."

Daniel struggled to find the right words. "What does the feeling of spiritual gladness and blood ties with Tesla teach us?"

After a prolonged silence Bogdan offered, "We have been discussing the great man and have failed to feel his spiritual power. Perhaps we have already failed."

Daniel said, "In Christ's eyes we have all failed and been forgiven. Slavskozhitore reminds us 'except a grain of wheat die, it cannot rise again'. Great men such as Dr. Tesla will continue with us. If we do not feel gladness it is only because we are sad at his departure. I am sure some day each friend will feel great joy. We can speak to Tesla through Christ." He stopped to look con-fused at his own words and turned towards Kosanovic to ask, "Was Dr. Tesla a believer?"

The question surprised Kosanovic "His father was a great man and a priest. Nikola, I believe, became more focused with the practical matters of ending war."

The references to realistic subjects made Daniel feel like a naive altar boy who asks, "What is more practical than eternal life?"

Kosanovic said, "I meant no disrespect. Dr. Tesla was baptized and raised in the church. He devoted his life to building a better world."

"Dr. Tesla believed in stopping capital punishment and was dedicated to spreading peace." Boris added.

"He was a pacifist." Kosanovic nodded.

All four men became uncomfortably silent. After a moment, Daniel apologized, "I did not mean to disturb your mourning and must return to my duties. I will pray for Dr. Tesla." He turned and walked out to the vestibule.

After an awkward moment Rado reminded everyone "Tesla had long since renounced the church."

"He had a firm belief system, scientific yes, fatalist perhaps. How he worked it out with god is, no doubt, a sight to behold and one continuing to this moment. God never created a greater brain. Now, God has the irony of Tesla's creation to challenge him."

Rado asked "I certainly mean no disrespect when I say perhaps our friend is not superman."

"If I were to have one criticism of my brilliant uncle, it would his belief the inventor was God-like. Surely, harnessing the Niagara Falls was a great feat but..." Kosanovic pulled out his handkerchief and removed his glasses to wipe his brow before continuing "Well he did make lightning strike the earth at Wardenclyffe, and yes he... he's on record creating that earthquake here in the city." Staring at the crucifix, Kosanovic's voice faded.

"He understood his gifts and what the Almighty expected of him."

Italian Savings Bank
SE Spring and Lafayette

Betty looked above the Colonnade street facades of Corinthian columns standing in front of the thirteen-story bank, from across the street. Standing alone, she stared at the one lit window on the third floor. It was after 7:15 when the light went off. A few minutes later the street level door opened and George walked out.

He smiled and quickly crossed the empty street to hug her. "Forgive me, my blossom. How terrible of me to stay so long. Money is such a burden, wouldn't you say?"

She asked, "Why does a German save money at an Italian bank?"

Laughing, he answered, "Here in New York, the Nazis use Chase Bank and J.P. Morgan. They help Nazis transfer money. We use different banks for different reasons."

They walked down the street. George recited.

'Tis by thy Name that is my Enemy What's in a Name?

That which we call a Rose, by any other name would smell as sweet.

With her head falling slightly to his side, she cooed "Is that Shakespeare?"

George said "No my love it was Thomas Otway who contributed greatly to every actor who understood him. I admire a man whose only desire was to clean up the imperfections of Shakespeare. The artist's burden is to recognize what is truly important. My sweet flower, one must master his image, his articulation, and his mastery of his profession. Beyond that names are no more than roles or occasions best understood as scenes. I create my opening and own the world as a stage."

"I love that about you." Betty hugged his arm. They walked toward his car. He opened the Cord's door and while getting in she asks "What is your real name?"

His character changed in a flash "Why do you ask such a question of a man?"

"Because you are a man" she teased.

With mock self-effacement George agreed, "Such is true."

"This is so exciting and would have never happened in my little town. You are the dream I always lived for. What can I call you?"

"Claudius."

"Do you have a last name?"

"You must understand how dangerous it is for Italians. Everyone feels pity for the Germans when this government harasses them. Did you know the American's have arrested over 1,500 Italians? It is a crime for my mother to be Italian. Claudius is my stage name and a testimony to my talent." He patted her hand

"You, as an American have no such idea how innocent Italian businessmen are persecuted in your country."

Betty pleaded "Please stay with me."

"I am but an Italian artist. Would you want such a life?"

"What an interesting life." She said.

Claudius had the ability to add or subtract emotions from one sentence to the next as he pronounced "I have decided to maintain two homes, one in Rome and one in New York. This is merely a matter of practicality. My home will be with you. I must warn you those tinctures we indulged ourselves in last week was in deference to George. He was my role, not my problem. I want you to give me what you have, and never play with something so precarious again."

With a smirk she offered "Maybe together?" With the tone of a patriarch he demanded "Only if I suggest it. Do not forget the temptress Eve cost her man's kingdom. I must not indulge myself foolishly from now on. I have to pay attention to a most serious business and my woman must listen."

Betty slid her hand inside his coat to slowly squeeze his nipple between her fingers. Claudius studied her as she cooed, "When can we go back to the room?"

Claudius pulled her hand back while reminding her "I must go back to my apartment and cannot take you. Here is money. Go rent us our own place for a month until my business is finished. Soon, I will be free to secure us the penthouse." Claudius pulled out a roll of cash and handed her five American C-notes.

Betty said," I'm scared, must you leave?"

"You must understand that this world is much larger than both of us. My homeland is collapsing. I will lose everything when my people revolt against Mussolini. My contacts in Europe tell me deteriorating conditions put us in grave danger."

She hugged him with both arms and pleaded "It is cold, can we sit inside the car for a minute?"

Claudius opened her door and she slid inside. He hurried around, jumped in and started the engine. "The heater will have you warm in a *momento*."

While snuggling next to him Betty explained "When I worked at the library, I would read what those politicians in Washington are doing against innocent people. You are right. They are persecuting your people because of their race. That violates our constitution, you know?"

"That is true. Every race contributes to America. We stimulate your economy."

She cuddled close to him. "The men at the funeral frightened me."

"They are greedy. Their fear will keep them in control. I will be one step ahead because I understand them and they need me to explain... what they must do."

"Should I be afraid for you?"

Claudius wrapped his arms around her and kissed her hair. "You have brought me great joy. I could hardly have handled the stress were it not for your warm bed."

"Who do you work for?"

"I work for myself. It is foolish to ally one to even one's own country. It's only a matter of time before our industry will be dashed into chaos. This war has created a very difficult climate."

Betty reached over and tenderly played with his ascot, "How do you pay yourself silly?"

"I work for the greatest inventor of this century, Marconi."

"I am confused, is he alive or did he pass away six years ago?"

"Seven to be precise, his memory is alive in my heart. He knew how to create good opportunity. He was all that is good, *Bene*."

"You must be proud to work for his company." Claudius lamented "His Company is no longer his company. Now it is profiteers who seek their greedy interests over their namesake. This insane war is changing everything. In 1935 the U.S. court invalidated Marconi's claim of inventing the radio in favor of Tesla. Now, this ridiculous matter is going before your Supreme Court. Perhaps I could have advanced our interest then but, now... the war certainly is changing Marconi, my stage and my plans."

Private Forces

Airlines Terminal Building,
East Forty Second St and Park Avenue

A stretch limousine delivered Prime Minister Jovanovich to the Airlines Terminal Building. Entering the streamlined vision of the aviation oriented future he saw conveyor belts to transport luggage an extensive pneumatic tube system for rapid circulation of tickets, and oil-hydraulic lifts to raise automobiles from basement to street level. The terminal was able to fully load and dispatch six limousines every eight minutes. The Yugoslav Prime Minister complained continuously to his chauffer about the noise and the crowds.

Kosanovic was walking around the building waiting for the appointment. Pedestrians were awed by the huge structure's façade, with its' decorative carvings and sculpture, including two stylized eagles triumphing the building, flanking the oblong light fixture and flag pole. Inside, the walls of the large waiting room were embellished with the famed Chamberlain's mural depicting flight. A restaurant had a mirrored back bar and a curved stairway with metal balusters leading to yet another dining room. Across from Grand Central stood an imposing symmetrical doorway with a centrally located main entrance and Kosanovic walked in from the southwest corner.

The building housed a 528-seat newsreel theater. Donald J. had prepared for the theater with his setup in the projection room. His guess work was only exceeded by his ability to wing what he could not jury rig. Connected by a fishing line, his receiver was weighted and on small rubber wheels. He was able to quietly role the mike down beneath ten rows of seats. Kosanovic made it easy by sitting in the back.

Prime Minister Jovanovich's emissary Simic, found Kosanovic sitting in the theater. Simic sat down quietly next to him before asking, "What indignity has brought us here?"

Kosanovic said, "Thank you for responding to my communiqué. This is a matter of utmost discretion."

Simic became preoccupied with the theater newsreel. He silenced Kosanovic by raising his forefinger.

The newsreel announced each news bulletin in a black and white snippet allied leaders hold a Conference in Casablanca.

"Have you considered the impact of this conference on Yugoslavia?" Simic asked.

"This problem I refer to could provide for our role in future conferences."

"Our role? I understand you believe you have some... silver bullet. I trust you did not receive such a revelation from your uncle and his annual flights of fancy."

"It does concern my uncle. I should point out he passed away last week."

"I read about it. My deepest condolences."

"The family deeply appreciated Dr. Tesla's funeral was attended by the King's envoy."

They stopped to listen to the newscaster explain "Yugoslavia's kingdom was created by World War I. The government fell apart the first fortnight of the Nazi attack. The defeat was the lack of leadership. After the Yugoslavian government signed a 'Protocol of Adhesion' with Germany, Italy and Japan on March 25th, 1941, Petar was overthrown and the teenager Petar II became the king in exile. His pathetic challenge against the Italians ended up with 9,000 Slovenes being executed. The Serbs and Croats were left to fight for themselves and racial divisions took over. The worst conflict between Croats and Serbs occurred the following autumn, when the news of the massacres of Serbs by the Ustashas reached London. The feckless King Petar II was dependent upon his ministers. The Croatian minister's reluctance to condemn or even discuss any reports of genocidal atrocities outraged the Serbs. The government compared this massacre to the Croatian teacher accused of nationalism."

Each time Kosanovic attempted to speak, he was quieted with the wave of a hand. The reporter on the screen continued "The Serbs sought revenge. The army led by Mikhailovich attempted to develop a pact with the Germans, who demanded total surrender. Mikhailovich abandoned his headquarters and scattered his forces. In 1942 Churchill was willing to believe the exiles stated position, the underground was aggressively resisting. The only resistance was from Tito's partisans, the Communists. The government in exile who has accomplished nothing has stated its Croatian members were firmly opposed."

With the report finished, Simic dropped his arm down onto the armrest.

Patiently Kosanovic asked, "May I continue?"

"Of course" Simic had a habit of stepping on his underling's last word.

The underling sat up a head taller. "We are busy men. Allow me to present my message."

Simic arrogantly flicked a hand.

"Dr. Tesla left behind his discovery of the most powerful weapon ever invented" Kosanovic carefully explained.

"Of course" Simic looked at him for the first time. "You brought me in this place to announce news discredited years ago?"

"What are you saying?"

Simic lectured "Surely you know your uncle disclosed his far-fetched ideas to the ministry before the war?"

"He built a working prototype" Kosanovic countered. "Before the war, when our ministry was in exile."

Simic continued to focus on the newsreels while speaking. "Of course, this war is in all our lives. How long since you have visited Belgrade?"

"I believe this weapon would speed along our return."

Grabbing his attention the emissary turned red with indignation. "My poor countryman, why must I come down to such a place and discuss this, well, you really cannot blame me. This is a fantasy. We do not possess millions of dollars to build such a weapon. Tesla offered this weapon to the English and he was turned away."

"Not exactly" Kosanovic protested

"What do you mean?" Simic asked.

Kosanovic welcomed the opening "The only reason the government ministry in England and the Americans rejected this weapon was one of control. My uncle insisted on overseeing its' development and, every government wanted to take his control away. Their rejection was never one of challenging the validity of his claims. Their rejection was one made by bureaucrats during the Depression." It is difficult to remain passionate presenting to someone who yawns.

Kosanovic continued with ever greater fervor. "Have we learned anything? Do you not think Prime Minister Chamberlain would have wanted such a weapon in his dealings with Hitler? He was never told his war department was looking at it. What impact shall each weapon have on the war?"

Simic gave Kosanovic's hand a patronizing pat "Please, we are in a public place and you have become quite worked up. You arrange for a demonstration and I shall arrange to have it properly attended. If this weapon is a fraction of what you suggest we shall all be grateful."

Staring blankly at the screen Kosanovic spoke without emotion, "I am not prepared to demonstrate the weapon. I have invaluable documents enabling us to build it. With the completed weapon we can ask any price."

"Do you see these newsreels?" Simic asked "Do you see the war turning. As we speak the allies are in Casablanca dividing the world over dinner. The Russians have turned the tide. Hitler's defeat in Stalingrad will spin the wave of history against him." Sitting forward he turns for a condescending hold on Kosanovic's arm. "This is the beginning of the end. Forget that we have neither the development staff nor resources. The war does not afford us the time. Did you want to announce your sale after the war has turned? You must agree the end of warfare is a bad time to start selling weapons?"

"Should the allies be given a choice?" Kosanovic quickly countered, "Can we use the money? This breakthrough could bring us into the discussions at the conference. Now what are we, Yugoslavia is nothing more than an access point to Berlin for the Allies? Is this the time to attain their respect?"

Simic crossed his arms and said "We have their respect. And the reason I, not you reside in London is because I am aware of the critical nature of this international war. Again, you choose to ignore the newsreels and would rather stare at your shoes attempting to lecture me. Do you have any idea of the embarrassment we could suffer with the preposterous proposition? I, for one would not forward anyone that we should begin the development on a project the major powers have long since rejected."

Simic stood and lectured him, "You have a promising career in the government, I suggest you remain focused on your immediate duties and let others fight the Americans for your uncle's belongings." Simic's wide girth lumbered awkwardly down the aisle to the exit.

Remaining behind Kosanovic stared at the screen where the newsreel announced, 'The Russians captured Karpovka airfield.'

He pulled out a notebook and wrote down, 'Are we so behind the times, the bastard Simic's right? Am I a fool? Yugoslavia will soon be led by Tito. Today, Stalin is enjoying Yugoslavia over dessert with Roosevelt. And Churchill is about to recognize Tito's army for winning the hearts of all countrymen. I should be raising money to send home. That bigheaded bastard is right. It is not for me to think I can decide the war. Yet, the weapon is invaluable.' From this A.I. concluded Kosanovic always managed to appear in control by venting his anger in his notebook.

The theater's newsreels provided historical footage of warring countries. The next newsreel announced the Russian army's immanent victory in Leningrad. It was a very different riddle wrapped in mystery inside an enigma for Churchill to appreciate the Communist Tito. It was expediency.

After looking at his watch, Kosanovic stood up and walked out of the theater into the lobby of the terminal. He noticed a concave indenting into Otto Bach's polychromatic stainless steel mural map of the world. Kosanovic stared at the map. Wearing a full length fur wrap NKGB Chief Akhmarhov moved like a spy next to Kosanovic "Your meeting did not appear to go well."

Startled, Kosanovic took a half of a step back. "Pardon me, have we met?"

"Forgive me. Allow me to introduce myself, my name is Akhmarhov. I represent the interests of the Soviet Union."

This huge man was a different Russian. Kosanovic looked unsure how much to fear this bear of a man. Why would the Soviet Union be interested in a low level dignitary from an occupied country?

Akhmarhov was a frank man "You are very interesting to us. You must understand what we must all focus on now is the map of the world after the war." He pointed to the wall atlas. "I assure you after our victory in Stalingrad, Secretary General Stalin is invited to Churchill and Roosevelt's planning Conferences."

Kosanovic could only wonder if this is a coordinated Russian effort to steal the weapon or does the left hand know what the right is doing. "My only concern is how that map will change Yugoslavia."

Akhmarhov continued to look at the stainless steel mural diagram. "The map will no longer be measured by national borders. Ideology will rewrite how maps are interpreted."

"Where is Yugoslavia's interpretation?" Kosanovic asked.

The Russian reassured, "Comrade, your hostility is unnecessary. What is important is the International. That is how the new order will be organized. Your fears are absurd. After Hitler falls, the Russian army wants to go home to their families. Our economy is growing. Do you know we are the only country in the world that has increased their international trade fourfold in the last decade? How did capitalism fare during this long depression?" He turned to the map. "We are confident our economic model is inevitable. This war is an earthquake shaking history but nothing will change the inevitable. The socialist model offers the only hope for the warring races in your country. Socialism is what people are going to demand. Did not capitalism create the Depression? Is not royalty collapsing? What is the option? The social revolutions of this war will have returning solders wanting equality."

Kosanovic asked "Do you think your Tito is going to let them have equality? Be serious. Tito demands obedience."

Even when he spoke English, Akhmarhov's tongue rolled his words. "Tito is the only one in your country fighting the Nazis. Why would you criticize him, for your fears or for the facts?"

Kosanovic turned to face this Russian Faust. "Does Tito take his orders from Moscow?"

The bear's face contorted "You give us too much credit. We are busy fighting the greatest evil of this century, as are your people. I assure you the only thing Secretary Stalin will be telling Tito is, 'I deeply regret we cannot give you more aid.' The Russian continued, "You have been involved sending aid to your homeland. Have you seen the Soviets killing your people or sending them weapons and food?"

The cynical Yugoslav, Kosanovic had always presumed an evil motive and had to ask himself for the first time, what if the Russians were allies?

Akhmarhov's hand swept across the map "Think comrade, what it will mean to have the Slavic people living in peace and thriving through mutual economic pacts. We won't prevent you from trading with England. You will prefer to trade with us by providing economic benefits for your people."

Kosanovic face wrinkled with the accusation "This does not erase my memory. Just a few years ago, Stalin was purging his people by the millions."

Akhmarhov turned to look at Kosanovic "Propaganda, comrade. I cannot deny millions of my countrymen died. I also know this; we suffered through long draughts, unforgiving winters, and the worldwide economic depression. And, we came out stronger."

"It is the stronger that I fear."

Putting his hand on his heart Akhmarhov explained "Fear the West. They are the one's plotting to rewrite your borders. The allies are the one's directing your government in London. How will your government appear after this war? Are you depending upon your young king to save your country?"

The day was wearing on Kosanovic, "What do you want of me?"

Extending his hand to grip Kosanovic's shoulders, Akhmarhov softened his voice. "I want you to join the international brotherhood."

"And deny God?"

"Comrade, when is the last time you read the Bible? When is the last time you sought divine intervention to protect against the slaughtering in Yugoslavia? Where is God during this damnable war? What will be the system of government chosen by your people after the war? You know the only answer is socialism. You are dedicated to your country. I have no doubt of your love for your people. What will you do after the war?"

"Return to Belgrade."

"Spoken like a man we would proudly accept into the international brotherhood. The rebuilding is all either of us will care about. What are you doing with your life now? You go to your little office and shuffle papers hoping that it helps one of your countryman. Let me show you what you can truly help your people."

Kosanovic asked, "What could you possibly suggest?

"You are a leader among your people and you have a passion in your heart" Akhmarhov explained with an offer "You should not be hidden deep in the bureaucracy. You should be raising support for your people in Belgrade."

"What can I do?"

Akhmarhov recommended "You can raise money to send home and help provide medical care and food for your countrymen."

"I am not sure if I can accept Marxism."

"Do you have to understand today or do you only have to continue caring about your people. Work with me and if I have lied, spit on my words." Wagging his forefinger hard Akhmarhov offered "If I show you something you have never seen then would you do this for Yugoslavia?"

Pupin Physics Laboratories
Columbia University
Broadway and 120th St.

In the garden outside the thirteen-story mass of stone known as the Pupin Physics Laboratory, Fitzgerald paced back and forth. Fitzgerald admitted he was angry at being afraid of the Nazis. A.I., people were a different game of chess. Every move required a counter move but this was no game but the only path to the development of Tesla's brilliant electrically accelerated particle beam. Fitzgerald was one of the few who understood how the pieces could be developed into a Hypersonic Tactical Weapon.

The rumors had haunted Fitzgerald all night. Being a physicist and understanding better than most the discovery of neptunium and plutonium was punctuated confirming plutonium is fissionable and thereby suitable for an awesome bomb. Fitzgerald understood weapons were all about dollars and the Office of Scientific Research and Development would be the only channel available for funding. The rumors about everything going toward this secret super bomb were disturbing. There were the rumors about the radar and the uranium bomb being the last major weapon development projects needed or capable of being completed before the war's end. Fitzgerald was angry and wrote 'How in the hell do bureaucrats know when the war will end'?

Fitzgerald believed there was one last play. The nature of government programs demanded a reputable professor to provide the congressional weight for the weapon's proposal. This was not going to be that meeting. This was the kind of meeting required to set up that real meeting. That should be with one of the prodigies from Columbia's SAM Laboratory.

Albert was a bright grad student who had started his doctoral studies when Fitzgerald did. Some students shunned Fitzgerald for renting a room to a Jew. He was Fitzgerald's best friend on campus even though the last time Fitzgerald promised him a government check. Three months later Fitzgerald paid him the money out of his own pocket. Albert was worth it in Columbia, where the smartest people in the world do research. Maybe because he was short, Albert had a distinct bounce to his step. He walked like he spent high school at the ballet. Only Albert was no ballerina. Moxie taught this Bronx Jew his moves.

Albert said "How is my government scholar, my oxymoron?"

When Fitzgerald put his hand out to shake Albert, he grabbed the wallet tucked into the binder and held it away until they both laughed.

Fitzgerald asked, "Keeping ahead of things? How about yourself?"

"Always moving my noble patriot always moving" Albert asked "So what brings you to the dregs of academia?"

"I was wondering if you could use cash."

Albert laughed easily. "Not that I would know what extra cash means. However, I definitely know what cash means to a starving grad student. What do I have to do, write a government report on bureaucracy?"

Fitzgerald worried about being beguiled by his charm and shtick. His life had become serious "What I need is discrete inquiries for anyone interested in working on charged macro particles."

Bringing his hand up to his face in mock wonderment Albert smiled, "And so, does he have to be from this campus?"

"No, I will take anyone in the country doing exploratory research. I need someone with great credentials. The literature is sparse. This will take some digging and networking."

"What does this schlepping all around academia earn these days?"

A.I. had no stateside budget. Fitzgerald tried his patriotism. "This is for the war effort."

Albert was quick to say "So is finishing my degree. Get down to tacks, what are we talking about?"

"I pay a bonus for speed and discretion."

"I am always for bonuses and for guaranteed base pay, too. So, do you want to dance or what are we talking about here? How long, how much, and what now?"

Fitzgerald explained "I want you to stay on this until completion and I want you to report to me each week and, I want it yesterday."

"Do you think I'm a schlemiel? Am I so foolish, such a clumsy person, a born misfit?"

"I'll pay cash."

"In advance?" he said finishing Fitzgerald's unintended sentence.

"Later." Fitzgerald remembered that word because it was so weak.

With a smirk Albert talked to some imaginary friend next to him, "Why am I asking questions if he's living elsewhere?"

Fitzgerald hated a project of this import being without a budget. "What is the right question? I will pay more if it is faster. I am not interested in giving salaries. It removes the motivation." Fitzgerald was rationalizing, knowing this payment was coming out of his pocket.

Friends were entitled to getting bent. Albert argued "So does starvation. Nobody is going to give money 'later' to someone of my persuasion. I have learned to live with that. I still learned to eat and I am definitely going to finish my doctorate. Quit beating around and get to making this worth my time."

Fitzgerald offered "Bring me three names next week and I will have $50."

Having already been burnt by the government, Albert half joked "Are we talking a government IOU, war stamps or cash? You're not going to do that to me again. It took me six months to get paid. You know what cash is? It is the stuff the regent's demand of my short ass."

Fitzgerald said "It was only three months. No, I won't let it happen again." Authorization on this weapon project was thin and money can never be issued in a week. This was an entire paycheck Fitzgerald promised away and so he demanded "Just be here."

Fitzgerald walked away and noticed Sandy behind a newspaper, down on the left side of the corridor of trees. The Englishman disappeared down the walkway.

Albert put both hands out "So what?"

Yelling over his shoulder Fitzgerald ran down the parallel walkway. "Just do it."

Leaving Albert with a slight smile on his face and extended arms, joking out loud to no one, "So what is with the goy this time?"

Sprinting, Fitzgerald sped around the corner, directly into a flock of pigeons. They flew up and across everywhere. With his hands covering his face Fitzgerald sprinted through the chaotic congregate and never lost sight of Sandy, who passed into view at the corridor crossing. "Sandy."

The Englishman looked around repeatedly, as if he was not caught. "Why, laddy, I should say it is a small world to see you here. You are quite the fast bugger, are you?"

Fitzgerald slowed to a fast walk "What in the hell you doing following me?"

Sandy raised his open palms "Let us not stretch this matter out of proportion."

"I asked you a question."

Sandy kept his hands and forearms up in a defensive position "One of your bloody generals is creating grave problems."

Fitzgerald stopped and asked "Who?"

"Do you know a bloke by the name of Brigadier General Leslie Groves?"

"No what about him?"

Sandy smiled at the two co-eds walking past. He waited until they were far enough away. "As you know, we Brits had a developed atomic project before you Yanks started yours. It was more than ironic that your good president started your atomic project the day before Pearl Harbor."

"What are you saying?"

"Now, now my friend what we are talking about here is rapidly becoming historical fact. Let's not get testy. I didn't mean to offend you. It was Roosevelt who asked Churchill to join in a mutual interest pact where we could develop the bomb together. Perhaps you have heard of it. The project is called 'Tube Alloys'?"

"What about it?"

Sandy explained "Then you may have heard that on January 7th your chairman of the National Defense Research Committee advanced the general's wishes. After sharing in our work and catching up you Yanks decided the exchange of views was limited only to the extent this information helps you. Your arrogant ass cut us out, as you say. Or, should I say, your mutual agreement now means only what the paranoid your General Groves needs for your Manhattan project. Are we all wet?"

"How do you know about the Manhattan project?" "You bloody Yanks would not have a Manhattan project were it not for the free run we gave your physicist at the British laboratories. Who do you think proved to Roosevelt that a bomb was feasible?"

The fact he knew proved there was a certain depth and breadth to the project. Fitzgerald lacked both and did not have any number of supporting scientists or the heavy commitment of resources the bomb did. "What does this have to do with you following me, arshole?"

"No need to become profane old boy. Were you working with members of the Metallurgical Project?"

"Who's running that?" Fitzgerald asked.

"Professor E.A. Long."

"Should I know him?"

"Your schools have been recruited for the bomb's metallurgical work. Didn't you know about the Berkeley Radiation Laboratory, the SAM Laboratory here at Columbia University and the Metallurgical Laboratory at Chicago? I thought that's why you are here." Sandy uttered the last word realizing his own mistaken assumptions.

"What in the hell's going on here?"

Sandy explained "You blokes have poured your brains and pocketbooks into developing some sort of uranium bomb. I have been assigned to find out what we will be missing, now that you are cutting us out."

Fitzgerald complained "I invited you to work with me on Tesla's electrically accelerated particle beam?" When a fellow researcher pledged to work on it, should that became a friend's assurance. This English spy was hardly cut from the same body of science. His word was not his reputation.

Sandy challenged "You have no funding and little or no authority. Can we be honest here? You are free lancing the project, right?"

Fitzgerald looked over at the lab building. "Not exactly I report to someone higher. I have authority to pursue the development of this weapon. Do you think I could have access to what I know without authority?"

"Is your authority with the Office of Scientific Research and Development?"

"Why do I need their authority?"

"You need their money." The realization for Sandy proved a friend's reaction. "Without the OSRD you will not have funding, will you?"

"They are only planning on funding radar and the uranium bomb," Fitzgerald explained. "Every such project had a hard beginning. Look at this bomb idea; we were ahead of you in physics until your President Roosevelt started spending money. All you need is money and you can develop it, right?"

"Stop patronizing!" Fitzgerald glared. "I hate being patronized."

"You are in quite a fix then old boy being against both your detractors and supporters."

Fitzgerald realized the project needed allies and needed them quickly. "You know the Russians started their atomic program?"

"The only way they can catch up is if they figure out how to steal it. We can't stop their science but, maybe we can depend on their ignorance."

Fitzgerald explained, "That's the difference between the bomb and the electrically accelerated particle beam. They have no body of knowledge to develop a hypersonic tactical weapon. Tesla's weapon is our best hope."

"History is on the side of the bomb. In Chicago a chap named Fermi demonstrated the world's first controlled and sustained nuclear fission reaction. That's what you need. Even Tesla understood the important of an announcement, some sort of a breakthrough to attract the money. Can you give us a demonstration?"

"Tesla gave a demonstration and the bureaucrats rejected him."

Sandy offered "That was then, but now is a completely different world and Tesla is not here to stifle." It was obvious Sandy was seeking answers as he explained. "Good God man, we are in the middle of what could possibly be the destruction of the Anglican race. Have no doubt the Teutonic tribes would pillage and enslave our people. Get a grip. You may very well be carrying the ability to save our race."

Fitzgerald said "You mean you were not following me and were here because of this uranium project?"

Sandy pretended to be mortified. "Well, not exactly. It was more of a case of me following the location you happened to show up on."

Fitzgerald realized the brutal truth, "You were not even following me?" The sinking feeling of personal neglect seemed to add to Fitzgerald's weight of this collapsing project. "I am not sure if I should be insulted, somehow."

"Nothing personal we are not following you. Instead, look at it the other way; you were hot enough that you made my surveying worthwhile. I could have scouted there all day and not come up with a lead. You made my day, as it were."

"Are you patronizing me again?" Fitzgerald fired back.

Sandy seemed to enjoy the moment and interpreted anger as an act of friendship. "You Yanks are a testy lot. Tell me about this young Jew of yours."

"What Jew?"

"The short one wearing the *Yamika* you were speaking with five minutes ago."

"*Yamika?*"

"Yes, that one."

"He researches for me." Fitzgerald's explanation felt confusing but in retrospect the moment of collapse had appeared.

Sandy said "Sounds enterprising."

"Do not get ideas about my patriot." Throughout the war, Fitzgerald experienced racial questions. Tesla had good reason to believe his race was persecuted.

Sandy asked "You really think any Jew is loyal to you?"

"You are starting to believe your own hooey." Fitzgerald was not sure about Europe but was sure about Albert.

Sandy spoke slowly, "Look at it this way you have a source and I have a need."

This was taking Fitzgerald off track and certainly redirected Sandy. "I cannot go against stated policy."

"You know it is acceptable policy to work with an ally?" Fitzgerald suggested "You said General what's his name, Groves issued an order. But it is hard for me to understand how a one star general can override a presidential treaty."

"You are not going to listen to a paranoiac general? He is a fountain of misinformation. He is worried about Roosevelt fears of the ability of German engineers."

"That's not paranoia," Fitzgerald said. "That is good country sense."

Sandy asked "What about the million dollars our oily friend is demanding?

"I'm working on it. Notice I have not asked you or suggested the British government?"

"Do you expect your English allies to pay in advance?"

"Your credit's good."

"Problem is you do not have any money either, do you? Let us work together on both?"

"Hold on I need to find out more about what you are talking about. You know I cannot go on unauthorized projects."

Not being anyone's fool Sandy challenged, "Such as you have done with the particle beam project?"

Fitzgerald felt the jab "What do you need?" The English spy showed more emotion than anyone ever expected from him, when he raised his hand in a fist. "I need to know why this uranium project has eliminated the working partnership between our two countries."

Out of necessity Fitzgerald nearly begged "One Week and we work together on the Italian."

"Fair enough" Sandy nodded.

Fitzgerald said "Don't be too quick to agree. That means you will not do anything to embarrass me or spy on my government? And this means you will continue to help me." In war it had become necessary to cover the truth with lies, to protect its' sanctity and legitimacy.

Sandy asked "Is that all?"

"Tell me everything you know and where I need to look."

Fitzgerald felt an ever greater weight pressing down and had to find a way up soon, real soon.

Sandy hesitated before explaining "We were doing pure research before the war in neutron induced fission in uranium. After the war resources became increasingly scarce. Then a couple of our university chaps, Frisch and Peierls, outlined a method for a fast chain reaction and how this could be assembled into a weapon."

"Were they describing a weapon or a bomb?" Fitzgerald asked.

"Their first thought was a weapon but, there were many problems delivering such a delayed explosion. That is one of many advantages with Tesla's electrically accelerated particle beam. It has the advantages of both and the limitations of neither. It was Frisch Peierls report that received attention. And that was how the MAUD Committee formed."

"What's MAUD?" Fitzgerald asked.

Sandy explained "Frisch remained in Copenhagen after the Nazi occupation and the blokes deciphering the message mistook his reference to his governess, Maude. He was giving the cryptic name for uranium."

"You mean they thought they were naming uranium and chose some woman's name cleaning his house?"

"Exactly." Sandy explained with a smile.

"That is nuts."

"Too true but the MAUD committee coordinated our universities and companies to advance the research. Three years ago, we came to Washington to share our notes. When you Americans realized we were farther along, they wanted a mutual agreement. We didn't have your money and were happy to bring you up to speed. "With Churchill's approval, we bypassed bureaucracy and created Tube Alloys." Fitzgerald listened intently "Meanwhile your academics remained aloof until Roosevelt set new priorities. Our work together progressed quite well until this bloody general of yours decided the British were a security risk."

"Why are you telling me?" Fitzgerald asked. "The point is, my good man, the only way the inferior product is ahead of your superior weapon are the right contacts jumping over the bureaucrats."

He did appreciate the insight and Fitzgerald regretted snapping at him, "I know that. I need a working model. Even if I did I do not have a body of work from a group of scientist sanctioning the damn thing. I need a supporting assemblage capable of explaining the conceptual framework. Tesla did not build his weapon from mounting wave of related works like that damn bomb, he created a new paradigm."

Sandy agreed there was no other choice.

Federal Court Building
Foley Square

Even though it was raining sitting on the park bench in the middle of Foley Square, Claudius stared at the Supreme Court building next to the Federal Courthouse. The park was made up of sidewalks and benches. Claudius had just heard the news.

There was a possibility the real George Viereck could be released from his cage by March. In all of his writings Claudius loved the role of George and hated the Supreme Court decision to review Viereck's conviction. Claudius had to consider how this would affect his transaction. He was not bamboozling the Nazis but maybe the Americans and Russians were best left with their foolish fantasies. Claudius knew this latest complication meant all transactions must be consummated and the money secured in six weeks. On one page he rhetorically entered into his diary, 'how can an actor be expected to focus if the damn script keeps changing'?

Because the surrounding offices belonged to the Federal government, Donald J. had no trouble requisitioning a 'work space'. A.I.'s gizmo man had positioned his two translators with binoculars and telescopes mounted on tripods. Donald J. was worried the slight drizzle might obscure their lip reading.

George had problems with his umbrella, and he was wet and tired. His comb raked the oily water through his black and gray hair while his eyes followed the leggy blond wearing dark nylons. The black line went up her leg and his ogle followed to her bum.

The harsh German accent startled him. "Are you continuing to use the name George?"

"What are you doing here?"

Under a large black umbrella Von Haak walked around to the front of the bench to face Claudius. "You did not answer my question." His suit was straight and movements too aggressive for a contented predator. Without a drop of water on him the Nazi looked from under his cover, down at his prey.

Seeing the passing federal workers, all in their blue suits, white socks and brown shoes, the public square gave the wet Italian some measure of courage. "I hardly work for you. You are in the wrong place to try any rough stuff with me."

With a look of pain Von Haak asked, "Why are you being hostile? We are on the same side."

"What do you have to offer?" The image of the old man walking down the road of the radio station never left Claudius' mind. He repeatedly wrote he moved from Europe to avoid violence.

Von Haak explained, "History is on our side. You will enjoy the glory of fascism and the fruits from our basket."

"Your troops are taking Yugoslavia from us." Claudius said "Is not Italy your ally?"

Even with his thick brows pushing toward each other, Von Haak was a handsome man. "Unfortunately as we speak, Yugoslavia does not belong to anyone. Not them, not us and certainly never Italy."

Standing up Claudius lowered the umbrella to the level of Von Haak's face. "What do you want from me?"

Von Haak effortlessly pushed it aside. "I am following my assignment which is you. I would hope we could meet and discuss our common interest, like gentlemen and allies."

Claudius' eyes darted around the park for security, any sign of authority. Most people had already shown enough sense to get out of the rain. Claudius tried not to shiver, "Shall we go to a restaurant?"

Von Haak's head clicked twenty degrees sharply like a tank turret, to look straight into his target's eyes. "We are better served by remaining discrete in our meetings. We need to be professionals who can have a discussion. Here is good,"

"I have been in contact with Dr. Kurt Kiep." Claudius's voice wavered. "I thought that meeting was what you wanted for assurances." Claudius looked around again. There were fewer people than before "He assured me I could work directly with him. Have you anything to report on the materials I gave him?"

With some disdain Von Haak explained, "You are part of this and know how long it takes a submarine to cross the Atlantic."

"What are your allies doing to take care of your own George Viereck?"

"He will be released on his appeal."

Claudius asked, "are you going to pay to keep him out?"

"He has had his wife sell everything so he can claim a pauper's defense. If the American government wants to spend endlessly to prosecute him then let them pay endlessly to defend him as well. We have more vital targets to expend resources on."

"Very well then, this is what you need to tell Herr Kiep. I have decided I will need $1.000,000. in cash within one week from today. I will call you because I have other offers."

"What other offers?"

"My employer is in this business for profit. I am on a business assignment. You must understand the predicament you put me in." With a swipe of his hand he expected the German to apologize.

Looking confused the Nazi challenged, "Is not your employer the Italian government?"

"Corporate interests guide my choices." The Italian sign requires two hands but with only one free Claudius twisted a gesture.

The German's muscles rippled across his cheeks before he spoke. "Where do you think we can raise that amount of cash in New York?"

"Everyone in Europe knows you have hidden stashes of gold outside of Germany."

Von Haak's thin lips tightened "You can speculate with the old women. We need to see and verify exactly what you possess before any serious offer can be submitted for approval." He appeared angry.

Claudius has seen this assassin kill an innocent stranger out of expedience. "The arrangements are made and every party will have an equal opportunity to own the most powerful weapon ever created. Do you think I would sell it too cheaply? Never mind. I am giving you the opportunity to usurp the auction." The accelerator was his protection so he lied, "If not then I have both English and American companies offering substantial sums. I'm offering my ally, you an advantage. How good am I to you?"

"I will forward your requests to Herr Kiep."

A smile slowly came to Claudius. "In the interest of discretion I recommend you walk past me and not turn back unless you care to meet my woman who is approaching. She is about three hundred feet and closing."

Seeing her Von Haak walked past Claudius, while promising out of the side of his mouth, "I will be watching you."

Betty waved and George waved back. She was under a floral umbrella. The way she carried herself the opening in her jacket revealed a soft white sweater and the gold cross he gave her last night. Claudius never forgot great passion for a woman only blesses a man perhaps once a decade.

Betty continued walking, allowing the rain to hit her face until she was under his umbrella. They kissed.

She asked, "Who was that man? It looked like one of those bad men at the funeral."

"He is frustrated because I want him to pay a proper price for my products."

"What do you sell?"

"I provide companies and countries with innovative products. What is invented in Europe is worth extra money in America and of course, vice versa."

"Show me sometime?" she teased.

"Of course my precious doll what would you like to do today?

"George, did you find out what you needed from the courthouse?"

"I did. Have you ever visited Italy?

"No but I would really, really like to... your invitation?" She stood on her toes out of excitement.

"I will show you how the privileged travel. Would you like me to do that?"

"More than anything" She appeared to jump without ever really leaving the ground.

He asked, "I mean to ask you: what did you learn about science in your librarian classes?"

"I was an engineering minor in college. No one would hire a woman engineer. My graduate degree is in library science."

Claudius smiled at his good fortune. "How would you like to do some research for me? Perhaps you can help move this transaction a little faster."

"I would love to help. My savings are down to nothing. You are a blessing George."

"I know. It is a burden I must live with." He laughed. "Let us move out from this cloud."

Betty tucked her hand under his arm. "Where would you like?"

"The closest place is the courthouse steps. It will clear in a moment."

He held his attaché case under one arm and Betty under the other, they huddled, sharing a laugh as they trudged up the stairs under the mammoth Roman columns.

After walking over to the secluded side he pulled out two pages from inside his jacket and handed her a drawing.

Betty pulled the schematic close to her face and then held it out at arm's length. "It looks like a big penis. Is this yours?"

George snapped it out of her hands. "No, this is most serious matter."

"I am sorry, I will be serious" Betty hugged him, "Let us not get huffy now." She kissed his cheek. "Now, let me have a second look." With a smile she removed the drawing from his reluctant grip and explained, "This is a building providing the controls and powers for this huge ball on top of a column. What is it?"

They walked over to the far corner of the outer foyer.

Quickly scanning George answered "I know very little of such matters. From what I can understand this is a particle beam generator capable of shooting large electromagnetic energy into a small space."

"How does it work?"

Holding out to her the second sheet Claudius read "One continuous thin, impenetrable hemispherical shell of energy is discharged over a large specified area. A shell is created by interfering two scalar patterns so they, the pair-couple into a come-like shell of intense, ordinary electromagnetic energy. Anything hitting the shell will receive an enormous discharge of electrical energy and will be instantly vaporized." His English stumbled with every scientific word.

Covering her frustration Betty kissed him before gently removing the paper from his grip and continued to read, "Stress waves can affect either space or time individually, or both space and time simultaneously or even oscillate back and forth between primary's affecting time and primary's affecting space." Looking up slowly Betty sincerely wondered, "Do you know what you have here?"

"I will have a Villa on the Mediterranean." The well-dressed man boasted.

Speaking cautiously she looked around "Do you think Tesla understood? I mean understand he is rewriting science. I knew he had arguments with Einstein but, this…"

"Einstein was a Jew," Claudius scowled in broken English. Seeing her flinch the dapper man took a loving hold of her arm and paternally explained "My blossom, Tesla was discovering new science. It has been Italian businessmen such as Marconi, god rest his soul and Westinghouse to turn them into money."

"Is that what you do? You're selling Tesla's invention." Betty immediately regretted her accusation sounding personal in this treacherous world.

He grabbed the sheets out of her hand and stuffed the larger pile back into his black leather, attaché case.

Betty's eyes started to tear. "I am so sorry it came out all wrong. Please pardon me?"

There was no forgiveness in his voice "Your duty is to secure the apartment and call me this evening."

"You are angry, please forgive." Gently reaching out to hold his arm, she was surprised by the speed he brushed her off.

With one finger in her face the neat little man explained with some force. "You listen. I had authority to sell these documents before he died. It was unfortunate he died. However, he did. What would you have me do? Throw them away?" It never seemed to matter about the truth Claudius could deliver believability better than anyone we ever witnessed.

Betty grabbed him, only to have him look down at her hand. She explained "I am sure you had authority. I only meant to… be with you. Please understand I was awestruck by what I just read. Tesla had utilized the fourth dimension to manipulate the first three dimensions. The possibilities are limitless." She let him go.

"We will continue this evening" Claudius picked up the sheets and placed them back inside his suit jacket. There was a tense silence.

They started to leave together when suddenly from around the corner, Von Haak was the first attacker.

One huge hand picked up Betty while the other put a thick cloth over her nose. She struggled briefly before falling limp. Claudius clutched at her and was knocked away by the German's flicking elbow.

Two men wearing white uniforms guided a gurney in between Claudius and Betty. From the ground the little man grabbed a muscular leg and was kicked hard.

Von Haak's instructions were succinct, "Dr. Kiep invites you to meet him."

The two German paramedics lifted Betty onto the gurney and pulled the sheet over her. Von Haak said "You can have her back when you cooperate with your allies. This is your fault."

They hurriedly guided the small wheels down the two dozen steps. One man ran ahead and opened the ambulance's rear door.

Claudius could see Kiep waiting in the back seat of his nearby limo. Betty's cart was slid into the ambulance. The disheveled Italian stumbled down the stairs. Von Haak grabbed Claudius' arm and shoved him into the back seat with Kiep. The big German followed inside, sandwiching Claudius in-between the two Nazis.

"By what right do you have to steal my woman and shove me around?" Claudius looked back and forth at their hard faces. "You have no right to touch me."

The Nazi emissary crisply explained "Last week you were calling me Kurt. I thought we were friends. Now, you do not call me. Today I receive this most disturbing news you are being rude to Wilhelm. What is this all about?"

"I gave you pictures and whatever you wanted." Claudius explained while straightening his suit. The Italian demands "Why is this goon pushing me around?"

Kiep looked at Von Haak "He obeys my orders." Kiep ordered the chauffeur, "Drive around to the far side of the square."

The long black "K Type" Mercedes pulled out into traffic. Claudius cleared his throat. "Have you heard back from Berlin?"

Without looking Kiep said, "Unfortunately my sources have not proved reliable."

Claudius asked "How is this possible?"

"Moral confusion will always affect history." Quietly staring at two, high heeled women, Kiep explained wartime reality "Our leading physicist Werner Heisenberg won a Nobel Prize by predicting our progress. Then he refused to develop nuclear fission. He called it safe science. If I were in Berlin, it would be called treason."

Claudius said, "Why are you telling me?" Watching the ambulance turn towards the Bronx Kiep was perturbed he was expected to answer "The Italian traitor, Fermi, immigrated here to help the Americans a few years ago. Our scientists chose to stay and do nothing. Shameless Heisenberg declared his loyalty to Germany but, solicited only for his private causes."

Claudius asked, "What causes?"

Kiep had lost interest in this discussion. "He should have been identified early for his Jewish physics.

Einstein, Bohr and the rest of those Jew bastards continue to plague us. Even our theologians side with the Jews. Bonhoeffer had no moral right to conspire against our Fuehrer. When Heisenberg convinced our Nuclear Physics Research Group there was no need for researchers to work together, we should have recognized his treacherous beliefs."

They pulled slowly to the curve. After the car stopped Claudius became nervous. "What are we waiting for?"

Von Haak answered, "Confirmation."

"Of what?" Looking back and forth there was no answer.

Watching from across the street Kiep explained,

"When I went to school, Heisenberg was on the first rung of the German academic ladder. He was a *Privat-dozent* back then and majored in mathematics and soon the Professors struggled to grasp his matrix mechanics.

His brilliance and influence spread through universities. It was his 'Uncertainty Principle' that should have been the telling clue. His Jew defense should have alerted the authorities. I will never understand what fool failed to see what this rat faced bastard was doing to us?"

Looking back in forth in vain Claudius asked "Should I know this Heisenberg fellow?"

Kiep turned to face Claudius "You should know about the two types of scientist in our country. Then you need to resolve our problem."

"I am honored to bring my skills to your service," Claudius declared reassuringly. "Tell me of your quandary with your scientist. You will find me most adept at such matters."

"You have set my mind at ease," Kiep cynically agreed. "Doctor Heisenberg is a proud German, a testimony to the superiority of our race. We have learned Heisenberg paid a visit to the Dane, Bohr to discuss the possibilities of nuclear fission. He worked to undermine the Fuehrer's policy and convinced many others not to seek the development of the bomb."

The actor fell out of role and spoke faster, "That means you need Tesla's weapon."

"That means many of our scientists will not pursue nuclear weapons of any magnitude. Cadres of trustworthy scientists are working with Dr. von Braun to build the weapon necessary to secure one victory... a rocket." studied the street. "Our Fuehrer is pouring research monies into his revenge upon the English. As we speak the Engineers of the Todt Organization are looking for a good supply of electricity to build our base. We will be able to build a V1 robot bomb in only 500 man-hours. We are far along developing the V2."

"Are you going to gamble the future on one program?"

Offering a slight smile, Kiep asked, "What are your motives for such an insight? It does not matter we are developing a series of rockets. With von Braun, his allegiance and desires are ruled by expedience. He is dependable."

"How can you put all your future in one technological basket?"

"The Fatherland will make available resources and the body of scientists necessary to begin development of any new weapons, much less a new technology."

"Then you are sure the Reich will win this war and want to continue with all new technology?"

Claudius asked "They acted as if they heard nothing."

The Nazi said "We will continue to develop our future." He continued to scan outside.

A.I. men with binoculars thought Kiep spotted them but it was not the case. A.I. took comfort knowing Kiep never discovered Donald J's recorder.

Claudius glanced at the door. "Perhaps we can do business later, no?"

"We can do business now." Kiep's words were deliberate.

"You said... you just said you didn't need a new program."

"And neither shall anyone else." Kiep said. "You must have us hold this box for your own safety."

Pulling out his handkerchief and dapping slowly for effect Claudius freely lied "It is not my decision."

After removing his spectacles Kiep slowly asked, "You have this weapon?"

Claudius expanded his lie "No, not at all. It was you who warned me of the threat. I forwarded the weapon and documents to my employer in London."

"He is lying." Von Haak said.

"When have you done this?"

"What do I have to lie for? You pay me and I would be onto my next project." Claudius continued, "Tell me more about what projects you have available. Perhaps we can help with your war effort. We sympathize with your cause we are loyal to Italy. A little gold will go a long ways with us. How can I help?"

Von Haak's massive right hand grabbed Claudius' arm. "When did you send a box to London?"

Claudius said "This strong-arming is not necessary."

Not receiving any relief the little man asked, "Von Haak here needs to explain what he was doing when I was at the Coenties Slip, Pier 5, East River yesterday morning."

Kiep stared at Von Haak before returning to Claudius. "I need to see your shipping docket."

The actor continued with his impromptu story. "I mailed the crate to myself. It should arrive tomorrow. Listen gentlemen, we can do business or we can be paranoid. It would seem during this point in the war, you would accept my support. I cannot address what decisions will be made in London."

Von Haak snapped, "Why did you speak of what you do not have?"

"I can deliver, can I not?"

Scowling at his lies Von Haak recited, word for word, Claudius' original statement, "'I have decided you will need to deliver $1,000,000. to me in cash in thirty days because I now have other offers.' That is what you said."

Claudius agreed "Yes, I am going onto other projects. Yes I can deliver in 30 days. What can you do?"

Kiep repeated, "I want you to give the shipping company's tare sheet to confirm the container your crate is on."

"If you do not believe me, send your goon over. I will enjoy his embarrassment. In fact I do now, is there anything else?" He jutted his jaw forward in defiance.

Kiep signaled Von Haak with a glance. "What time does your mail arrive tomorrow?"

"Stop by in the middle of the afternoon. It should be there by then." Claudius sat forward and was allowed to exit. "Your goon is not invited to hang around. His stench will bring the FBI around. I do not need the harassment."

Von Haak opened the door for the little man to step out. Claudius offered his hand to Kiep, "May we work together soon. I'm only considering my next project. I can trust German gold better. Don't you agree?"

Kiep's words always had a double meaning. "We always pay."

Enjoying the confusion Claudius started to slide out and then stopped. "One more little item, if I may. How can I get my bib back?"

"What is a bib?"

"My doll your men stole."

"We will deliver her after you honor our request and, will continue this discussion tomorrow."

With a small bow Claudius slipped out while leaving the warning. "You better not have hurt her."

Von Haak smiled thinly "I will see you before tomorrow." The bigger German shoved Claudius out of the way and darted into the limo.

Exhausted Claudius walked to the closest bench and rested for quite some time, while staring at the ground. Pulling out his silk handkerchief he patted his eyes. Claudius looked up at Rostarchuk wrapped in a large coat of pelts. The communist fur hat was too small to cover his enormous head. The Russian's words were cumbersome. "What a poet face for a sad man. Are you pleased you found your friend?"

With his mouth left open Claudius looked around before answering. And in a flash, changing into character George asked, "How did you find me?"

Laughing the Russian bear sat next George, who neatly reinserted his handkerchief in his front suit pocket and started to move away. Rostarchuk quickly extended his left arm around the smaller man, securing him. "We have not spoken days, have we not?"

Pulling his handkerchief back out he held it over his nose to screen the Slav's alcohol breath. George explained, "I have been quite busy. How can I help you?"

"Help me, help you and help each other. This is the communist way. Where else are you going to go? George asked, "Do you have authority to purchase a weapon?"

"What weapon are we discussing?"

"Tell your superiors they should be interested in the most powerful weapon ever created by the genius, Dr. Nikola Tesla. They can have this secret to winning the war, when they deliver one million dollars… a fraction of your Lend Lease money."

"You are not serious?" His face wrinkled together hiding his eyes. "Are you playing a joke on your friend?"

Carefully pulling the papers from inside his jacket Claudius cautioned, "You do not touch, you look. You do not touch." He held the patent application carefully.

Rostarchuk grabbed the document out of his hands. "Don't worry me not steal. I cannot read from afar." He then slowly read aloud, awkwardly stumbling over each word. "Project Concentrated Non-Dispersive Energy through Air. What does this mean, George?"

"This means Tesla invented a weapon able to electrify the air from hundreds of miles away with a shield so highly charged an airplane would be vaporized." Whenever he was excited George's face would slightly flush. "Do you think Stalin would want that? I think not. You will become a national hero."

Rostarchuk lips spread to his ears. "This is good. We will be partners."

George snatched his paper and quickly put it in-side his suit jacket while explaining "Not partners, businessmen."

Rostarchuk asked, "When can I see this weapon?"

"When will you have the money?"

"Our department controls the distribution of American lend lease. We have a billion American lend lease dollars. I'll have them requisition what you ask."

Quickly standing up George said, "You need to arrange this before next week."

January 21-28, 1943

Final Forces

Theater District 52nd St & 7th Ave

The Theater's billboard flashed a banner for the long-running James Cagney movie. Fitzgerald whistled "I'm a Yankee Doodle Dandy" while walking around the corner and froze. Five Hispanics wearing Zoot suits were struting towards him.

Fitzgerald was not going to run and certainly did not want to fight anyone wearing high-waisted wide-legged, tight-cuffed trousers. They swaggered under their long coats with wide lapels and padded shoulders.

The newspapers were full of the fights. Every week the blue or white clad sailors on shore leave fought these well-dressed Latinos. More than a few sailors bled and a lot of Zoots ruined their suits. The racial fights were part of New York. Hearing Cagney's tune, the Zoots whistled some bastardized bolero loudly. They walked past, each glancing twice.

The newsboy yelled loudly "Frank Sinatra's opening at the Paramount Theater." Fitzgerald saw Hoover's documents on Sinatra. Few people understood Sinatra turned on the band leaders who made his career. A passerby yelled along with the newsboy, "The Russians have divided the German army at Stalingrad!" Fitzgerald heard a couple of hoots. Everybody excited about Sinatra cared less Russia.

Grabbing a copy, Fitzgerald read about the German army collapsing. The article predicted the loss of those 300,000 Germans who went into Russia. Hitler had demanded his soldiers fight to the death. Their forthcoming fatalities were not destined for battle. Everyone knew the Germans would never get out alive. In the last three years the Teutonic invaders had slaughtered over nine million Slavic civilians. The ancient enemies were ancestral and would seek blood retribution. The reckoning would lead the frightened young men to achieving their penitence by dying a slow and miserable death. Over three hundred thousand German mothers will never see their children ever return home. For all of the Slavs justice is racial retribution. This was the beginning of the end for those tribal invaders; those Nazi clans assaulting the Slavs in the East were destined to die. The totals were preordained. A hundred thousand German soldiers would freeze and suffer cold and hunger draining life away. Another hundred thousand young men would bleed a slow death from their wounds, and the hundred thousand survivors of the march would die slowly in Russian prisons. Statistics were a German in a Russian prison camp had less chance of survival than a Jew in a German camp.

Crossing the street Kennedy from the Office of Naval Intelligence waved. Fitzgerald returned the gesture. A common myth was the Army and Navy could not work together. The services worked together. It helped if they had first met at a party in Washington. Now buddies meeting in New York proved connections were the name of this game. Everybody knew the unwritten rules and played.

Fitzgerald had a bad surprise and needed the Navy. His question was why some bureaucrat within the National Defense Research Committee, inside the Office of Scientific Research and Development, chose Prof. John O. Trump to evaluate Tesla's 88 trunks, boxes, cabinets, cans and barrels stored at the Manhattan

Storage? This was a political blunder of the worst order. Fitzgerald knew Trump was jealous of Tesla and his work. Fitzgerald needed quick answers and willing contacts, offering Kennedy a mock salute.

Dressed in civvies and with drooping shoulders, Kennedy made a half effort to return the salute with only his middle finger extended. He smiled under the bird. Kennedy walked over and Fitzgerald offered, "You look like a man needing a drink."

"Don't tempt me," Kennedy answered. "I have to head back to the office and waste the rest of my day and probably tonight, writing up this report. I'm told this testimony is a high priority. It would not bother me if my work was to mean anything. But no I have to get this review out by tomorrow 8AM. Why I spent the day sleeping with my eyes open, and plan on doing so throughout tonight." He looked longingly at the bar "That and more before tomorrow, all this, so someone will look at it and wonder why we did this in the first place. Are you with me?"

While tapping his own Lucky Strike, Fitzgerald offered him a fag. Kennedy took one while his right thumb flicked the top of his lighter open. He lit up and snapped the lighter shut before taking two long drags back to back while asking, "Do you know Dr. Trump?"

"No but I've read his reports. He is an egomaniac. I was a large party when we met at a hotel conference and Dr. Trump didn't pass a mirror he didn't admire. Whoever picked Trump to review Tesla's work sure threw undermined any assessment."

Fitzgerald asked "Did he look into any specified topics?"

Kennedy shrugged "I doubt it. I know he did not want to find anything."

"I know he pursued this with hardly any methodology beyond the hope of personally gleaning some way to discredit Tesla or credit himself."

Fitzgerald exhaled angry puffs. "What do you mean? Are you telling me he failed to find anything on Tesla's particle beam or Teleforce?"

"You said Tesla started his work decades ago, right? This arrogant fool declared with one swipe of the deck, any of Tesla's work more than 15 years old was not worth reviewing. Can you believe him?" Kennedy was visibly irritated with his own report.

"The fact is Tesla revived his work after the people from his country started shooting at each other, and that was years ago."

"From the start Trump discounted the entire lot of Tesla's work as being speculative," Kennedy explained.

"Did he look at any papers in storage?"

"He only looked at materials from Tesla's apartment."

"The problem" Fitzgerald explained "is that someone got there before we did and stole the accelerator and the prototype. There are other key elements to the puzzle. We must secure these two critical items to prioritize the investigation of his materials."

"Do you know where it is?"

"Better, the British are sending him to me." Kennedy half joked

"Him? Tesla's invention is a human?"

Fitzgerald bragged "He is carrying it."

"How convenient."

Fitzgerald confessed, "As hard as this case has been, nothing is expedient."

"Is there anything I can do?"

"Give me details on what went on in there."

"Fair enough, pal," Kennedy answered. "When the four of us arrived, the first thing Trump did was complain about there being too much material to assess. Trump decided to review only those papers in his immediate possession. We were helping him select only Tesla's most recent work. During the entire time, he complained Tesla received too much credit in radio, robotry, and, even alternating current. He never addressed any of Tesla's hundreds of patents. Here, look."

Kennedy opened his attaché and pulled out a document to read out, "As a result of this examination, it is my considered opinion there exist among Dr. Tesla's papers and possessions no scientific notes, description of hitherto unrevealed methods or devices or actual apparatus which could be of significant value to this country or would constitute a hazard in unfriendly hands. I cannot see a technical or military reason why further custody of the property should be retained." Kennedy looked up.

"He is worse than an idiot; he is dangerous and stupid" Fitzgerald concluded.

Kennedy pulled out a few neatly stapled papers and read the titles. "In Trump's abstract, he has 'Art of Telegeodynamics', the 'New Art of Projecting Concentrated Non-Dispersive Energy through Natural Media' and the tract 'A Method of Producing Powerful Radiations."

"I do not want to criticize your report or anything like that but did you know this is Tesla's weapon?"

"How do you know?"

Fitzgerald leaned forward "I worked with Dr. Tesla."

"Is that right?"

"If you are right old buddy, I need to see those papers."

"I absolutely cannot release them to you. You know better than that." He started to slide the papers back into his case.

"I was only suggesting I review them before you submit them, to be sure they are complete."

He tossed his cig before pulling the papers out and challenging "Prove it."

Fitzgerald recited "Art of Telegeodynamics is a type of method for the transmission of large amounts of power over vast distances by means of mechanical vibrations of the earth's crust. The second paper 'New Art of Projecting Concentrated Non-Dispersive Energy through Natural Media" describes an electrostatic method of producing very high voltages and very great power. This generator is used to accelerate charged particles, electrons. In Tesla's next paper 'A Method of Producing Powerful Radiations, a new process of generating powerful rays or radiations' Tesla outlined his new simplified generation of projecting rays. These consisted in creating through the medium of a high-speed jet of suitable fluid a vacuous space around a terminal of a circuit and supplying the same with currents for the required tension and volume."

Kennedy nodded "Damn, where in the hell did you learn to talk like that?"

"I assure you, Dr. Tesla would not have spent time with me unless he was sure I understood his work."

"Where were you in today's circus?" It was a fair question and Fitzgerald did not know the answer "Because whoever went into there today would be publicly registered as endorsing that lunatic Trump. I have read enough of what that pompous geezer wrote. The fact of history is Trump was publicly embarrassed by Tesla. There was no way this 'authorized assessment' wouldn't turn out to have the decisions made by political interests before they started. Tesla's materials had no chance of a fair assessment."

"Why would anyone in the government want to know what he left behind?"

"The only thing I know for sure is there are certain people who have a vested interest in contracts with the government right after the war who would pay to take attention off what is really there. They will be back in a couple of years for what is in those stored files."

"Damn, that makes too much sense after what I saw going on in there today. What are you going to do?"

Taking little solace from his concern, Fitzgerald had to take advantage of his trust. "Let me look at the papers for a minute."

"I will give you one minute and then I draw my pistol."

Fitzgerald smiled "I have no weapon. Listen these are the papers you are releasing anyway, right? Would you like to hear an educated review first?"

Kennedy looked around at the pedestrians. "Let's walk to a place away from hundreds of people."

Fitzgerald reluctantly followed him into the entryway of the nearby empty store. Kennedy reached in and carefully handed over 'The Art of Telegeodynamics.'

"One minute." Fitzgerald sped read the twenty-odd pages and handed the stapled pack back to Kennedy.

He asked "What did you find out?"

"In a nutshell, Tesla used his reciprocating engine invention. He first wrote up a patent fifty years ago. What he reviewed was when he made a machine clamped onto an I-beam and the engine found it is own sympathetic resonance."

"Did it work?"

"He fastened it onto his own building and started an earthquake in New York."

"Are you serious?"

"The police came and the landlord evicted him. The whole incident is recorded in public documents. Now let me see the New Art of Projecting Concentrated Non-Dispersive Energy through Natural Media."

Kennedy cautiously passed it over. Again, Fitzgerald sped read every page.

The naval officer seemed entertained. He took the document back before asking "What does it all mean?"

Fitzgerald said "Tesla had patented a spiral flow turbine. Again he is advancing yet another one of his inventions. This was a complimentary technology of using a turbine as a turbo compressor to extend his valvular conduit."

"What does that mean?"

Fitzgerald explained "It means he created a weapon as an open-ended vacuum tube to shoot fire-balls."

"Fireballs?"

"Tesla devised a second weapon made out of lava requiring no more than twenty horsepower to continuously shoot 15,000 watt fireballs." Recognizing the confusion, Fitzgerald tried a different tact, "Tesla created an offensive weapon for his defensive shield. He developed his shield and left the weapon in the realm of theory and, by the way, he was a world class theoretician."

The Navy man appeared dazed "Why in the hell would anyone not want that?"

"They did. They also demanded to take control away from Dr. Tesla. In the last years of his life he wanted respect they were unwilling to give. The short response is time and money. Like I explained earlier, the long answer is more complex."

"Did he make it work?"

Fitzgerald answered carefully "I saw it."

He froze for a moment. "Shake it off, buddy. This is no good."

The Army man explained "The problem is far more complex because the communists and fascists are both trying to get their stinking hands on it. The tide has turned. Hitler has refused to allow his Sixth Army to break out from the Stalingrad pocket. Instead, he ordered the army to fight to the last man. And there they will die. We are beginning our bombing raids into Germany this week. The tide has turned. The war has reached its' intellectual end. From now on planners and funds will be directed towards exit strategies."

Kennedy asked "What is going to happen?"

"The communist army is hell bent on killing Hitler then destroying us. There is going to be fascists running around after the war, redeemed and living out their years in the southern hemisphere. Give guys like that weapons like this, and what do think we are in for? Tesla designs destroy anything within hundreds of miles. It would only take a couple of guys to obliterate New York!" Fitzgerald's sincerity made it sound plausible.

Unnerved Kennedy secured the documents inside his attaché. Placing the case under his arm, he scanned the horizon before looking at me. "Why would Dr. Trump say something?"

Fitzgerald explained "These papers are the concepts, not the schematics. Somewhere there are detailed drawings and working units. Trump had his mind made up about the inventions before he arrived and he is necessarily closing the door on everything else."

"Why?"

"His reasons are petty. What bothers me is the critical notes are missing."

"What accompanying notes?"

Fitzgerald said "Tesla wrote concepts as well as the very foundation for those models of reality. In other words some of his ideas were so utterly ingenious that he had to design a theoretical framework for them to be fully appreciated, much less function and his ideas always worked."

"Why in the hell did you tell me about his work before Trump's dog and pony show started?" He sounded like an officer who knew Fitzgerald's rank was as an enlisted man.

Recognizing the magnitude of his blunder Fitzgerald explained with the credibility of a truant "I expected you to be sent away with Tesla's work. I only thought they wanted to set it aside until the attention faded."

Kennedy asked "I am confused? I thought there was only one weapon. How many weapons did Tesla invent?"

"He conceived cannons to shoot fireballs but never built a production model. Later Tesla invented Teleforce which he demonstrated with a prototype and accelerator but he never shielded an entire city." Fitzgerald said.

"Again, you're doing this crap. How did he demonstrate without building it?"

Sounding like a graduate student Fitzgerald presumed everyone understood "He devised a new framework for controlling nature."

Kennedy had no answers only deadlines "Fair enough I have to file this report."

"Did you hear what I said?" Fitzgerald asked. "Did you?"

"What do you mean?"

Kennedy said "You already explained they want to bury this report fast. The operative term here is 'fast' and those are my orders. Sorry." Kennedy offered his hand and he walked quickly around the corner and down the street.

Fitzgerald went to the coffee shop and read the newspaper and checked his watch every five minutes until six. Walking out, Fitzgerald spotted George pacing back and forth across the sidewalk. Sandy stood casually near the wall, watching the well-tailored Italian use a cane to steer his abrupt turns.

When Fitzgerald crossed the street and approached them George complained" You are late." Fitzgerald snapped back, "What are you talking about? It's six and we are all here." George looked around and all three walked under an extended window sill. He demanded, "Where is my money?"

Fitzgerald countered "Where is this accelerator you say you think you have?"

George had an aristocratic air and pulled out his handkerchief to dap his lips before concluding "Let us not play games. You are young men and think like children. It is time to speak like men. You have seen pictures of the accelerator, yes? You know I have notes too."

"What notes?" Fitzgerald asked.

"The price goes up for the notes. I have sets of notes from different papers Dr. Tesla wrote."

"When did you steal those?"

"I will not stand here and be insulted. You are only angry because you failed to secure them first. Am I not correct?"

Sandy asked, "What papers were these notes taken from?"

"You take me for a fool?" Claudius countered. "If you have no money then you must admit the truth and allow me to get along with my business."

Fitzgerald lied, "I can requisition money as necessary. But, I must first know exactly what papers you have."

"Are you familiar with the terms Telegeodynamics or Concentrated Non-dispersive Energy? Does it have any meaning to you two?"

Fitzgerald was never one to hide his disdain "I know what they mean and what they are. I suspect you do not."

Raising his chin Claudius explained, "I do know by the degree of your interest the price for both can be arranged."

"How much?" Fitzgerald asked.

"A million dollars American and I must add there are other suitors. The first one with the cash wins. Will it be you two or perhaps will competition be too difficult for you Americans?" He tapped his cane and looked over at Sandy.

Sandy studied his quarry.

"When can you deliver?" Fitzgerald asked.

"We can arrange for the transfer tomorrow. I would insist we meet at the bank near the guards. You understand everyone must be comfortable for this to work peacefully. When I see the cash we can go to the weapon and its documents."

"How do you want to handle the transfer?" Fitzgerald asked.

"When I see you with the money then you will see your weapon, fair enough?"

Sandy asked, "Where is the beautiful lady you have been with lately?"

"I beg your pardon."

"We were watching them steal her away from you."

The one consistent character of a drug user is they are always on the edge of stability. The question threw George over the side. He stammered his words "You must be mistaken."

Sandy had professional motives and was personally enjoying the moment as he taunted "They took her away in a gurney. Is that what a woman of yours deserves?"

George's voice rose with each word "Those German bastards kidnapped her."

"Let me understand this old chap," Sandy challenged, "You are dealing with the Nazis? Are they the other party we are bidding against?"

George blinked before answering, "It is hardly any of your business about what company I keep."

Fitzgerald interrupted "It is our business if you are putting weapons into the hands of the enemies, especially those who are here to kill us."

Aiming his cane at each, in turn, George struggled to regain his composure, "There is nothing innocent about this business. Save your righteousness for those who are not in our business."

"Do not misunderstand us," Sandy offered. "We could help you regain her and you could very well end up with the cash. All we want are the papers and equipment." George looked at each of us. "Why would you do such a thing for me?" His face squeezed.

Sandy acted as if this was nothing more or less than a day's work "Not for you, for us. We would rather help everyone win here rather than risking a silly bidding war with thugs who will only cheat. We cannot compete if they are holding your woman. We simply want to assure our position and able to intervene on your behalf."

Gripping his jaw with his thumb and forefinger

George concluded "This could be good, good for us all."

"You do want her back, do you not?" Fitzgerald asked.

George was confused enough to mumble options he was starting to consider "Women are a considerable effort. I shall not let my heart interfere with my work..."

Sandy snapped, "Have they told you what they wanted for her?"

Refocused by Sandy's question George again tapped his cane. "They want everything for nothing, of course."

Sandy offered "Perhaps we can assist you and you us."

"How?" George asked.

When Fitzgerald nodded Sandy offered, "If you were to lead us to them, then we can give you the edge you need. Your enemy is our enemy."

Eternally suspicious George asked "And then what will happen to me?"

"You shall deliver all the documents in your possession."

"What about my money?"

"Very simple" Fitzgerald explained "You shall demand the Nazis show you their payment. Our security men will make sure you receive their money and your woman.

After a moment George offered, "I am scheduled to meet them tomorrow."

"Bit of a rush I must say," Sandy paused in thought before reassuring George. "We will be ready. Where are you scheduled to meet them?"

"They were not gentlemanly enough to inform me of their plans."

This was the break Fitzgerald needed. "What time are you supposed to meet them?"

For the first time George relaxed his cane. He explained, "They are scheduled to pick me up at four in the afternoon."

"When it is near dusk," Fitzgerald knew the time was significant.

Sandy looked at me and said "I believe they will expect to transfer the package off shore quickly as possible, just before sunset when submarines prefer to approach the shore."

Relaxed for the first time George said, "Now we have an agreement here. I will not release my documents or the accelerator until my money is secured."

Not to lose the moment Sandy wondered "What about the safety of the woman?"

Visibly agitated George lectured us "Do you think because I am old or I am a fool for I'm sure you are not close to representing a competitive corporation. Just as I am sure you have men with weapons that are able to take care of such problems. Correct?"

Sandy nodded. "We will talk later."

"Today!" George demanded.

"But of course" Sandy answered. "We must worry about the more immediate problem of when they will come for him."

George insisted on knowing "Who are you talking about? If you speak of me, speak to me. I am right here." Again, he started with the cane taps to make his point.

Sandy asked "Can we depend on you?"

"Can you deliver $1,000,000 tomorrow?" George tapped close to Sandy's shoes "You take care of those goons and I will make everyone most happy. I must go."

"You do not have to worry," Sandy assured him. "You are being followed by our men to protect you."

Looking down his long nose George demanded, "I will expect you to remain outside of my apartment until they pick me up tomorrow."

He walked away, discretely glancing at the two men following him from across the street.

I grabbed Sandy. "What the hell is going on here? You have a team working this case?"

The Englishman explained "I was contacted for background information."

"If you saw them kidnap her then what did you do about it?"

Sandy explained "Have you heard about your own people? You should be proud that somewhere in the Bronx there are two smoldering bodies inside a burning ambulance. She was rescued that afternoon… This is war."

Fitzgerald complained "Why am just hearing this now?"

"They already had your written reports. They needed mine."

"What are you talking about?" Fitzgerald asked.

"If the Germans get their hands on any of Tesla's documents then you most assuredly will not be able to keep them."

"And with you, we will?"

Sandy explained like this was all normal channels even though it was not. "It could be a sanitary place to park them."

"I notice you forgot to mention everything to that greasy salesman. What makes you think we can de-pend on him?"

"I'm sure the old boy is quite untrustworthy. That is neither here nor there. The fact is we presume him to be a liar and a crook. We would be quite disappointed if he was not. It would interfere with our plans if he were to show some bit of integrity. Sandy concluded with a broad smile and ugly English dentistry.

Claudius' Suite
1001 Madison Avenue

Mr. George Sylvester Viereck maintained the subleased Manhattan suite during the countdown. He planned on being moved out before the end of the month. There was no reason to bother with forged identification; cash always worked around the brown-stones. There were rumors the real George might be out on parole soon. At this point it hardly mattered; Claudius would be paid and gone by then. Claudius preferred traveling as George. Acting put him in control. His diary held up the character as his favorite of the decade.

A knock startled him. He expected someone later and he was hardly ready. Looking in the mirror he checked his image and contorted into a characterization before opening the front door.

He opened to see a tall, bespectacled and well-dressed Slav who said "Good afternoon. I'm looking for George Viereck."

"I'm George. May I help you?"

"My name is Sava Kosanovic. I came to visit on a matter of great importance. May I come in?"

With a wave of his hand George stood aside. "How can I be of assistance?"

After walking in Kosanovic waited until the door was closed before speaking. "Forgive my ignorance. By which name shall I call you?"

"You come into my home to insult me?" Kosanovic challenged

"The name registered here is George Viereck and I have verified that he is in prison.

Perhaps you would be so kind as to enlighten me?" George asked "What is of so great importance that you barge into my home and question my integrity? Has it ever occurred to you there is more than one George in New York?"

Kosanovic ignored the little man and explained "My uncle Tesla recently passed away and I represent his interests."

"Fortunately, you came to the right George. I knew your uncle and he was a great man." Recognizing the man had continued with his deception Kosanovic felt free to lie as well. "Perhaps you could assist me in my pursuit to gather all his materials for the museum we intend on building in his honor."

"Why would you believe I have such materials?" George looked around his own room.

Kosanovic sensed something profoundly dishonest about this well-dressed fraud. He later wrote George's German-American accent was excellent. Kosanovic said, "I only know that a large fund has been made available to, shall we say, compensate anyone with materials complimenting the Tesla museum."

George changed tones. "During a war, it is quite difficult for one to determine what materials are appropriate for museums, you understand the difficulty?"

Falling out of character Claudius mocked slapped himself, "Oh, forgive me. Please have a seat. Can I offer you anything?"

"Thank you." The Slavic diplomat followed George across the expensive array of colors decorating the living room. Kosanovic sat next to the yellow pillows and studied the décor; intent on understanding the man who would chose this furniture.

George sat on the red leather round swivel chair turning to Kosanovic and explained, "Please understand the delicate position I have here. I must maintain appearances for my friend and my employer, all while Mr. Viereck is being unjustly imprisoned."

Kosanovic answered, "I have access to a considerable amount of cash and am in the market to recover my uncle's estate. There will be no questions asked. Of course any contributions will be duly honored."

George picked up his glasses. "Help me understand what you are saying."

Kosanovic leaned forward. "I have cash available to purchase any and all items relating to my uncle. Forgive me but, I have little time and considerable money. How clear can I be?"

"I understand. I simply need to appreciate how these items will be used."

"What items?" Kosanovic asked.

"Weapons of course for we are at war."

Ignoring the obvious Kosanovic charged forward "How much do you need for what you have?"

George said, "Again, my answer is dictated by your explaining how this weapon will be used."

"My Uncle Nikola wanted to give at least the Slavs and Croats each such a weapon with the full knowledge the other had such a weapon. I believe a third, perhaps the Montenegrins as well." Kosanovic continued to explain "My uncle's intentions were to develop hypersonic tactical weapons with and without the accelerator. Do you understand what this achieves? This would provide a balance of power because each side could not attack the other with this ultimate weapon, designed strictly for defense. This weapon had no mobility beyond a certain range and with the Accelerator assuring two hundred mile bubble perimeter shields, safety would be guaranteed for every major city in Yugoslavia."

Sitting back Kosanovic continued, "Were you to realize exactly what this weapon is capable of then you would know it is a static weapon, one for defense only. My only concern is that my people stop killing each other.

This design would be only to stop anyone from attacking them. Each party to the conflict would have one or two weapons. Our problem is that part of the weapon is missing. I would secure it for my people."

"You must understand the predicament you are placing me in." George had never been propositioned this blatantly before. It caused the actor to pause for a moment before returning to his German accent "It is my understanding, you evidently know your uncle entrusted such a weapon to my benefactor. What you must understand is in order for me to secure this weapon on his behalf I would need to assure him the cash is available. You should also be apprised that a gentleman – your competitor – is arriving tomorrow with the money for this weapon."

"Who?"

"This is my business and your problem"

"How much?" Kosanovic snapped.

Smiling broadly George announced, "One million dollars. Are you prepared to compete in such a league?"

Kosanovic had only one concern and that was to do whatever necessary to secure the documents. He lectured George "What should concern you is who truly is paying that amount of money."

"Why?" George picked up a cigarette.

It was common knowledge that Kosanovic explained "They are scavengers at best! They will turn on you the first time it becomes convenient."

George took a long drag before answering. "I understand there are unsavory people in the world. That is why we must work well together. When can you produce the cash?"

Kosanovic asked, "What time tomorrow?"

"Meet me here at this time, noon. If you would be so good to give me your telephone number I will keep you up to date."

George went to the writing desk.

Kosanovic removed his billfold received the number from George and placed the note inside.

George declared "I look forward to our successful conclusion of this matter tomorrow." The shook hands and the Slav left.

The scheming Italian knew the Americans would arrive early and the Germans would appear promptly at four. He decided to rest and fell asleep on the sofa.

When his eyes opened Sandy was bent over him with a hand on his lapel.

George demanded, "How did you get in?"

"What matters is old chap, is that I did. I look forward to working with you."

"You have no right to enter my home." He started to sit up but Sandy's quick hand on his chest prevented him from moving.

The English spy said, "I will let myself out." George listened carefully but could not hear him leave. He announced to no one, "British theatrics will not intimidate me."

An hour later the knock was distinct and punctual. Von Haak always had a heavy hand.

Claudius opened the door. "Welcome Herr or do you prefer Von Haak?"

The German scanned the room and said. "I am pleased you feel more comfortable. We must work together from now on. It is important we explain every-thing and get that weapon to Germany immediately."

The nervous looks made Claudius smile and he offered Von Haak a seat before explaining. "I will be pleased to have this discussion with anyone of your organization. Of course, it must be someone with authority to negotiate for the weapon".

Remaining standing Von Haak demanded "We will drive to meet Herr Kiep. He has your money. We need to hurry as sunset is 5:13. Bring your items and documents for delivery."

Claudius stood his ground. "Again, I must see the cash and your authority to decide on such matters before I expose my position."

The Nazi's knuckles cracked as he clinched his fists. Von Haak took an intimidating step toward Claudius while his voice courteously offered. "I will drive you there and assist in whatever decision you two agree upon."

Carefully putting on his mink-collared jacket George was followed out the door by Von Haak. A.I. had a radio transmitter in the trunk of their sedan. They drove to the southern coast of Long Island. This was a different road from last time.

Kiep was parked in the 1937 LaSalle coupe. Von Haak drove past and turned in, behind the two-tone. He parked and motioned Claudius to follow him. Germans despise Italians who despise Germans and they both knew it.

Claudius walked up to the car, whispering to himself.

Upon opening the door, Herr Kiep offered, "Come, sit down and let us talk."

Claudius demanded, "What are you doing in my car?"

"I wanted you to know we work together."

"Were you to pick me up yourself?"

"It seems the FBI has become ever more attentive to our affairs. The precautions are for your benefit.

Why did you want to see me?"

"I brought you an offer. I have both of the vital parts of the weapon and the documents defining what and how it works. Given that I am not involved in the Nazi Party, I will give you the first right of refusal. You must be aware, I do have other bidders."

"What other bidders?" Kiep demanded.

"The Tesla estate has been endowed and it approached me. And then there are those boys with the deep pockets from General Electric." Claudius ignored the ferocity of the glare.

Kiep spoke carefully. "Are you suggesting you would turn against your ally in the middle of this war?"

Claudius moved from one foot to the other. "I am a poor business man and all I ask is that I be paid. Do you want to pay me for my work?"

"What about your woman friend?" Kiep asked.

"I trust you have taken good care of her. May I see her?" He held his smile.

Kiep said "Not until you produce the records you claim."

George felt secure enough to be glib "Are you going to be able to pay in cash or gold?" The tone of his voice had changed to the delight of the Italian and the anger of the German.

The German asked "What do you need?"

"I believe the greatest weapon ever devised should be worth $1,000,000. Would you say that is fair?" George obviously expected the offer to be quickly satisfied.

With a glimpse towards Von Haak, Kiep probed "What are Tesla's people or GE offering?"

"I told them my first choice is to the allies of my people, the Germans. Should I repeat your pledge?"

Sitting back Kiep said, "I do not remember me pledging anywhere close to your figure for an unproven weapon."

Claudius said, "Mussolini himself has seen Marconi's version."

Von Haak asked "Where is Mussolini's weapon?"

George confessed "Marconi's had limited power. It had a range measured in meters. You saw a picture of the accelerator. This weapon can destroy airplanes 250 miles away." Once he became excited, the Italian sounded like he was selling them the auto they were sitting in. "If the Fuehrer knew about this, he would pay tens of millions of dollars. You will be awarded the Iron Cross for your great contribution to the war effort."

Kiep spoke slowly "You are quite a used car salesman. My problem is, I am a loyal soldier. I give orders and obey orders. I do not have to worry about the games businessmen play. You must deliver what you have now."

Claudius asked, "What do you expect me to do give you a weapon worth great money? And then what do you do? You get the glory for bullying around an honest businessman? I think not. You think because you brought your goon and drove me out here where he killed innocent man, I should be afraid of you? You think I am a fool?"

Kiep's tone remained dry. "I think you are quite stupid if you believe you are going to sell this weapon to my enemies."

"I knew you would resort to threats over honor." Claudius dropped any pretense of his German accent and spoke like an Italian speaking English. "I am not the fool you play me for. Right this minute the Americans are following us. I knew you planned on taking me out here to intimidate me. You are wrong. I will not be played for a fool. If you try anything, they will fall on you this moment!"

Kiep believed Italians were pathological liars and challenged him "Where are they, these American guards of yours?"

"Not of mine, they only want you. I told them everything as they have a vested interest in me too. Now, what do you propose?" He sat up straight, folded his arms and extended his jaw.

"You make up many stories, George or Claudius or whoever you are today."

"Am I?" Claudius again surprised himself with his confidence... acting as himself, not a role. "You want to risk everything for nothing. What do you have here, a picture and nothing else? You risk a fight for nothing?"

Kiep ordered "Get out and you will have the money tomorrow." The German opened the passenger door.

Claudius smiled and got out.

Bending to the window Claudius offered, "I am a businessman. If you want to purchase the weapon, you really must show up tomorrow or I sell it to the Americans or the Yugoslavians. I would advise you be at my house tomorrow morning by nine with the cash. You keep the woman."

Kiep turned on the engine before signaling with his emergency blinkers, flashing brightly once before being turned off.

"Come up with the payment." George said. Kiep drove off.

Claudius walked back to the Von Haak's car and got in. "I trust you are civilized enough to drive me back to my home."

Von Haak started the engine and ordered "Lock the door". As Claudius turned to push the door button, the Nazi reached over with his Lugar and pointed it at Claudius' temple. He pulled the trigger and the bullet drove straight through the Italian's brain, blowing out bone and gray matter onto the door. Von Haak put the pistol inside his jacket and shoved the body over.

Slightly behind him through the driver's open window, a standard issue Army Colt slipped silently behind Von Haak's ear and fired. The 8mm bullet shattered Von Haak's cranium and blew a bloody mass across the dashboard. The body fell forward onto the steering wheel. The horn blasted until the Nazi's body was shoved over on top of Claudius' legs.

Betty put her pistol back into her holster. She turned and found herself looking directly across the street at Sandy giving her a nod and Fitzgerald stood in shock.

She charged towards us. "Hit the road, Limey. We have a sanitation crew on the way. You are one foreigner who definitely cannot be here." Before he could answer she added, "Do not say a word. Leave immediately."

Turning Sandy jogged to his car and drove away. Fitzgerald stood frozen half behind the tree. Betty turned back, just as a brown Ford pulled up alongside the two corpses. An agent stepped out and walked directly toward the parked car, opened the door, shoved the German over on top of Claudius, got in and drove away.

Looking at Fitzgerald frozen in place she offered "It is a long walk, come on if you want."

On the drive home Betty told Fitzgerald "I first identified Claudius through an admiral and naval attaché at Italy's Washington embassy. The meetings were very fruitful. I let him make love to me as often as he wanted since this guaranteed the smooth flow of political information I needed. Wars are not won by respectable methods."

Fitzgerald sat silently for the ride, afraid of a woman like he had never imagined real. Then Fitzgerald's mind imploded with the realization A.I. did not know where George had moved the Accelerator. Panic struck at the revelation. Fitzgerald concluded she hardly cared if he was in the car. She was talking herself down after the shooting. Betty drove to Fitzgerald's and promised, "I'll see you tomorrow."

Sokol
71ˢᵗ St

A.I.'s tail picked up Kosanovic walking slowly to the Sokol and called Fitzgerald. The Slavs immaculate, black worsted suit was the same one he had worn yesterday, before losing his tail less than a mile away. The white powder on his pant legs below his top coat appeared to be cement. His slouching shoulders marred his dignified stature. He no longer had the tightly wrapped package he was carrying.

His journal made reference to a rented basement to the west. Kosanovic wrote daily how deeply distressed he felt possessing proof Tesla's shield worked.

The invention was his uncle's and they never agreed on any political argument. It hurt Kosanovic that Tesla never would understand the pragmatics of diplomacy. It no longer mattered Tesla's personal papers are controlled by the U.S.

The nephew was pained by their political differences. He felt persecuted by Tesla's side of the family. There were deeper issues. Tesla had been naive about the depth of the fratricidal civil war. The lines of disagreement overlapped: the many shades of truth were grey at best, and the complications were innumerable. How could Uncle Nikola, an inventor understand the fleeting hopes and intertwining conflicts of this war?

Kosanovic regretted leading Tesla away from exclusively supporting the Serbians. The diplomat would never live down his words. Last year, when he defended Mikhailovich against the rumors of genocide, he told everyone, including uncle Nikola, "This is Nazi propaganda to which some people have lent them as naive accomplices."

Everyone remembered later that year, Dr. Sekuich brought to London documents attesting to the criminal persecutions of the Orthodox Serbs in Croatia. The damning testimony against bigotry was horrendous. The new, overwhelming evidence forced the Serbian Orthodox Church to appeal for the Nazi generals to intervene In halting the racial massacres. The truth came out that the Italian Clergy helped administer the deportation of thousands of Serbs to concentration camps. Orthodox priests and their families were arrested. Their birth, marriage and death registers were handed over to the diocesan authorities to assure their conversion. The Ustashas tortured and executed members of parliament, including Orthodox clergy and bishops. The relatives were sent to concentration camps or forced to become Catholics. They died and Kosanovic was wrong.

What happens to a diplomat's word when the truth rises against him? The answer is different between members of the family and countrymen of the profession. Surviving politics was his stock in trade. Kosanovic became Chairman of the Yugoslav Economic Mission because his people needed a new federation. He was the architect. Kosanovic's uncle never again mentioned the massacres.

The exhausted cultural attaché left his national headquarters and walked down the sidewalk. From the shadows Fitzgerald and Sandy appeared in front him. Kosanovic recognized Fitzgerald. Sandy had the cold eyes of a mountain wolf and surprised the Yugoslav into stepping back.

Fitzgerald stepped up, within inches of Kosanovic.

He asked, "May I help you?"

There was nothing about Kosanovic Fitzgerald trusted or liked. "We have information regarding your activities."

"What activities are you referring to?"

"We need to talk," Fitzgerald demanded.

"I am really quite busy. If you must speak to me then, I suggest you contact my office and make an appointment." Kosanovic took a step.

Sandy side stepped into his path.

Fitzgerald explained "I do not need an appointment to talk to a foreigner in my country." Kosanovic repeated "What do you want?"

Looking at Sandy, Fitzgerald waited before answering "I want what you removed from the Tesla estate."

Kosanovic had worked in diplomatic circles long enough to recognize an empty threat. "You have yet to prove your standing."

By now A.I. had debriefed the Clinton Hotel manager and learned Kosanovic had switched the packages. "Would you tell me the truth?"

"Must I remind you, I enjoy diplomatic recognition by your government?" Kosanovic explained.

Fitzgerald fired back "That does not entitle you to threaten the country you live in."

"What do you think you will accomplish? If you want to fight, I invite you to my homeland. There you will be able to truly test your mettle. What are you, two government thugs?"

Sandy calmly explained "We know you have been in contact with the Russians. Have they caught you with their promises of utopia?"

Kosanovic looked at me first then over at Sandy.

"I presume you're British. I'm Yugoslavian. My only fight is with those who occupy my country. The Russians are allies of Britain, not Yugoslavia."

"We were watching you during your encounter with the NKVD." Sandy explained.

"I am a diplomat whose primary directive is to develop trade with every country able to assist Yugoslavia. I believe we are free to pursue such interest with Amtorg." He stared long and hard at Sandy "Why are you in America, Englishman?"

"Because I asked" Fitzgerald snapped.

With not so subtle disdain Kosanovic said "If you will allow me to pass."

Fitzgerald took a side step in front of him. "Listen, we can make this easy or we can make it hard. I need to know what exactly you removed from your uncle's apartment. You may have diplomatic privileges but stolen weapons are not covered. Am I making myself clear?"

"What do you expect a confession?"

"What I expect is that guests in my country act like they are allies in this war. What side are you on?"

"I'm against the fascist who has invaded my country. I'm for the liberation of Yugoslavia." Kosanovic paused. "We've already covered this ground. I only took from my uncle what belonged to his family."

Fitzgerald took a breath. "Look, you know and I know this weapon can win the war. We have common interest and should not be arguing. We should be working together."

"How would you suggest we, as you say, work together?"

Fitzgerald attempted a different tact "We can combine all of Tesla's materials and give a demonstration that will shake the world." Fitzgerald would never forget looking into his eyes. Knowing what we both knew Tesla's shield is technically possible, he had key elements and working together would never happen.

"I believe you imagine far more than really exists," Kosanovic explained his half-truth "I have nothing and, evidently you have very little. How can we shake the world?

"I'll give you credit for not blinking." Fitzgerald answered.

"I have nothing. You have nothing." He looked down the street. "I gather we have nothing further to discuss."

"Can we negotiate?" Fitzgerald asked. Kosanovic was tired and his ploy sounded sincere

"Yugoslavia has very little to offer this war. Given numerous countries are willing to brutally abuse my country for their own ends, I would prefer to remain outside any politics other than trade policies."

"You give yourself too little credit," Sandy offered. "After the Nazis invaded your country a true hero emerged. Mikhailovich delayed the Wehrmacht's time-table and the drive on the Soviet

Union was delayed three months. The Nazis failure to reach Moscow before the Russian winter set in doomed their mission. Hundreds of thousands of Germans who had expected to garrison in the shelter of the Russian capital died in the icy trenches a few miles away. All that, lead to the German surrender at Stalingrad last week. You see, you cannot underestimate what you do."

Everyone knew Mikhailovich's actions had delayed the Nazis; the Yugoslav also knew this British agent hated his people. Yugoslav could never trust the English, even if their king lived there. If the British armies decided the shortest route from Africa to Berlin was through Yugoslavia then Churchill would choose British expediency – Tito.

Kosanovic also knew the Russian armies could come to Slavic Yugoslavia's rescue, driven by their ancestral hatred of the Teutonic invaders. The answer must come from within, the only belligerent fighting the Nazis; Tito would again be the choice. No one cared about Mikhailovich's past collaborations or had little concern if Tito was a communist. What this diplomat knew for sure was Tito's resistance was the future of Yugoslavia and the British will always serve the British.

Kosanovic answered, "We do what we can. My country is cursed with foreign armies."

"We are at the war's turning point and the Nazis will never recover from their defeats in Africa and Russia," Sandy said. "You must make some choices. I trust you are loyal to the monarchy in London?"

"Again gentlemen, I reiterate my duty and loyalties are only for my country."

Fitzgerald said "That's a diplomatic answer and you need to step up and take a stand."

"My only position I must take is to sit inside the Sokol. Would you be so kind to excuse me?" Kosanovic walked past.

Fitzgerald said to the departing diplomat. "We will be constantly watching you from this point forward."

Kosanovic turned. "If you care to waste your time then the choice is yours."

He then turned and walked into the Sokol, shaking. The cold morning did not stop him from sweating. We monitored the Sokol telephone. Kosanovic walked to the pay phone and dialed the number, calling George. No answer.

Looking carefully around, Kosanovic wandered through the foyer and from nowhere the large Russian walked alongside.

"I see that you had company?" NKVD Chief Akhmarhov spoke softly.

Kosanovic snapped "Why must you do this? Can you allow us to meet in a room without you approaching me from behind?"

"Forgive me, comrade."

"I would prefer you call me by name, Sava Kosanovic if you don't mind."

"Very well Kosanovic, I am honored you telephoned. Why don't we go to a room and discuss our common interest."

The two walked quietly around the perimeter of the large gymnasium floor, filled with teenagers practicing flips across the mats. The gym instructors' commands and compliments echoed off the tall, sports hall walls.

Before they reached the top bleacher, Akhmarhov stopped and, breathing hard put his hand on Kosanovic's shoulder. "What we old men must go through for a little peace and quiet."

Kosanovic checked his own smile. He never stopped watching the Russian.

They finished the climb and went into the small booth. Sitting down, the two men looked at each other for a troubled minute.

Akhmarhov was first to break the silence. "What did the American want?"

"Who was the other one?" Kosanovic asked.

Staring, assessing and then deferring to the need for an exchange Akhmarhov explained, "We know he is British intelligence and has been sanctioned by the Americans. He sails has own sloop and been sighted working in the West Indies. What did he say?"

"They want what you want." "What is that?"

Kosanovic answered "Materials from my uncle's estate."

"What materials do you have?"

Kosanovic countered, "I am the legal heir of my uncle's estate. I intend on pursuing my rights in the American courts." He looked out the window, rather than at the Russian.

"And so you shall," Akhmarhov leaned forward. "How can we provide assistance?"

"I appreciate the offer but, you understand these Americans. They can ally with Russia but if anyone else forms such an alliance, he is a suspect."

The Russian spoke a perfect Queen's English. "Kosanovic, you must understand we are not at war with you. Russia does not want to conquer or divide your country. Your strength protects our southern flank. Understand the International wants only a united and strong Yugoslavia."

"You cannot honestly suggest Russia will support our Prince." Kosanovic sat back.

The Russian was correct in pointing out "And you do not believe for one small moment your young prince will lead your people after the war." The Russian's fingers interlaced and he lifted his clasped hands off the table, almost in some perverted prayer. "You must understand that historical dialectics requires Yugoslavia become part of a Federation of peoples. No one in the West sees or speaks such words to you. Why? They want you divided, like a good colony. Your only choice is Tito. He will unite you and make you strong. He will stop the genocide and demand everyone sit at the table. You know this to be true. Do you not?"

Kosanovic chose not to answer quickly. He headed trade missions and ideology was always a negotiating issue and a common ploy. His journal recounted these challenges to his principles for one reason and one reason only – the ideology of peaceful coexistence. Sure spies turn but, not those of Kosanovic's patriotism. He was honest, only deeply burdened by his country's emerging conversion and those who continued to threaten Yugoslavia's future. With authority he explained, "Of course I have no doubt the English will decide our postwar fate as much or more than Tito."

Akhmarhov said "Sava listen to an old man's wisdom. You will have to make a decision. The love-struck prince will not survive any more than Mikhailovich will unify your people."

"I must continue to represent Yugoslavia's interests without incurring the wrath of the Western armies."

"Will you agree to travel across the United States and remain in contact with us?" Akhmarhov leaned forward. "Allow me to forward Tito news of your support?"

Kosanovic said, "The communiqué must come from me."

Akhmarhov again asked, "Is there any help you need from us? We can provide you with ongoing communications with Comrade Tito?"

"I have means of contacting Tito. I look forward to developments between us."

Akhmarhov said "Again, I am honored to work with you, comrade. Forgive the question but, understand I must ask: would your uncle's weapons further our efforts?"

Kosanovic "Of course, you read about the force field weapon. The problem is the jackals picked apart his apartment before securing his technology. I must confess I only possess limited documentation."

"Do you know who the scavengers were?"

"I'm sure the American who attempted to roust me out on the sidewalk perhaps has some parts of the weapon. I doubt if they have significant materials. I am at a loss of who else may have the rest. I would have suggested Tesla's friend George Viereck but, he is in prison." Evidently Kosanovic saw no need to give the Russians any leads about Claudius.

"I am sure you recognize we paid your uncle for his work and did not receive our complete product," Akhmarhov said. "Are you able to make Tesla's work… honorable?"

Kosanovic smiled at the passing gymnasts before answering "Akhmarhov, you of all people certainly should know I do not control my uncle's estate. The American government asserted jurisdiction over Dr. Tesla's property. They know their own laws are being broken to enforce their will. They also know until this war is over, they can."

"I appreciate your situation" Akhmarhov said. "Would you be so kind as to share the documents you do have?"

Kosanovic explained "My authority here is limited as the sole representative of the family. I am a mere guardian who needs to discuss the American's seizure of my uncle's property. A representative without portfolio, from a government without a country would hold on to what little there is until all of the legal challenges are resolved."

Akhmarhov said, "Should we not evaluate the possibilities offered by documents in the meantime?"

"Give me time to understand the legal issues." Squinting and obviously tired, the tousled Kosanovic removed his winter coat. He attempted to brush off the cement powder remaining on his pant legs and held his coat in front. "This weapon will not be built in a day or a year. This will not be used in this war. There is too much resources required and the fighting has already turned against the Fascist."

Akhmarhov asked "Are you qualified to make that judgment?"

"I am only qualified to serve Yugoslavia." Kosanovic knew the prototype was safely buried far enough away in a place of permanent safety. Once it became obvious to Kosanovic there is no power in Yugoslavia capable of building the weapon anymore, Kosanovic prepared to commit his life to a Marxism-Leninism-Stalinism-Titoism form of government. The question is: will it cross the moral line set by Uncle Tesla, knowing the nephew would never receive approval. Kosanovic concluded "I am serving a simple custodian with a disappointing few papers and a personal memento."

Akhmarhov pushed the thought to "And moving from the ideal to the real is called Praxis, the progressive truth of the human condition, from each according to their ability, for each according to their need."

Kosanovic explained "Marx plagiarized his most famous line from Jesus." They both smiled and he shook Akhmarhov's hand. "It would be premature to distribute my uncle's work at this time. It is not legal for me to hold my uncle's possessions."

Akhmarhov wrapped his enormous left hand around Kosanovic's to keep him from pulling back. "Comrade, let us understand each other. We are all part of the International. This means we work together. Let me bring a friend, an expert in such matters, to view the documents, nothing more."

With a bow to the church and the future Kosanovic pledged "I will continue my struggle for a federated Yugoslavia. I will fight for a federated Europe. I will do nothing to interfere with our future leader, Tito. Besides the jackals have already picked my uncle's possessions clean by the third day. What is left?"

Releasing his grip Akhmarhov asked, "When you travel across America raising money for your people, I trust we can work together from time to time?"

A.I. was surprised to hear Kosanovic's tone change. "We shall leave the work for later, for now you and I may have a civil discussion, on occasion." He paused to look down before finishing, "My contributions will be measured by diplomacy; and I'll leave your rather dangerous business to experts."

Looking out the window of the judge's box seats, Akhmarhov pointed to the tall teenage girl's graceful series of flips across the mat. "There is the future of our countries, the youth. The Soviet Union has developed the best gymnast in the world. After the war, we will share our country's finest teachers."

"The children are the future," Kosanovic agreed before explaining "We cannot meet here anymore. We are drawing American agents into our children's playground."

"Perhaps..."

"Perhaps not for now, we simply ask that our country be allowed to survive the war. We must coexist amongst larger and hostile forces."

At least in his words the Russian agreed "You know how to locate me at the Soviet trade mission?" They stared at each other before sharing a second hand-shake. Akhmarhov smiled and walked carefully down the bleacher steps.

Waiting until the Russian had left the building Kosanovic went to the telephone to call George. There was no answer. After five calls since last night, Kosanovic was left to conclude the Italian chose the Germans.

When he returned to the bleachers his eye caught the graceful young gymnast speaking with her coach and repeatedly looking over at him. After the coach turned away, she retied the twine holding up her oversized gym shorts. Adjusting his glasses Kosanovic focused on her long left leg. The bullet had gone clean through, leaving her calf with round scars on both sides. They looked straight at each other. He smiled at the young lady, gliding gracefully across the mat towards him with a slight gimp.

"Hello, my name is Lepa." She gave a respectful bow before adjusting her pants to cover the worn hole in her black t-shirt. "My coach says you are a diplomat. I am a Croatian. Have you ever been there?"

Sitting straighter Kosanovic introduced himself "Hello, Lepa, my name is Sava Kosanovic. Yes, I have been there many times and will surely return. Actually I am not well-known but, my uncle was a very famous man. His name was Nikola Tesla."

"Yes I know" she said, "In American School they teach us Edison gave us electricity but, we learn the truth about Dr. Tesla from our teachers. We know our lights and motors come from alternating current."

"Your parents taught you about Tesla?"

"My mother and father were killed. I came to America with my cousins."

"I am so sorry I did not realize..."

"It is okay, I miss them but now I have gymnastics." Looking over to the practice floor Kosanovic watched Lepa swoon at the muscular boy's swinging circles on the high bar.

After watching the young man do a perfect flip dismount, Kosanovic lamented, "Yes, I know I miss my uncle. Please sit down and I will tell you about a great inventor."

Lepa sat on the bench before asking, "Was it true your uncle could have stopped all war?"

Looking at the future of his country Kosanovic said, "He could have if one national leader would have championed his genius. War is complicated. Kings and President's declare war and think they know the outcome but are incapable of controlling opposing forces."

"Are you really a diplomat?" "Let us just say, it is my struggle."

Lepa asked "Why must there be this war?"

"As with all wars countries use it to resolve their differences both real and self-serving." Kosanovic gave her a pained glance.

She had the same bright blue eyes his uncle had. "Why do they need to kill each other?" He shook his head, perhaps to clear his thoughts. "It is a very complicated matter. Some are trying to conquer yet most people are killing for... confused rea-sons." Stopping in a pained moment, Kosanovic rubbed his temples. "Not even that explains the terrible things happening in Yugoslavia."

"Why must our people kill each other?"

"That is the most difficult question of all." They sat silently for some time before he offered, "We can speculate about their fears or ancient hate of race or religion but, ultimately it is about who can force who." Her smooth face wrinkled as she continued asking. "I just do not understand what gives them the right to kill each other. Both sides say they believe in God and then kill in the name of God. If they do not have the government telling them to kill, they blame God."

"Do you believe in God?" Kosanovic was startled by his own question. He then found himself rubbing his neck in a futile attempt to relieve his rare headache.

Lepa's thick eyebrows furrowed. "I will believe in God when He takes me to my parents."

"Do you enjoy being in America?"

"Here people are rude because of my accent but, at home there was no gymnasium," she explained softly. "I am most happy at my Sokol. Why do you come here?"

"To feel at home... and, to see our people... living with their pain. I find being here, helps me experience the feeling of our nation. I... I wonder sometimes what life has thrust upon us all.

What is my life if not diplomacy? I am above reprisal. If not for our future, old men must not attempt anything which may prove the destruction of innocents."

"What does that mean?"

"New York has brought you and me a sanctuary. Our families are left behind. And I carry this burden."

"What is your burden?" The young lady with notable maturity said, "My friends say I am a good person to speak with."

Kosanovic opened up to her "We all struggle with the challenges the war has thrust on our lives. We are in the middle of the harshest fighting civilization has ever endured. In the end, we must understand what principles we live, yet never lose sight of civilization. We struggle to discern what these governments and weapons will do to our children. Does this make sense?"

Lepa said "In our history books, there is always war... somewhere. Why?"

"I have asked same question every day for the last few years." Kosanovic was quiet for a moment before continuing," We must hold the government responsible, not the people. No peace can stand when there is a matter reserved for future war. The French forced the Germans into a doomed accord that preordained this horrendous war. As evil as Hitler is, he could not have succeeded were it not for the Treaty of Versailles. The French wanted to eternally force their way and now tens of millions are dying." He looked up, energized by her focus before continuing. "A government must realize hostilities are insufficient. Peace will only be established when we remove the sins of man. I often wonder what the natural state of humans is. I do not believe for a moment, there is a perfect balance; the accepted condition for any country is one of unceasing change. The dynamics of peace will forever be eternal struggles. The solution is politically fluid fields between governments."

"How can we establish anything when we do not even have a real government inside Yugoslavia?" Lepa asked.

"In a perverse form, war is a government. It just adds insidious and malicious policies. Warfare forces the new order."

"I thought the communist stages demand change. Are you a Marxist?"

"I believe history is clear. The days of royalty have ended and the people must create new government, one allowing a forum for discussion and resolution. We must issue regular bulletins and tell people about the concerns affecting their lives. The form of government is based on the way the state makes uses force and those who are ever ready to support it."

Lepa pointed to young woman staring straight ahead. She crossed the balance beam, "Her equilibrium is in her mind."

Kosanovic asked "If you had a weapon so powerful it would guarantee victory, what would you do with it?"

Lepa explained "I would make sure each country knew about such a power and then never let any single country have the weapon. Give everyone the weapon or give no one the weapon."

Kosanovic stared at her with wonderment. Lepa stood. "I need to return to practice." She gave a ballerina's curtsy.

He smiled. "So you do. Please rejoin your friends. It has been most interesting speaking with you."

She started to leave then hesitated "will I see you here tomorrow?"

"I will not be able to return. I must walk away from one choice and head towards a new one. Perhaps someday we will cross paths and I will tell you how it worked out."

She offered him a parting smile. "I am sure you will make the right decision." In spite of the hole in her slipper, she skipped across the wooden floor towards the other teenagers.

Kosanovic walked out of the Sokol for the last time. He knew Akhmarhov was out there hiding somewhere. Instead, he caught a glimpse of the hawk eyed Brit, standing across the street. The Yugoslav cultural attaché turned away and walked directly east to never risk his people by returning.

Federal Court Building
Foley Square

The next morning Fitzgerald bought a cup of coffee and bag of pigeon feed from the street vendor to Sandy met at the park bench in the middle. Fitzgerald had to file an accurate report and so did he.

The symbolism was obvious, facing the Supreme Court building next to other federal traditions. The popular park was made up of sidewalks and benches. While tossing the grain across the ground, Fitzgerald noticed the pigeons had a strict pecking order. "Have you ever studied pigeon's foraging patterns?

Sandy looked at Fitzgerald as if he were mad. "Not only have I never studied pigeons, it is quite likely I never will."

Fitzgerald said "I understand why Tesla liked to feed pigeons he was entertained by their mathematical patterns."

"You sure he was looking for meaningless diversion?"

"Tesla did not have so much as one meaningless diversion."

"Are you feeling bloody guilty?"

"You mean about the Italian?"

"About the weapon," he asked.

Fitzgerald had to come to grips with the last month and harder than that, realized how this will affect the rest of history. He came clean, "Tesla's shield… sure, I feel guilty as hell. I feel guilty I failed to secure the ultimate defense for my country and maybe end this damn war."

Sandy offered "Look at it this way; neither did anyone else."

Fitzgerald wondered out loud "The ultimate defensive weapon to stop all war will either appear in the next few years or is forever scattered among thieves."

"Are you sure it was divided?"

"Absolutely, the force field weapon had critical parts stolen by more than one agent. The fact is Tesla proved the shield worked and, unfortunately kept the technology in his suite."

"What are you going to report?"

"I think this search is over. Sure, the scavengers grabbed portions and prevented each other from having the superior weaponry. I doubt the essential pieces will ever be put together again..." Fitzgerald emptied the bag of pigeon feed and sat back; noticing Sandy had tucked his thumbs in his belt, like a swabby.

"What the hell America wins all of its wars," Sandy said.

Fitzgerald feared "After this war we will never stop preparing."

Sandy asked, "What good is a weapon that prevents combat?"

Fitzgerald explained "Weapons are getting bigger and more effective. I suspect we will lose our choice to fight. This is the second world war of this century.

The military will have a free hand to defend from a third world war."

"You are never going to stop America or England from building more weapons and you are not going to stop the next war." Sandy's sage insights sounded true yet his premonitions were typically British. "If we build it, you will want it. If England has it, then a third country will build a bigger one. We cannot seek terror as a lasting strategy."

"Atomic energy will be developed instead of Tesla's harmonic technology and the world's fighting fields will be mutual terror, not protected cities. Why would we want the fun of destroying an enemy's country?"

Fitzgerald wanted to follow this thinking because he was not sure about what to report. "Then, everyone will want it and build their own."

"If you blokes end up building this super bomb you are not talking about, then no one will dare want to war against you and, of course, we will have secured it too." Sandy was cocksure.

Fitzgerald was not "Unless we become a country willing to watch the massacre tens of thousands of civilians" His head dropped and voice was forced, "If we build it, others will, too."

"We British have been playing this exercise for centuries. War is a game of chess, not men. Each turn in this war ripples change and alters decisions across the world. War demands new weapons. Without enemies, how would we justify financing the next weapon?"

Sandy concluded. Fitzgerald hated Englishmen who thought Imperialism cute.

It was nearing eight in the morning, and being late was not an option. Fitzgerald was not looking forward to reporting the disappearance of the greatest weapon ever created, during the middle of the war when our Country needed it the most.

What else could be said by a man true to his heart? Fitzgerald lost the world's one chance for permanent peace. In the bottom margin of his report Fitzgerald handwrote "I will never forgive myself."

Epilogue

Sava Kosanovic spent the remainder of the war working in the Royal Mission on Fifth Avenue publishing bulletins of peace. He hired Philip Wittenberg from Wittenberg, Carrington & Farnsworth to prosecute his claim on the Tesla estate. A decade passed before Kosanovic recovered his uncle's remaining papers. Tesla's ashes were transferred to the Belgrade museum.

Fitzgerald was transferred to Wright Patterson airbase in Ohio.

June 21, 1943: U.S. Supreme Court ruled Tesla must receive credit for his fundamental contributions inventing of the radio. See, 'Marconi Wireless Telegraph Co. vs. United States'.

July, 1943: Drew Pearson papers, Nadya Gardner and Sandy Griffith testified against George Sylvester Viereck during his last appeal before the U.S. Supreme Court. Viereck spent the remainder of the war in prison.

15 December 1946: United Nations Security Council -Yugoslavia's Ambassador to the U.N, Sava N. Kosanovic develops a peaceful resolution to the Greek question.

After the war, Kosanovic was instrumental in guiding the strong arm of Tito into a federation, a forum for trade and peace throughout the Balkan region. Dr. Sava Kosanovic became Yugoslavia's Ambassador to the United Nations under Tito.

PARTICLE BEAM RESEARCH

April 17, 1950, FBI Memorandum [FOIA], Colonel Duffy of Air Material Command, Wright Field, con-firmed Tesla materials by the military.

February 7, 1962 p. 9, Christian Science Moni-tor, 'Fireballs for Defense'.

May 2, 1977, Aviation Week, pp 16 – 27, 'Soviet Push for a Beam Weapon'.

May 27, 1977, Science Magazine, 'Charge Debate Erupts over Russian Beam Weapon'.

April 1980, Specula, "Possible Soviet Test of a Tesla Weapon".

July 28, 1980 Aviation Week, Soviet's Build Directed Energy Weapon.

Sept, 1981 – Omni, pp 52 – 55, 'Zeus in Orbit' 1986 Tesla Conference Proceedings "The Fundamental Concept of Scalar Electromagnetics.

August 11, 1987 – U.S. Patent 4,686,605 – "Method and Apparatus for Altering A Region in the Earth's Atmosphere, Ionosphere and Magnetosphere" issued to Bernard Eastlund.

August 13, 1991 – U.S. Patent 5,038,664 – "Method for Producing a Shell of Relativistic Particles at an Altitude above the Earth's Surface", by Bernard Eastlund.

Fiscal Year 1993 The Committee on Armed Services Hearings National Defense Authorization Act, Research and Development Subcommittee on Research, Development and Evaluation. P458, Funding for Particle Beam Research.

Printed in the United States
By Bookmasters